PRAISE FOR *BRAND STORYTELLING*

D0023926

Miri Rodriguez's *Brand Storytelling* is an engaging and insightful must-read for all digital marketers and storytellers. Plenty of ah-ha moments for brand storytellers seeking to infuse their communication strategies and tactics with empathy and vulnerability that will resonate with their customers, but in the most authentic, emotional, and immersive way possible. *Brand Storytelling* provides an essential journey for brand storytellers that truly does put the customer at the heart of the story.
Michael Raymond, Senior Writer, The Walt Disney Company

Miri Rodriguez's *Brand Storytelling* is bound to serve as an essential practical guide for anyone seeking to harness the power of the brand journalism movement that has revolutionized communications over the past decade. Whether it's benchmarking, waving the 'magic wand of vulnerability' or amassing an army of storytellers, Rodriguez's methods will electrify the town square of any organization. And who better to guide us than an influencer with an international reputation in the field of storytelling?
Mark Ragan, Chairman and Owner, Ragan Communications and *PR Daily*

Miri Rodriguez's demonstrated experience in the technology industry, with a marketing and multicultural background, plus her personal and professional experience, have positioned her as an authority in the storytelling field. With this gift to the world, she inspires us to be the best, by being story designers driven by the power of empathy, vulnerability and authenticity. A must-read for generations to come. Having spent quality time over the past five years, reading, researching, trying, failing, executing, teaching and successfully creating a Visual Storytelling Studio, I can tell you with no doubts in my mind that Rodriguez has created a masterpiece with a profound, delicate and fascinating equilibrium. This book is for readers of all ages, in any industry, for any role, for entrepreneurs and business leaders, students and anyone interested in using a guide to understand, value and apply the power of storytelling to awaken and inspire emotions and transform them into meaningful actions.
Dieter Avella, General Manager, Zebra Technologies

Storytelling is the foundation of all communication, but is often overlooked. Miri Rodriguez is not only one of the best storytellers out there, but is also able to give practical, reliable, easy-to-implement advice for the real world. Well worth the read.

Craig Stilwell, EVP and GM of Consumer and Small to Medium Business, OpenText

Rodriguez's insights and advice on brand storytelling are critically relevant for both public and private sector organizations alike to survive, succeed, and stand out in a crowded social media landscape of noise and distractions.

Chris Hsiung, Deputy Police Chief and social media influencer

We know how important storytelling is – it captures the hearts and minds of your consumer in a way that no other type of marketing can. After seeing Rodriguez's dynamic presentation about brand storytelling at my conference in Sydney, I could not wait to read her book. And Rodriguez does not disappoint. She delivers so much valuable content. Rodriguez helps you to discover your story and provides a template to help you craft it and share it with the world. It is a must read for every business.

Mireille Ryan, CEO of the Social Media Marketing Institute and award-winning entrepreneur

Brand Storytelling

Put customers at the heart of your brand story

Miri Rodriguez

First published in Great Britain and the United States in 2020 by Kogan Page Limited

2nd Floor, 45 Gee Street
London
EC1V 3RS
United Kingdom

122 W 27th St, 10th Floor
New York, NY 10001
USA

4737/23 Ansari Road
Daryaganj
New Delhi 110002
India

www.koganpage.com

ISBNs
Hardback   9781789660586
Paperback   9780749490478
Ebook   9780749490539

British Library Cataloguing-in-Publication Data

A CIP record for this book is available from the British Library.

Library of Congress Control Number

2020931782.

Typeset by Hong Kong FIVE Workshop
Print production managed by Jellyfish
Printed and bound by CPI Group (UK) Ltd, Croydon, CR0 4YY

*For Luis, Alex and Isaiah – you are my best story.
And to all of you storytellers daring to find stories
and the courage to tell them.*

CONTENTS

List of contributors x
About the author xi
Foreword xii
Preface xiv
Acknowledgements xv

Introduction: The science and art of storytelling 1

1 **Brand storytelling: What is it?** 4
   The power of storytelling 7
   Your brand mission and the story arc 9

2 **Where do I start?** 20
   The Robin to Batman effect 21
   Design thinking applied to storytelling 22
   Finding your story's universal truth 23

3 **The magic (and magic tricks) in storytelling** 39
   Magic trick 1: Don't just define your story setting. Find it 43
   Magic trick 2: Visual elements are not a nice-to-have; they
      are a must-have 45
   Magic trick 3: Shape your brand assets to help you tell the story 48
   Magic trick 4: Keep your conclusion inconclusive 50

4 **IMC Reimagined: Building an integrated marketing plan
   with story** 51
   Incorporating brand storytelling into your IMC plan 53
   Reimagining the brand message 56
   Resetting your goals 58
   Identifying your design (not just target) audience 59
   Measuring success 61

5   **The brand story hero: Put your customers at the heart of your brand story** 63

Non-obvious trends in customer-centricity 64

Steps to unveiling your brand story hero 70

6   **If story is magic, vulnerability is the magic wand** 76

Vulnerability in storytelling 78

Waving the magic wand 79

7   **Ethics in storytelling: When to use your secret weapon** 89

The importance of ethics in storytelling 92

Ethical perspectives 93

8   **Immersive storytelling: Exploring the story experience** 100

What is immersive storytelling? 103

Immersive storytelling trends 105

9   **Your best brand storytellers: Employees and influencers** 113

Building a storytelling army 115

Designing the story persona 122

Employees and influencers: The good, the bad and the ugly 126

10   **Marketing (actually, testing) your brand story** 131

Defining key assumptions 132

Story concept testing ground rules 133

11   **Benchmarking your brand story** 146

Main indicators for benchmarking story 148

Leveraging existing metrics 149

12   **Villains and antagonists: The bad guys who want to tear down your brand story** 161

Why villains and antagonists? 162

The bad guys archetypes 164

Your offensive weapon 172

Attack mode: training internal stakeholders 173

13   The future of brand storytelling: How AI, machine learning and automation can tell only one side of the story 177

Enter: the machines 179
The race against the machines 182
AI technology trends 184

14   Inspire your brand story: Interviews with leading storytellers around the world 188

Interview with Dux Raymond Sy, CMO of Avepoint 188
Interview with Luz Maria Doria, two-time Emmy winner and
    Executive Producer of TV show *Despierta America* 192
Interview with Derek E Baird, writer, social media expert and youth
    culture trend spotter 195
Interview with Greg L Witt, youth marketer and public speaker 198
Rapid-fire questions with Cindy Coloma, bestselling author and
    storyteller at Microsoft 201
Rapid-fire questions with Park Howell, advertising industry veteran
    and owner of Business of Story 203
Rapid-fire questions with Candy Rasmijn-Reino, marketing and PR
    agency owner 204
Rapid-fire questions with Dona Sarkar, author, fashion designer,
    engineer and principal manager of Windows Insider Program at
    Microsoft 205

Further reading 206
Index 210

CONTRIBUTORS

Candy Rasmijn-Reino marketing and PR agency owner

Cindy Coloma bestselling author and Storyteller at Microsoft

Derek E Baird author of *The Gen Z Frequency: How brands tune in and build credibility*

Dona Sarkar author, fashion designer, engineer and Principal Manager of Windows Insider Program at Microsoft

Dux Raymond Sy CMO of AvePoint

Gregg Witt author of *The Gen Z Frequency: How brands tune in and build credibility*

Jose Camacho Social Media and Employee Advocacy Program Manager for Adobe

Luz Maria Doria two-time Emmy winner and Executive Producer of TV show *Despierta America*

Park Howell advertising industry veteran and owner of Business of Story

ABOUT THE AUTHOR

Miri Rodriguez is an award-winning digital marketer and storyteller. She has dedicated the last four years of her extensive marketing career advocating for and evangelizing brand narrative across many sectors and industries around the world. Rodriguez' mission for imparting storytelling techniques entrenched in vulnerability and empathy began when she worked as a creative journalist in the engineering discipline at Microsoft Corporation. There, she recognized the immediate need to help educate and inspire engineers and colleagues across functions on designing distinctive narratives that help define and drive immersive and emotional customer engagement experiences, while navigating the uncertainties of the digital age.

Basing her storytelling techniques in design thinking and user experience (UX) principles, Rodriguez has successfully bridged the contentious gaps between traditional business practices and creative communication strategies, crossing the brand storytelling boundaries from simple narrative design to a culture activation blueprint.

Rodriguez' thought leadership in both the digital marketing and tech worlds, as well as her passion for leading diversity and inclusion efforts, has made her one of the top sought-after speakers and business consultants in the industries. Clients include Walmart, Adobe, McKesson and Discover. Rodriguez holds a Master's degree from Georgetown University in Integrated Marketing Communications and certification in Design Thinking. She is also a NASA Social and MySkills4Afrika Programs alumnus and has served on the board for Africa and Middle East sector social enterprise association Trade + Impact and US marketing conference Social Shake-up.

Rodriguez was born in Caracas, Venezuela, and currently resides in the state of Washington, US, with her husband, two sons and American Bulldog.

FOREWORD

'You have to meet Miri,' my friend Jack stated, and it wasn't a request. Jack and I had developed a close friendship while working on his book, and have remained so in the years since its publication. He had been on a book tour and was in the Seattle area speaking at Microsoft when we met for a quick lunch that turned into a half day of catching up, and that included his Miri statement.

Jack is a former KGB spy (now US citizen and patriot), and when someone with KGB training tells you to do something, you generally listen. At least, I do.

Days later, Jack introduced Miri and me over email, and I dove into the usual social media 'research' to find out more about her, while we tried matching schedules to meet in person.

At that time, Miri's title on LinkedIn stated she was a Storyteller at Microsoft. After 25 years of writing stories, I was immediately intrigued. What a great title. And at Microsoft? I wasn't sure how those two worlds – tech and art – co-existed without some major marital issues.

Then, I met Miri.

We met in front of the Microsoft Visitor Center as designated. She had her Bosch headphones around her neck, a chic outfit that looked more appropriate for someone in fashion than in tech, and her tall stiletto heels impressed me to say the least. She called my name and rushed towards me with a huge smile on her face. I was immediately enveloped into a heartfelt embrace and into her energy and charisma. She's the type of person that makes you feel better than you felt before seeing her that day.

After a whirlwind tour of Building 92, we headed to lunch in the Commons. I was impressed by everything I saw on campus and felt drawn to the world of Microsoft, though mostly I was impressed by and felt an immediate connection with Miri herself. We laughed a lot, talked about our shared faith in God, and discussed our love for stories and how she was bringing them to life in the corporate world.

Over the next two years, Miri and I spent more time together, and I was able to attend several of her Storytelling workshops and keynotes. That's when I was able to see exactly how she was marrying art and tech in a way that could shape people, products and companies if they followed her advice.

I could see why she was such a sought-after speaker in locations all around the world.

I was also excited that Miri touched on an area that I've long felt passionate about, and that's to not follow the trend of 'platform building'. To create a platform, you are seeking to have a product or person, or company, stand above everyone else. Instead, Miri talked about embracing people in a brand through storytelling to build trust and a loyal connection. I loved how she emphasized linking humans to products and companies through stories, and how empathy is the core of that connection.

Now, as I've become part of the corporate world, I've discovered how much storytelling has become a buzz word and trend. At first, I loved this. As an author and writer, stories and storytelling have been a core part of my world for nearly three decades. I'm always asking how I can tell a story in the most compelling way to my particular audience (or readers), and how to best leave them with the most impactful takeaways. But in the corporate world, I discovered how often the words 'story' and 'storytelling' were being misused or misunderstood. People just weren't getting what a story is! While these topics are being talked about and taught in workshops, they're not often being used correctly or in an impactful way.

Meanwhile, Miri has become an amazing story evangelist, speaking around the globe and working hard to change these story abuses and perceptions. I was thrilled when she shared that she was writing a book to reach more people. After all, you can only impact so many on a stage. In book form, anyone can discover what storytelling is, its power to connect, how the craft should be used, iterated on, and how humans should be at the centre of brand development, always. She also provides innumerable tools to guide in the brand storytelling process.

I have a staple of writing and storytelling books I return to over and over again. Miri's book will be added to that small stack, and it should be added to yours.

So now, hear my voice as I emulate Jack's spy tone and say to you, 'You have to meet Miri!'

Just as I am, you will be grateful that you did.

Cindy Coloma

PREFACE

There are stories. Then there are great stories. A great story is one that reaches beyond the narrative, unsuspectingly grabbing you by the hand and immersing you into a newfound storyworld, never to bring you back again.

Are you a storyteller? Of course you are. We all are. At the cradle of our humanity lies the intrinsic cognitive ability to connect with other human beings through the most powerful medium that successfully influences our behaviours and decisions: story.

But, are you a good storyteller? *That* is the real question. We know a story is made of three basic elements: a character, plot and conclusion. In other words, you can say that if you are able to introduce these three elements to any type of content, it will inevitable become a story. However, does that make it a *good* story, or you a *good* storyteller?

We've all been exposed to dull, uninspiring narrative. Stories that pass us by inconsequentially and leave us at the same place where we started. Today's digital age – also known as the *information* age – has forged a modern path for the way we engage and connect with one another and with content. We are savvy consumers, parents, friends, siblings, children with access to an unprecedented plethora of information available at our fingertips – and now, voice command. We are driven by passion and enthusiasm to do something significant, purposeful; to leave a mark in the world. We have little or no time to waste on lifeless, useless content that provides no value to our lives or business. So why should we expect our customers to be any different?

In *Brand Storytelling* I want to offer practical tools to help you become a skilled brand storyteller, both at the personal and business levels. These narrative schemes have proven successful in turning *any* content into compassionate human experiences where stakeholders and audiences are inspired into action and where your allegory alchemy will turn *words into worlds*.

ACKNOWLEDGEMENTS

I will never be able to put into words the depth of gratitude and appreciation I have for every person who has in one way or another influenced, supported and inspired this epitome. This book is a result of countless hours spent not only writing, but sharing insights with incredibly smart industry experts, acquiring wisdom from extraordinary mentors offering guidance, celebrating small milestones with friends and family who have seen me through the entire process, and saying intimate prayers with my husband and sons on the days I felt I couldn't keep going.

I want to begin by acknowledging Jesus Christ, my Lord and Saviour who has given me the health, endurance, capability and a platform to share my lived experiences and knowledge with a worldwide audience. It is He who prepared a table before me, providing me with the ultimate direction of strengthening my empathy soft skill to become a human-driven communicator and servant to others.

Thank you to my husband, Luis. My eternal support and better half, who prepared rose and camomile hot teas on demand, coffee shots made of very specific beans at odd times in the mornings and ensured I was taken care of mentally and physically at all times. Thank you for keeping Team Rodriguez thriving and extending yourself to our house and the boys while I sat perpetually in front of the laptop. You are the cornerstone of our family. I love you.

A special thanks to my sons Alex and Isaiah for not only putting up with Mom being 'away' for a while but collaborating with me on this project. Alex, thank you for taking time to illustrate some of the concepts. You are a gifted artist. Isaiah, thank you for always letting me run ideas by you and offering insightful perspective. You are a great storyteller. Most of all, thank you both for inspiring me every day to find and tell better stories.

An equal amount of thankfulness goes to my sister, Eli, who spent countless hours letting me decompress from the day's demands, listening to my rants and worrying about my sleeplessness. Our FaceTime routine and your prayers saved me.

I also want to thank my mom and dad for believing in me, for bringing our family to the United States of America so we could make dreams like this one a reality. Thank you for your sacrifice. I hope you're proud.

My dear tribe of extended family, friends and mentors, you are my accomplices in all I do and have undoubtedly challenged, shaped and loved me into the person I am today. Thank you for being there for me all these years. I wouldn't be here without you. The list is long, but you know who you are.

I owe a deep gratitude to Microsoft Corporation. When I made the choice to join this company many years ago, I really had no idea how empowering and fulfilling it would be to me. Thank you to the leaders, including my immediate managers, who not only encouraged me to pursue my passions, but launched me on many platforms. Thank you to my colleagues from the different disciplines who spent time listening to, teaching and doing life with me. You are family.

I'd also like to thank Cindy Coloma for writing the stunning foreword as well as everyone who enthusiastically jumped in to collaborate in the midst of their very busy schedules.

Finally, a special thanks to the Kogan Page team, and specifically to my commissioning editors Lachean Humphreys and Charlotte Owen for having faith in me and in this project and supporting me to the end. Charlotte, thank you for reaching out to me and presenting the idea. You started it all.

Introduction

I was in London speaking at a marketing conference about the power of storytelling when a commissioning editor for Kogan Page publishing house introduced herself – along with the idea of me writing this book. I must admit, I wasn't immediately sold on this proposal. The opportunity couldn't have come at a worse time in my life. My mother was not doing too well. I had recently uprooted my immediate family three thousand miles from our home state of Florida to Seattle and was dedicating every ounce of personal extra time I could afford to relocation, personal matters, a new job and finishing my Master's degree. However, as often happens in life and against all logical reason, my heart stirred for a brief moment when standing in front of this opportunity, and began to whisper softly. It began to tell me a story about *you*.

My heart spoke about your struggles as a marketer and communicator and the many moments in your career that may have felt like wasted energy when you fervently tried to create and relay compelling messages that could inspire your internal and external audiences... yet you counted on minimal support or scarce resources. It painted the grim picture of your daily frustrations when trying to creatively incite other leaders or business partners within the organization to speak the language of empathy for the customer, while they brushed you away and remained focused on the product or the bottom line.

My heart went on to unapologetically expose the ugly battle scars I had collected over the past 20 years in the industry to poignantly remind me of the shortcomings and failures I had experienced in my quest to drive real human connection between my stakeholders. It then took out a life-size mirror and discerningly planted it between the commissioning editor and me to faithfully expose a truth I seemed to have forgotten: the reality that I was once you.

My dear reader, if anyone can understand the arduous (and often under-appreciated) unwinding journey that communicators and marketers have been forced to take within the past decade in attempts to successfully keep customers engaged and the brand thriving through the digital *chaos formation*; and if anyone can recognize the slightest pain points, mundane nuances and countless unseen *hats* the role of a marketer or communicator affords, it is yours truly.

You may not know me personally, but those who do can firmly attest that I do business with and lead with my heart. And it is that same heart that came up with the notion of me becoming vulnerable and empathetic – just as I lately invite others to do – to share my stories of failures, fears and learnings so that perhaps you will be saved from additional future heartache and feel empowered to fast track your marketing and messaging passions and inventions.

It is for you that I lost more sleep than I care to recount. And for you that my family made a significant sacrifice to put my *wife* and *mom* duties on hold for a while. Because I understand how hard it can be to navigate this uncharted landscape. And even more so when there is no one to guide you.

My hope is that this book will lead you beyond the practical storytelling tools and techniques instruction and wondrously rejuvenate your energy and passion for communication and marketing by offering a fresh hope grounded on ingenious, low-cost ideas birthed from your reawakened soul. Here's what you can look forward to.

In Chapter 1, you will begin to explore the basic elements and structure of story and the importance of giving your brand story a mission, so that you can purposely design it to reach a goal and target audience.

Chapter 2 takes you right into the design thinking approach and breaks down each of the five design thinking phases as you begin the fun journey of prototyping stories. You will also learn to define the brand story's *universal truth*.

Chapter 3 will take you on a magic carpet ride to a new mind palace: that of a story *designer*, not just a *teller*. You will learn some cool magic tricks that will sprinkle some pizazz into your narrative and elevate it a step further.

Imagination is the key in Chapter 4, where you will be able to reimagine a traditional integrated marketing plan by incorporating storytelling practices. Your brand story is now taking on a new force beyond content.

Chapter 5 digs deep into today's market trend nuances and makes a compelling case for putting your customer at the heart of your brand story.

Get ready to get a little uncomfortable. In Chapter 6 you will learn the importance of practising vulnerability in order to tell authentic stories. This might be my favourite chapter.

Chapter 7 makes an important case for drawing ethical boundaries as you uncover just how powerful storytelling is.

In Chapter 8 you will be delighted with futuristic storytelling ideas that will take your brand narrative to the next level.

Chapter 9 begs you to consider building a well-commissioned army of storytellers as you get ready to launch your stories.

Then in Chapter 10 you will learn the best techniques and ground rules to take your story to market.

In Chapter 11, you will understand how to define success when launching your story.

But we can't forget the story villains. We welcome them in Chapter 12.

In Chapter 13 the machines enter, and we have a *heart-to-heart* about what they will do to and for our stories.

And finally, in Chapter 14, I introduce a group of incredibly talented storyteller colleagues from around the world who generously share their own experiences and leave you with invaluable wisdom that will be sure to inspire your brand story.

I'm really excited about the opportunity to take you on this storytelling design journey and hope you will find this guide valuable, memorable and insightful. Just as great stories should be.

1

Brand storytelling

What is it?

- What is storytelling and what is not
- The power of storytelling
- Your brand mission and the story arc

Google 'Storytelling' and you'll find a plethora of definitions, videos, guides and how-to's on what has become the hottest marketing sensation since influencer marketing. I don't know about you, but the more hype the use of story for brand marketing seems to get lately, the more confusion it appears to create for industry leaders seeking to truly understand what it is. In the span of two years working directly in this field, I've seen it all: someone creating a PowerPoint presentation and calling it a story, someone else posting 'stories' on social media channels and calling it storytelling, and many others adding 'storyteller' to their business profile on LinkedIn but never having designed or told a business story before. I see brands scrambling to figure out how to effectively implement this messaging alchemy as part of their business forward strategy. And I see a lot of miscommunication happening across business disciplines, organizations and industries, all in the sacred name of story. But... why?

Simple: because the machines are here. And they're here to disrupt everything we've ever known about effective marketing and communication in business.

I'm an 80s kid. I know. Lucky.

I walked around with a Cabbage Patch Kid doll (official certificate included) in one hand and My First Barbie in the other. It would take a supernatural event for me to let go of these prized treasures. Toys of this kind only came by once in a rare moon for our humble family of five. Plus, as the middle child, I learned very early in life to take all I could and never take anything for granted.

As you're probably already foreseeing, that fateful, extraordinary event did come to pass one day. I'm not sure how or when exactly it appeared on our tiny apartment balcony (often used as an extension of our modest living area), but when I think back to this instant, I distinctively see me standing next to my father and in front of this clunky, shiny intruder, inspecting every ounce of its peculiar metallic parts.

'What is it?' I casually asked my dad, making a superheroic effort to contain my excitement and underplay my freak curiosity. 'It's a computer,' he casually responded. Recognizing that his short answer would inevitably provoke a hundred more questions, he went on without hesitation: 'I'm talking to it.'

My eyes widened as far as they were physically allowed. I was instantly filled with wonder and my brain went into overdrive to try to make sense of this hard-to-believe piece of information. I quickly became keenly aware that I was exhausting (or had probably already exhausted) my child–parent pertinent questions quota for the day, and though I did have another hundred questions, I resorted to asking one last, very important one: 'Does it talk back?'

Three decades later and an MS-DOS 2.0 command has turned to voice recognition. We have smart buildings, smart homes, smart cars and smart customers. Customers who know what they want and how they want it. Customers who search for online reviews and request peer input before even considering a product. And customers who continue adopting new technologies without hesitation and expecting brands to do the same so they can have a seamless buying experience.

A rambunctious era of connectivity with customers has been born, and brands all over the world are not only having to take notice but put in double time to stay afloat and meet the savvy customer demands. Whether an organization is currently leading the digital transformation or just getting started, this technological journey for companies has not only forced a shift in core business operations such as moving data from on-premises to the cloud, but compelled a realization that, fundamentally, there is a need to begin deconstructing and unlearning the way we have previously communicated with stakeholders and start to 'talk back' to our customers the way they faithfully expect us to.

Digital transformation undoubtedly made every brand reassess business operational values, but most importantly, cultural and communication ones. The birth of social media alone brought on the perennial headache for traditional marketing strategies as companies struggled and continue to struggle with the who, what, when and where of effective marketing over these nuanced, ever-changing channels.

With social media also came the deformalization of content. A gross disintegration, if you will, of what we once knew as 'business talk', which became profusely altered by new visual expressions such as emojis and memes. Enter live streaming, photography, video-type forms and, more recently, robots, and the world of communication from a business perspective was inherently revolutionized, never to be what it once was: a way for brands to share whatever information they wanted, however they wanted, whenever they wanted, with a little – OK, a lot of – help from PR and the media.

And millions of marketers and communicators around the world began to get rightly nervous.

This is where I found myself back in 2014 when I embarked on a new adventure at Microsoft, moving from the operations discipline to the customer service one to lead social media support channels in global English, Spanish and Portuguese languages. This was also around the same time that Microsoft's current chief executive officer, Satya Nadella, was appointed. Having joined Microsoft a couple of years before that, I was an alumna of the 'Ballmer Days' (when Steve Ballmer was CEO) and was able to detect a recognizable change in the atmosphere the day Nadella took charge, but at the time couldn't tell you exactly what it was.

On this historic day, employees all over the world tuned in to the live webcast if they weren't fortunate enough to be able to attend in person. On that fateful day, on the third floor of the Microsoft Latin America headquarters in Fort Lauderdale, Florida, a small group of friends and I organically gathered around a colleague's desk and, with much anticipation, we glued our eyes to the screen as Bill Gates, Microsoft's founder and Member of the Board of Directors, standing next to Steve Ballmer and Satya Nadella, spoke and shared the reason Nadella had been selected: it was because of his 'engineering skills, business vision, and the ability to bring people together'. Unstoppable cheering and luminous smiles often interrupted the ceremony as Softies (the nickname given to Microsoft employees) around the world, new and old, cheerfully celebrated what seemed to constitute a cathartic milestone for the company. Thinking back now, and with a few years spent in the craft of storytelling, I can pinpoint the distinctive smell that saturated the air that day. It was the sweet smell of empathy.

It wasn't much longer after taking charge before Nadella set out to rewrite the company mission. 'To empower every person and organization on the planet to achieve more' became the new Microsoft mantra and for every employee in the company, this became an immediate mandate to rethink how the evolution of the brand's mission would catapult across every single geographical sector, business discipline, partner, customer and employee of the brand. Although, at its core, the Microsoft brand story theme had always been the same (empowerment), their savvy, connected customers wanted more than to see themselves as the enabler of the brand's success story. They wanted to become a central part of it. Nadella knew this. And he also knew that evolving the mission unquestionably meant an evolution for the entire company. It is story, after all, that conjures emotion. And emotion induces action.

The power of storytelling

Before storytelling became an actual profession for me, I too was puzzled about the use of narrative as a tool for business impact. As a mother of teenagers and public speaker, I habitually used stories to capture and keep my very particular audience's attention. What's more, I had known of its magical elements way before I could even articulate why story worked so well with stakeholders. Its sorcery had infiltrated my fledgling brain long before I could consciously recall specific moments of it. My mother was – and to this day remains – one of the best storytellers in the Chronicle realm and her enchanting oratories transcended time and space so swiftly that the ones I can still recollect to this day vividly make me cry or laugh with the same force they had on me over 35 years ago.

I was fascinated with my mother's stories. Her imaginary accounts were invisible time machines that unsuspectedly transported me to fantastical and forbidden lands of giant creatures and warriors. A devout religious woman, my mother ensured my sisters and I memorized an astronomical amount of biblical scripture on a weekly basis. And so, we did. Because of story.

Research confirms that stories can be up to 22 times more memorable than other types of information. And this is but one of the many infallible benefits of narrative. Neurological studies have also shown that when we're exposed to stories the brain produces the following transmitters or hormones:

- dopamine, which contributes to feelings of pleasure and satisfaction as part of the reward system;
- cortisol, also known as the 'stress hormone', which creates an effect that predisposes the person to act (fight or flight);
- endorphins, which are responsible for our feelings of pleasure;
- oxytocin, known as the 'love hormone', a hormone and a neurotransmitter that is associated with empathy, trust, sexual activity and relationship-building.

Not only that, but our auditory, olfactory, visual, sensory and motor cortices are also activated the minute we evoke a *once upon a time*. This means that, if told well, a story can make the whole human brain wake up and immerse the audience in it, making them feel as if they were the actual protagonist or any other active character in the story.

As marketers, we know that consumers do not make rational decisions when they buy. They make emotional decisions and then rationalize them with logic. Storytelling allows us to digest and remember content more easily because it helps connect information with emotions in a way no other form of communication can.

Another alluring power of story is attention-keeping. Stories unleash neurochemicals, such as oxytocin and cortisol, which create physical tension, and help in keeping the audience's attention. Even when presenting dry or boring content such as numbers and data, if you strategically introduce a character, plot and conclusion to the content, you have a much better chance to entice your audience.

Stories are also great at influencing and transferring values. We see it in all respects of history and since the dawn of time. Stories have been used from the genesis of mankind to teach guiding principles and shape behaviours that irrefutably enabled our survival as a race.

These are all assurances about storytelling you probably already know. And even if you didn't, you can still personally attest that story just works for some reason. You know it does because you use it every day when organically communicating with your family members, friends, acquaintances and colleagues... but only outside business hours! As social creatures, story has been embedded in us as a cognitive communication tool and, instinctively, we leverage it to connect and engage with others. So then, why is it so hard to bring this efficacious mechanism onto the business side? Why doesn't it feel natural to deliver a business presentation in story form instead of through charts and graphs?

Here's where this book can help. Storytelling for branding takes you beyond the coherence of the *why* for 'once upon a time' and meticulously spells out the *how* through poignant storytelling design thinking principles and growth mindset techniques that will enable you to pierce though ancient traditional marketing ideals and fast track you to emerge as an innovation leader in your own space.

In this book, you will find methodology, illustrative lessons and pertinent examples that will warmly take your hand and walk you through the first steps of story prototyping all the way to implementation of storytelling as a foundation to your business approach. Be it for corporate or personal branding success, this epitome will serve as a practical manual to help you become a skilled storyteller and tell your story in a compelling way.

And I promise you'll have fun while at it, too. So let's begin.

Your brand mission and the story arc

Because stories are a natural component of the human experience, it makes perfect sense that we consider integrating them as part of the entire customer journey. This simply means that we must cease thinking of brand storytelling merely as a process of crafting and delivering a set of brand narratives and begin to recognize it as an influential source that can be harnessed to diligently map out the end-to-end customer journey, both internally and externally.

Today's connected customer is inadvertently weaving together every aspect of your brand as a rich tapestry of the brand story. An ad, an email, a meeting with a salesperson or a customer service representative. These are all part of the brand story in the customer's mind and if not designed intentionally to be cohesive, there's a great chance that you may lose the customer somewhere along their brand interaction trip.

To begin building the basic arc for your brand story, we ought to first take a look at its conventional opening: your brand mission. Your brand mission statement is the exposition piece of the basic story arc (Figure 1.1) and what sets in motion the rest of the story (the rising action, climax and conclusion).

As you know well, every brand's mission statement serves to manifest the purpose and intention of why the brand exists, and though from a design perspective it may seem logical to begin the brand storytelling adventure here, I'm often perplexed to find the number of individual and corporate brands nonchalantly choosing to bypass this crucial and foundational piece of the puzzle.

FIGURE 1.1   The classic story arc

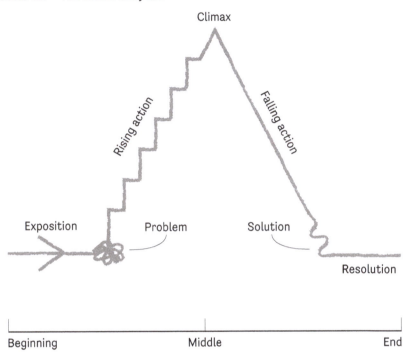

How can brands set out to write their story without incorporating their brand mission as part of it, or better yet, at the very outset? When I began teaching storytelling for branding, both at the corporate and the individual level, I realized that this is because people don't understand how the brand mission is the overarching *theme* of the story. You see, every story needs to have a goal, an intended reason for why the story is being told. Specifically, when it comes to brand storytelling, the main goal is to showcase to your audience why the brand exists (in essence, to elevate the brand statement of purpose). So as a first step, it is imperative you take a look at your company's brand mission statement and begin to decipher if and how it can be turned into the *once upon a time*.

As I said before, in my research and as a consultant it baffles me to learn how many brands, corporate and personal, big and small, do not even bother to align their brand mission to their storytelling. They treat them as separate entities without realizing the confusion this causes to their audiences.

The following is a prime example of a brand mission statement belonging to a world-renowned company which appears to be severely disconnected from their brand story. The brand name has been removed to properly illustrate the point.

> The mission of .... is to be one of the world's leading producers and providers of entertainment and information. Using our portfolio of brands to differentiate our content, services, and consumer products, we seek to develop the most creative, innovative and profitable entertainment experiences and related products in the world.

Can you guess what brand this is? Before I shock you with the answer, it's fitting to recognize that by simply swapping a few words here and there, this statement could really fit *any* brand. The mission statement is so broad and scattered that it's truly hard to deduce anything about why the brand exists, other than that it lives in the entertainment industry somewhere and wants to make money from its products and services. Admittedly, that is the ultimate goal for every brand. But as industry leads pioneering across the disruptive landscape of digital, we must recognize that mission statements (or brand stories' themes) like these are no longer effective when trying to reach internal and external audiences.

The mission statement above belongs to the The Walt Disney Company. (It was recently changed to something a bit more compelling but, nonetheless, equally non-spellbinding.) Many people erroneously attribute the statement 'to make people happy' to the Disney brand mission. However, this was never its official mission statement but a derivative of a quote from Walt Disney himself, who once said: 'My business is making people happy, especially children.'

It would make a lot of sense for 'to make people happy' to become Disney's mission statement. I presented Disney's actual mission statement, along with the 'happy' one, to my teenage son and asked him, if he had a choice, which company would he likely work for? There was no hesitation in his choosing of the 'make people happy' one because it immediately resonated in his heart. That is, his brain *lit up* at the sound of the word 'happy'. The statement spoke to a human emotion, which we can all understand. That is what I like to call a universal truth. A truth that we can all connect with, no matter our background, lived experiences, age or geographic location.

You may ask, why is this so important to consider? Especially for a brand like Disney which is an already-established leader in the market? The same reason why every brand should consider re-evaluating and ever-evolving their mission statement today: Millennials, Gen Z and the next generation after, plus robots.

With the rise of hyper-techy, always-connected and digital-friending consumer demographics comes a new set of challenges for brands: being meaningful to consumers. We keep hearing and reading all about it: in order to keep relevant today, brands can no longer afford to present only their products, services and who they are as a company. They must intend to connect and stay connected with their customers at the deep human level. What most brands fail to recognize is that this connection effort starts from within. It starts with reassessing why the company exists and how this reasoning permeates across the organization, igniting hearts and souls to continue driving it. It starts with the brand story.

Happiness. Empowerment. Inspiration. Embarrassment. Sadness. Loss. These are feelings we can all relate to as humans, and if a brand story can strategically drive these themes across its business functions, it will succeed in connecting and staying connected with its audiences.

Of course, in the case of Disney, there is no argument that the brand has been able to succeed in the market without a more emotionally driven mission statement. But the reality is that unlike most brands, Disney has thrived for over 90 years because it has been built on nostalgia, so its consumers are less prone to delve into the nuances of an impassive mission statement and the newer generations intuitively appreciate what the brand stands for at the organic level. In other words, my teenage boys are not googling Disney before deciding whether they want to go to a Disney park. They were introduced to the parks (and the brand) long before they had the opportunity to do what they do today: extensive research and peer feedback request prior to interaction.

Unless your brand has accomplished what Disney has, it's time to reassess the weight of your brand story against the demands of the market. Newer generations see brands as a potential extension of themselves. Whether for work or play, Millennials and Gen Z approach brands as 'individuals' and seek first to understand the 'why' before they make a choice to befriend and invest time and money in them. This is where brand storytelling can help.

Say you've taken that first step and looked at your brand mission statement or realized you don't even have one yet. What next? How can you get started without your 'once upon a time'?

Having helped a number of clients at different levels and types of organization, I realize there is a real struggle in taking that first step of developing

TABLE 1.1   Storytelling mission design template

Story topics
Who and what is this story about? Hint: this is where your brand mission statement goes. If you don't have one yet or the current one is outdated, simply write down why your brand products and services exist.

Story mission
What do you hope to accomplish by telling this story? Aside from your brand mission, the brand story also has a purpose. Similar to a marketing plan, here you explain the ultimate purpose of your brand story (ie, gain market share, brand recognition, rebranding purposes).

Brand attributes
List your brand guidelines (personality, archetype, tone, voice, slogan).

Key audiences
Who is this story for? You may have more than one audience.

Feelings
What feelings are you hoping to evoke from your audience with this story? Think briefly about how you want your audience to feel when they come in contact.

How can you make it believable?
Key points in the story to support your story message.

Tone and manner
The manner in which your story will conveyed.

the brand mission statement into a story theme. So, I developed a quick story mission brief that has proven helpful to me and I believe you too may find it useful.

The template in Table 1.1 on page 13 works for both personal and corporate brand storytelling and serves to gather the groundwork materials for your story arc. In other words, before you even begin to craft the story, this template will help you define the *what* and *why* that will become the main fabric in the narrative. We will delve deeper into each of these concepts in later chapters; but for now, the brief will provide a general visual of what brand storytelling looks like at the structural level, as long as you have a basic idea of what your brand stands for.

As you will note from this simple exercise, brand storytelling begins with your brand mission. This is the overarching theme of your story and any brand narrative told in any form should always tie back to this central theme. While we can't expect, or should hope, that every business discipline tells the same type of brand story (a marketer will tell a potential customer a different story from the one a salesperson will tell an established customer), if both the salesperson and marketer are embodying an unchanging story theme, the customer will always be able to recognize what the story is about, even if it's not explicitly revealed.

Let's dive a little deeper into the story mission brief to help you build the raw collateral you will need for your brand story.

Story topics

Your brand mission statement should be able to define *why* your brand exists as well as its core principles and values. These are the topics your story is going to highlight, especially the why, because the why gives your brand purpose beyond the product or service. Spend time listing the topics in your brand mission statement and this will help you map out storylines for the near future, when you're ready to start designing the narrative.

Story mission

Not to be confused with the brand mission, the story mission is the goal you want to give your story. Every story should have a mission of who you hope to reach with it and why. Are you hoping to inspire your audience to visit your website and learn more about your products? Are you looking to evangelize your product? As you learn more about story design, you will find that while there will be a main brand narrative, inevitably other mini-stories will be designed by your company's internal stakeholders who wish to serve their audiences. However, every story related to your brand should always tie back to the brand mission and the overall objective you have given the brand story.

BRAND ATTRIBUTES

It's important to list existing brand attributes in the brief to make sure you 'stay on brand' as you set out to design the brand story. Granted, you may also be leveraging this opportunity to complete a full rebrand of your brand. Either way, by listing your current brand's personality and other attributes on the brief, you can keep aligned to the brand identity and guarantee it is reflected in the narrative.

KEY AUDIENCES

In the story mission, you will likely list who the story is for. But this section is meant to get a little more specific about any and all audiences your brand has so that as you begin to design the narrative, you are mindful of these audiences. Don't spend too much time here, as we will do so in later chapters. Simply record what audiences come to your top-of-mind right at the moment.

FEELINGS

Notice the next story mission brief's record is feelings. What feeling are you looking to evoke in your audience? Again, we will spend more time learning about each of these notions further into the book and how to build them into the story design, but I believe it's noteworthy at this moment to begin thinking about the feelings you want your audience to feel because this will always be the key piece in good storytelling.

MAKE IT BELIEVABLE

The rest of the book will provide a detailed account of the very elements that make your story believable. However, just like feelings, it's good to take a few moments to ponder what assets, resources, elements you may already have in hand to support your story. Do you have customer testimonials at your disposal? Are there any case studies that speak to the feelings your brand story gives customers? These are great examples of copy points that can back up the narrative.

TONE AND MANNER

This is a very preliminary wish list of how you envision your brand story being delivered. Again, we will take a much deeper look into how to dress the story for launch once the fundamental structure has been designed. Nevertheless, listing initial ideas on the brief helps you visualize the direction you're seeking to take earlier in the process.

Taking but a few minutes to fill out the story mission brief can certainly get you thinking about what it takes to design a brand story and the intentionality behind it. And perhaps, help you avoid some of the challenges and bruises I experienced along the way, when this didn't exist for me.

My first three months as a Storyteller in Core Services Engineering and Operations at Microsoft were painfully terrible. With no engineering background, I was tasked to craft deeply technical stories about digital transformation for our IT professional, business decision makers and developer audiences that also needed to be personal and emotional in their essence so that we could reach a wider community. I failed miserably during my first few attempts.

Desperate, I decided to seek guidance from experts of all sorts, backgrounds and industries in the storytelling field (from CMOs to published authors, screenwriters and distinguished public speakers) associated with brands such as Microsoft, Hilton, Coca-Cola, Columbia University, Google and Disney.

In my quest to obtain a more profound assertion of story, I asked them all the same question: in your experience, what is and what is not storytelling?

As you will imagine, I received many different answers. Some were sort of expected, and others truly took me by surprise. I spent weeks mulling over these answers and categorizing them under three key areas: functionality, strategy and the human heart.

Storytelling serves all three of these areas distinctively and it's important to recognize how it does this, so it can be effectively applied to brand marketing. After working through categorization, I managed to summarize their answers in one statement.

> Storytelling is the emotional transfer of information (opinions, assertions, facts, data, ideas and arguments) through the introduction of a character, plot and conclusion.

I want to pause here for a moment and highlight once again that a good story serves to evoke emotion. Yes, technically we can write a story with just a character, a plot and a conclusion, and it will be constituted as such. But we're clearly on a quest to deliver compelling and memorable content. In order to make it such, the goal of your brand storytelling needs to always be driven by the emotions it can spark from your audience.

Now let's break down the three categories.

FUNCTIONALITY

We've established that a good story makes you feel something. Therefore, the primary purpose of story is to evoke emotion. As noted earlier, it is scientifically proven that introducing a character, plot and conclusion to any type of information will immediately activate parts of the brain that the information alone could never do. But taking it a step further, if you strategically focus on the feelings these elements can induce as the narrative unfolds, you will have a winning story in hand.

This is why it's crucial to nail down your brand story theme (the brand mission) from the get-go. If your current brand mission does not speak of a feeling that is universal, or that speaks to your audience in an all-inclusive way, it's time to revisit and change it. (I will explain what I mean by this in Chapter 2.)

Many of today's leading brands have already rewritten their mission statements in recognition of their need to adapt to the ever-evolving digital landscape – or the imminent *Robopocalypse*, as some are starting to call it. Here are a few good examples:

- **Nike:** To bring inspiration and innovation to every athlete. (If you have a body, you are an athlete.)
- **Coca-Cola:** To refresh the world in mind, body, and spirit. To inspire moments of optimism and happiness through our brands and actions.
- **Nestlé today:** Good Food, Good Life.
- Newer brands have had the chance to introduce their clever brand missions from the very beginning:
  - **Life is Good:** To spread the power of optimism.
  - **TED:** Spread ideas.
  - **Starbucks:** To inspire and nurture the human spirit – one person, one cup and one neighborhood at a time.

Notice that each of these statements holds within it a keyword, or what I like to call an underlying universal truth, which all of us can understand and feel. The functionality of storytelling is at work here because the theme of the story has been clearly defined.

STRATEGY

If we agree that storytelling is the emotional transfer of information, then we obviously need to understand how it can do this. In my definition of storytelling, I'm careful to mention that this is done via the basic elements of a story: character, plot and conclusion. Simply put: if it doesn't have all three of these, it is not considered a story. When thinking about how you are going to incorporate storytelling into your brand marketing, you must strategically define who the characters will be, what will happen to them as the story develops and what the conclusion, or end result, of the story will become. Just as the story theme (your brand mission), these three elements must be defined before even beginning to construct the story. This is why filling out the exposition brief can be very helpful.

HEART

As mentioned earlier, I was amazed to hear some of the unconventional answers I received from leaders in the storytelling craft. One of the most eye-opening responses was 'storytelling is not manipulation'. As the seasoned interviewee went on to explain: 'It is exactly because of its incredible power to persuade, that storytelling can be used to manipulate people.'

But wait, isn't that essentially what we *want* to do? The whole point of introducing storytelling into our brand marketing and communication strategy is so that we can showcase our brand as human, relevant, memorable and significant to stakeholders and ultimately persuade them to buy our products and services. Right? Sort of. Remember that the new generations are looking to attach themselves to a brand well beyond the product or service. At its core, storytelling intentionally displays the heart of the company (why it exists). Brands must be careful not to abuse this tool to confuse or deceive their constituents and should be able to back up their story with their actions. If the brand story speaks of empowerment, the brand's culture, products, services and customer experience must provide empowerment at all levels.

Therefore, storytelling for branding is much more than creating narratives that talk about the brand. It's carefully designing every aspect of the story to match it with the brand's core values and aspirations with deliberate intent to spark responsiveness.

But where to begin? Glad you asked. Come with me to Chapter 2 and I will explain.

2

Where do I start?

- The Robin to Batman effect in story
- Design thinking principles applied to storytelling
- Finding your story's universal truth
- Building the story structure

OK. You get it. Brand storytelling goes beyond 'telling stories'. It's the intentional design of a character, plot and conclusion coming together under your company's manifesto as the central theme to drive an emotional experience for your audience. By now you have probably completed the exposition brief to help you map out how these elements are going to come together, but that's just the story spine. The real work of dressing the story up with bells and whistles to successfully convey these ideas starts now.

To make a story exciting, you must employ narrative techniques that can help bring the brand story to life. At this point, you should have a good idea about who will be the characters in your story, what will happen to them (plot) and how the story will end to achieve its ultimate goal (conclusion).

A quick clarification point before we get into techniques: the story structure shouldn't be confused with storytelling techniques. Storytelling techniques are the methods that can be used to design a story, including details of how the story should look (ie how you might use visual elements such as a specific type form) and how it should go to market. Techniques can and should vary from time to time to adapt to your audience's needs. Example: if a new social media channel emerges, and your audience suddenly moves there, you will have to use a new storytelling technique to deliver the story to your audience in that particular channel.

The story structure is the foundation of the story, cemented in the elements we've been discussing so far (character, plot, conclusion, emotion, universal truth). These elements are non-negotiable when it comes to building your story, and while you might consider changing a character or twisting the plot, you should never remove character or plot as an element, as it will cease to be a story.

The Robin to Batman effect

Speaking of characters, I should point out that today's successful brands always seem to place their customer as the central character in the story. Going back to the Microsoft example, though empowerment had always been the brand's central theme, by switching the main character of the story from 'a PC' to 'every person and organization on the planet', Microsoft forced itself to live out that mission by diligently driving a customer-centric approach from the inside out. The result was inevitable: in 2018, the brand formerly known as 'a tech giant' in the industry earned the coveted title of Most Valuable Company in the World.

I like to call this the Robin to Batman effect. The brand takes on the role of sidekick in its own story, commissioning the customer to prosper with its help (product and services). The psychology behind making your customer the main character (and hero) in your story is simple: when the customer understands that your brand exists to make them better in one way or another and that you are positioning them to win, they become especially interested in winning. And when they win, you win.

I have dedicated a full chapter to making your customer the hero in your story, but before I go all *DC Comics* on you, I'd like to share the practical storytelling model that proverbially helped me break my first technical but emotional business story at Microsoft – and possibly helped saved my storytelling career.

Side note: I foretold this approach in Chapter 1 in the hope your storyteller skills picked up on it – did they?

I was completing my Master's degree for integrated marketing and communication when I took the role of storyteller. As luck would have it, the design thinking course was part of the curriculum and it required me to use a real-life challenge and design a solution for it.

'Could I prototype stories?' I asked my professor, secretly hoping for an affirmative response. 'You can prototype anything,' he responded matter-of-factly. And so I did.

I am sure many of you are familiar with the design thinking process. It's one that centres on empathy, seeks to understand the consumer, challenges assumptions and redefines problems to identify strategies and alternative solutions that may not be evident at first. As I delved deeper into the design thinking stages with my storytelling project, I was happy to find that it's not only possible to apply the design thinking concepts to storytelling, but that this is a great way to build the structure of a brand story.

Design thinking applied to storytelling

With this in mind, I'd like to walk you through each phase of design thinking for storytelling so you can begin your brand story design adventure (Figure 2.1). If you have it handy, the exposition brief will serve as a guiding tool.

Here we go!

FIGURE 2.1   Design thinking applied to storytelling

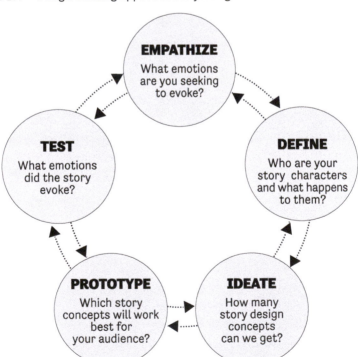

Phase 1 Empathize

The old adage by storytelling queen Maya Angelou couldn't be any truer: 'People will forget what you said, people will forget what you did, but people will never forget how you made them feel.'

The first stage in storytelling with design thinking principles is all about gaining an empathic understanding of your target audience in order to deliver a story that will make them have 'all the feels'.

In design thinking, this process begins by conducting research at many levels and in many forms with all stakeholders, including the design or target audience. The more research the better. Things like ethnographic observations, social media listening and pulse surveys are all great ways help gauge where the audience is and what type of narrative you should be telling them. Any research done with your stakeholders takes you one step closer to becoming more empathetic in your brand story, and empathy is the key that will unlock the human emotions you want to awaken in your audience.

Finding empathy in storytelling means understanding which needs the brand fulfils for the customer and, as a result, what feelings the brand story evokes. Think back to a wondrous moment when you first encountered a really good story. In your estimation, why was it so 'good'? Do you still consider it to be good today? Because of the master storyteller that my mother is, her stories continue to transcend space and time, no matter how old or cynical I get, because every one of her stories intentionally spoke to a universal truth, meaning they resonated with a feeling that reflected a core human need in me. As a young girl, I could never pinpoint or even articulate the foundations of this storytelling strategy; however, I knew very well how her stories made me feel, and that feeling is what I sought every single time I begged my mom to tell that story again. And again.

Finding your story's universal truth

American psychologist Abraham Maslow developed a theory based on fulfilling innate human needs. In his hierarchy of needs theory, we learn that humans have certain physiological, psychological and biological needs that seek to be fulfilled. When those needs are satisfied, we experience positive feelings. When the human needs are not met or satisfied, we experience negative ones.

Maslow explains that ideally, as an individual naturally grows and evolves, they will work their way up the needs pyramid. Chances are, however, that many of us have probably got stuck in one or two of the pyramid levels at one point or another in our life journey, and this means we have all experienced both positive and negative feelings. This makes us extremely capable of sympathizing, but better yet, empathizing with another person who has experienced the same feelings, even if the circumstances surrounding the events are completely different.

When I speak to live audiences about this notion, I often share old personal stories of embarrassment. It's very satisfying to see the crowd grimace with evident pain as a response to the mortification I've been subjected to at unfortunate times in my life. As soon as I'm done with the story, I bring them back to 'reality' where they have practically understood how to drive empathy through story.

This process is what I call 'finding the universal truth'. I introduced the term universal truth in Chapter 1 as a truth we can all connect with, regardless of background, age, gender, religious or political affiliation. In other words, a universal truth is an inclusive feeling that makes the story individually relatable to every person in your audience.

When I share my stories of embarrassment, I know there is a high probability that my entire audience will also experience feelings of embarrassment, because even though they may never have been through the exact same situation, they have presumably been through an embarrassing situation themselves at some time in their life and they inherently understand what it means to feel embarrassed. That makes embarrassment a universal truth.

> In this fiercely ambivalent digital era, only those brands that spend a considerable amount of time researching to truly understand which universal truth appeals best to their audience will remain competitive.

Please take the time to understand how your customers feel when they come in contact with your product or service and whether your brand story theme (mission statement) speaks to those feelings. Let's use an example to better understand how this process works, using the Prada brand.

As part of a group of luxury brands, Prada does not have a specific mission statement but does have a webpage dedicated to the brand history and identity, which provides certain keywords that help us identify why they exist as a brand, as highlighted below.

Since 1913, Prada has been synonymous with *cutting-edge style*. Its intellectual universe combines concept, structure and image through codes that go beyond trends. Its fashion transcends products, translating conceptuality into a universe that has become a benchmark to those who dare to challenge conventions, focusing on experimentation.

If we were to design the Prada brand story based on these key topics, we would first conduct extensive research to better understand how current Prada customers *feel* when they use their products. After gathering the research, we would then categorize these insights into human feelings in order to find the brand story's universal truth.

Let's hypothetically say research showed that satisfied Prada customers overall felt:

'classy'
'exclusive'
'powerful'
'happy'
'fashionable'

while unsatisfied customers felt the opposite:

'inelegant'
'inferior'
'unimportant'
'disappointed'
'unstylish'

These feelings help us understand what Prada customers are seeking to feel – and what they're not.

We learned earlier from the overall brand statement that Prada is committed to 'cutting-edge style, going beyond trends and transcending products' and that its target audience is 'those who dare to challenge conventions, focusing on experimentation'. We can agree that Prada's mission aligns well with the feelings their customers seek to have when they encounter the brand (ie cutting-edge style makes people feel 'fashionable' and transcending products make them feel 'powerful'), so the next step is to bring all these feelings into one universal truth which can be tested in the process.

When carefully analysing each of these feelings plus the mission of the brand and its target audience, several universal truths keeps resonating throughout, such as confidence, fearlessness and timelessness. One of these words should then be considered as the theme for the Prada story.

I realize this example showcases a well-established brand. If your brand has existed for a while, you probably already have some of this research in hand and can use it to determine your brand's universal truth. But don't skip this step and do take time to define your brand's universal truth as the foundation of the brand story. Without this empathetic approach, it will become much more difficult to design a successful narrative.

If your brand is just starting, this is a great time to conduct empathetic research and understand what your customers are feeling when you present them with your product or service.

After understanding and defining what feelings you want to evoke with your brand story, the next step is to define the characters and plot that will unfold them.

Phase 2 Define

This second phase focuses on defining the characters and plot of your brand story. By now you should have a good idea of what your brand story theme (brand mission statement), owing to the extensive research conducted in the empathy phase, the feelings you are looking to spark with your brand story.

During this phase, it is important to take time to draw up a list of characters for your brand story. There are main, secondary, stationary, dynamic, flat, static, observing, round and many other character possibilities in a story. Earnestly mapping out who or what moves the story along and how, where and when will bring much needed intention to how the plot develops.

When Microsoft decided to make their customer (every person and organization on the planet) the main character and hero of their brand story, they also set out to determine what that would mean to the character. Their brand character would be empowered through the brand's products and services to 'achieve more'. Because achievement can be subjective, four pillars of achievements were established, as shown in Figure 2.2.

Chief Storyteller Steve Clayton and his team also crafted and shared a little red book called *Once Upon a Time* to guide internal stakeholders on key elements to use when developing the brand story plot. For Microsoft, the brand story theme and universal truth is empowerment. It is the brand's mission 'to empower every person and organization on the planet to achieve more' and the feeling of empowerment can be universally felt and understood by everyone, no matter their demographic cohort or background. This little red book showcases the Microsoft brand story but also key pillars (or what they call the 5 Ps) that the brand wishes internal storytellers align to when telling the brand story. The five Ps are: people, place, pictures, personal, platform. Notice the first pillar is *people*. The brand is centring the story on the characters and reminding us that stories are about 'humans doing human things'.

Because achievement can be subjective, four pillars of achievements were established, as shown in Figure 2.2.

FIGURE 2.2   Microsoft's storytelling four pillars of achievement

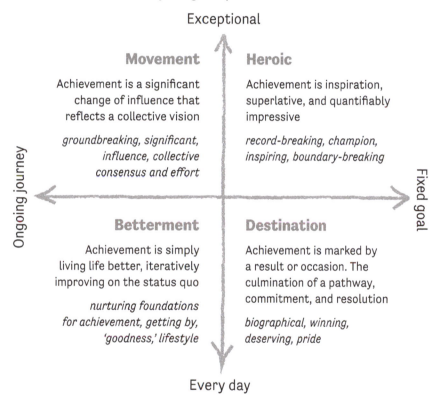

Thus, the plot of the Microsoft brand story became customers on a quest to achieve something great under any one of these categories with the help of Microsoft products.

Notice that the brand story plot is not necessarily stating the problem your product or service solves in the market, but the *conflict* the character is experiencing in the story and how this storyline is going to awaken those feelings we want our audience to connect to. Once again, empathy must be at play at every phase of brand storytelling design. And this phase is no exception. By spending time thinking about how your stakeholders want the story to unfold based on the feelings they want to feel, you gain better insights into how to best develop the plot.

Notwithstanding, designing the story plot is never easy, so to make this process a bit less challenging, I want to share with you another design template that has helped me strategically map out the story plot. As we have already been talking about Microsoft and you are now familiar with its brand story, I want to use it as an example, filling in the blanks with Microsoft's brand story information to illustrate how the template brings together the story plot.

Microsoft wants to *tell a story that showcases how Microsoft products make people feel empowered* (design goal), *can be told from a real person's perspective so it shows up authentic* (physical attributes) *and meets the customer need to: feel accomplished.*

You can now see how the brand story is beginning to take shape, and this gives you a better idea of what the story will be about and the direction it's going. For Microsoft, the story is headed in this direction:

- The story plot will showcase how Microsoft products make people *feel*.
- The story will not focus on the actual product or its features, but the *feeling* it brings to Microsoft customers.
- The story characters will be real people – not actors or influencers.
- The story characters will share their authentic stories of achievement and how they reached their goals because they were empowered by Microsoft products and services.

Great! We have a plot outline. But how does the plot actually develop within the narrative? What is the best way to reveal these characters, their journey of losses and ultimate wins in the brand story? Well, that will always depend on Microsoft's audience. And the same applies to you and your brand story.

It's important to recognize that there are many ways to tell a story and none of them are wrong – just different. Let's take a look at eight basic story structures, and as you get acquainted with them, think back to the exposition brief and the audience you listed there. Which story structure would resonate best with them?

> Remember, you want to take your audience through an unforgettable journey,
> so taking the time to assess what the journey will look like is a critical part of
> building the brand story.

There are many structures storytellers use to create different types of stories,
but here are eight of the most common ones.

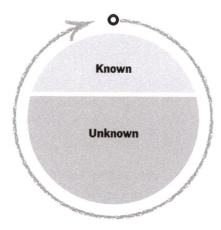

1   Monomyth

Also referred to as the Hero's Journey, this story model is probably the most popular
because we simply love heroes and their remarkable journeys. Many of our favourite
childhood stories as well as religious accounts have been built around this structure.
This story archetype introduces the character as someone who lives an ordinary life
but then through some unforeseen circumstance or conflict, they undergo a deep
personal transformation that brings a fresh perspective to them and those around
them.

In brand storytelling, this structure is often used to showcase the customer as
the hero as they share testimonials on how they were 'transformed' by the brand's
product or service. We are also seeing that brands are leveraging this approach internally to drive employee advocacy by turning employees into the heroes in their brand
story and giving them an open platform to share the 'transformation' they've
experienced while being part of the company.

At any rate, this model is very effective in inspiring audiences.

2   The Mountain

This story structure centres on building up the narrative conflict or tension to its high climatic point. Just as a mountain visually escalates in nature and then descends after reaching the summit, the plot in this story model exposes one challenge after the other, leading to a dramatic point and then to an equally sensational conclusion. In the Mountain structure, the ending of the story is not necessarily a happy one. Many people confuse this structure with the basic story arc because visually they look relatively the same. But the story arc, as shown in Chapter 1, is a general guidance on how stories should be crafted end-to-end. The Mountain structure, on the other hand, is an actual plot design that strategically and deliberately takes the audience through an intense experience immediately after the story begins.

This structure can be used to capture and keep your audience's attention in a very emotional way. Because it is intense in nature, it's important to measure how the story might land with your audience in the testing phase and be extra analytical of the responses you get when landing it to ensure it is successful as a technique.

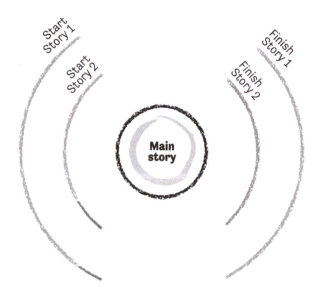

Start
Story 1

Start
Story 2

Finish
Story 1

Finish
Story 2

Main
story

3   Nested loops

In this storytelling technique, you build a number of narratives (loops) to finally arrive at the central story. This technique is practical for large corporations that have hybrid audiences because they can 'layer up' the brand narrative to eventually reach general audiences. At Microsoft, my team was able to use this model to accomplish the task of creating a technical story and matching it with one showcasing a personal angle in order to expand our audience base. In this case, we knew that our core audience (IT professionals, business decision makers and developers) wanted their content to be specific and not 'watered down'. They enjoyed reading technical white papers and case studies because this content delineated specific steps they were looking to employ within their own corporations. Clearly, we couldn't reach a general consumer audience with a white paper or case study, and of course, we did not want to take content away from our main audience. So we set out to create other narratives (or loops) that pointed to that main content. These other narratives were people-focused stories – stories about those engineers or team members who contributed to that specific task or project mentioned in the case study. But the narratives also served as stand-alone stories that highlighted a person or team and could be marketed all by themselves as feel-good stories. This proved to be a very successful tactic for us, directly contributing to significant increase in content consumption year over year.

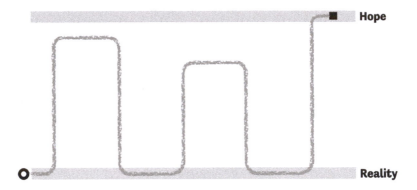

4   Sparklines

In this narrative, the audience is presented with a contrasting view of reality and utopian world and taken through a journey of 'what is' and 'what could be' to inspire the audience into action, often to help improve a specific situation. This structure is creative, dynamic and emotional in its essence and often used to draw attention to social activism, which we will speak about in later chapters.

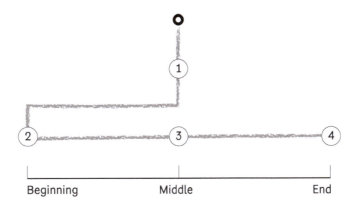

5   In medias res

From the Latin for 'into the middle of things'. This narrative begins in the middle of the action, often the climax of the story, to invoke a shocked reaction from the audience, and then loops around to give context to the story. This technique is very successful in capturing your audience's attention from the beginning, but you must be diligent in keeping their attention through the rest of the story by creatively bringing the beginning and conclusion together.

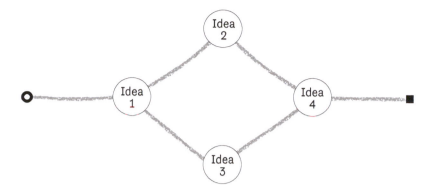

6   Converging ideas

Just as the name indicates, converging ideas is an amalgamation of different angles of a story that together unearth the story's main message. Similar to nested loops, converging ideas tells many stories (which may even seem disconnected if standing by themselves) that eventually come together cohesively. This technique is great for building stories from different areas or disciplines of a company. As we can't expect a finance lead to tell the same story as an operations analyst, both can build the brand story from their own angle, centred in the brand theme (mission) and showcasing the same universal truth. This allows for bigger and more diverse audience reach while at the same time keeping the story inclusive. In coming chapters, we will learn more about how to do this effectively with an integrated marketing plan... reimagined.

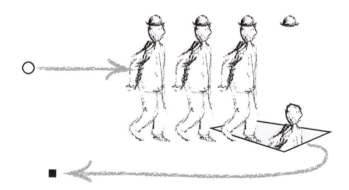

7   False start

This story technique is primarily used to show a flexible approach to a story and keep the audience wondering what's next. In this narrative, you begin by telling a story that can be easily foreshadowed (it's predictable in nature), giving the audience a false sense of control, before abruptly starting over with another narrative. This surprise element forces the audience to 'stay tuned' and pay close attention to the rest of the story.

8 Petals

Similar to converging ideas, this structure brings together other stories, but differs in that the stories are all connected by a central narrative. In this technique, each individual 'petal' culminates in the main or centre story. This technique is good for showing your audience how many interconnected stories can be told from one main narrative.

Thinking back to the stories that have had the most impact on you, can you identify which structures were used to tell them? A meaningful story lands well because it considers the audience's needs. While anyone can tell a story by introducing the basic elements of character, plot and conclusion, building an effective brand story structure intentionally contemplates how the storytelling will be received by the audience. Does your audience enjoy a sudden and explicit beginning? Do they rather see the whole story unfold first?

How can we tell what will work best? We don't really know, so the best way to move forward is by ideating story concepts (Phase 3 in the design thinking process).

Phase 3 Ideate

This is my favourite phase in storytelling design because it's the most creative. Now that you have a better idea of what storytelling is and what are the basic steps to begin building an effective brand story, and after you have done some research and defined the central theme, character and plot, you can have a lot of fun coming up with story concepts through brainstorming sessions that will help build the next steps in the story structure.

There are many creative ways to generate ideas for storytelling through activities such as sketching, mind-mapping, journey mapping and SWOT analysis, to name a few, but to ensure you conduct a truly dynamic and productive session every time, the following steps should be considered:

- **Establish and keep the goal for each session**. During brainstorming, it's very important not to deviate from the final goal: to find stories that resonate with your audience. Each brainstorming activity should be dynamic and creative, but if you fail to maintain controls around them, you may not reach the main goal and the sessions will become obsolete.

- **Establish the rules of the game**. To have a productive session, it's also critical that everyone understands the expectations and rules to play by during each brainstorming session. Whether there is a specific time to complete an activity or everyone is expected to share ideas without judgements at the end of an activity, game rules should be shared clearly every time.

- **Be diverse and inclusive**. The success of brainstorming comes from gathering groups of people with different lived experiences, personalities and talents who can contribute diverse opinions and skill sets during the sessions. Make sure that in every session you have a balanced and diverse team of contributors.

- **Inspire the team**. It's no secret: an inspired team generates more innovative ideas. Before engaging them in a brainstorming session, think about how you can inspire a creative environment through the introduction of games, foods, colours, art or activities that build an immersive and inspiring experience.

- **Choose your brainstorming tool**. As mentioned earlier, there are several brainstorming techniques you can choose from. My suggestion is that you conduct at least two separate sessions to get a good number of story ideas or concepts.

- **Remember that every story should tie back to the brand mission (story theme)**. While every idea should be considered when designing the brand story, always keep in mind that the central theme is your brand mission and if a story idea does not reflect the mission statement and universal truth of your brand, it should be explored a little further until it does.

There is no limit to how many brainstorming sessions you should have or how many story concepts should come out of each session, but the more concepts to explore the better, as you will begin to see some patterns that will guide the next step.

Phase 4 Prototyping

After conducting your brainstorming sessions, you should have a lot of innovative ideas to enable you to get started in prototyping your story concepts. Some of those ideas may even include the structures mentioned in the ideation phase, or various forms of story such as video, writing, drawings and even visual elements such as colour and typography, but this is not necessary at this stage as we're only looking to finalize the story structure. We already know that your brand mission is the theme of your brand story and that it must hold a universal truth that your audience can connect with. Through the prototyping process, you can begin to deduce what works, what doesn't, and why. The best part of this stage in story designing is that a prototype, by definition, is a low-cost, low-resolution idea coming to life and there is great flexibility in shaping stories this way, without spending too much time and too many resources.

A great way to prototype your story concepts is by using the 'napkin pitch' model. The idea of napkin pitch is simple: write the story concepts generated from brainstorming sessions on a napkin-sized, four-quadrant table that answers the questions in Table 2.1 to help determine if the story is viable.

After submitting each story idea to this process, you will have a better set of story concepts in your portfolio and should share them with your stakeholders (internal editorial team, partners, agencies and, if you can, current customers). When you present these story ideas to your stakeholders, listen intently to the feedback and, if available, observe closely their nonverbal cues. Are any of the story concepts being presented evoking the right type of feelings from your audience? Are the different stakeholders reacting the same way to the stories? Are any story concepts showing more promise than others? I once used this story-building technique for a millennial audience and was surprised to find that the story concept I thought would be least impactful turned out to be the one of greatest impact to the audience, and ultimately became the winning story.

Because storytelling is rooted in empathy, every part of the story creation process requires raw and unfiltered feedback from your stakeholders, especially during this phase. This enables you as content creator to design tailored narratives before spending large amounts of money on production and marketing. But most importantly, it serves as a North Star for your brand story to land best in the market.

TABLE 2.1   Napkin pitch model for story concepts

1. What is the central theme of this story?	2. What are the benefits to the stakeholders and what needs does it cover?
3. How can this story be executed?	4. What are the business reasons for telling this story?

Phase 5 Test

In the final stage of story designing, you get to test the story concepts that best resonated with your stakeholders. While you may have had the chance to include some customers in a feedback loop during the previous phase, at this stage you are now presenting the entire brand story to your entire audience, not just a few. Think of it as a soft launch project where you will get to evaluate what rings true with your audience at a larger scale. Just like in the prototyping phase, tools must be in place to capture and observe your audience's feedback and reaction. If you are planning for the story to launch on social media channels, be sure to have listening tools in place to gather metrics and sentiment. Remember that this is not a formal launch or rebrand, by any means, of your story. It is a test to see if you're on the right path to connecting with your audience in the best way possible. The beauty of this stage is that if the story does not land well, you can certainly go back to your other concepts, or even to holding new brainstorming sessions to generate more ideas. Chapter 10 will be dedicated to this phase and show you how to best launch your prototyped stories in the market.

Storytelling with design thinking principles is an art as much as a science and a good storyteller will diligently continue to iterate the brand story, recognizing that the act of perfecting it never really ends. Even when you think you may have arrived at a thrilling, meaningful and impactful brand narrative that speaks to a universal truth and excites your audience, given today's ever-changing digital world, you can't be sure this specific narrative will work years – or even months – from now. Always be ready to evolve your brand story, just as your customers do.

Now that you understand the principles of design thinking and how you can apply them to storytelling, let's take a deeper look at how you can sprinkle some magic on these story prototypes.

3

The magic (and magic tricks) in storytelling

- The story designer mindset
- Sprinkling elements and assets to enchant the story

I hope that, by now, you've started to put the design thinking principles for storytelling into practice and begun to build your brand story spine. It's now time to sprinkle a little magic on your narrative. While the design thinking approach is faithfully a tried-and-true methodology to help build a memorable brand story, there's always an open space to add a little more sparkle and make the story truly magical.

Earlier we learned that a story is not a story if it does not have a character, plot and conclusion as basic elements. We also learned that the story theme (brand mission) and its universal truth (relatable feeling it can evoke) are essential parts of a great story. But going from great to magical is another level of designing a narrative. It's the difference between becoming a storyteller and becoming a *master storyteller*. And it's also the difference between delivering a short-lived or a long-lived action-provoking narrative good enough to bait the audience.

Predictions about narrowing attentions spans continue, and by the time you've finished reading this book, we will probably have a ghastly new statistic in hand about people's inability to retain concentration for an adequate period of time.

This is why prototyping stories is a better storytelling strategy than the traditional prolonged, big-budget undertaking. If you spend too much time (and money) crafting a big production story, your most opportune moment to land the story, or worse yet, your most interested potential customer, may 'scroll by' long before the narrative is even ready to be shared.

Prototyping stories enables a quick, efficient and consistent way to produce and deliver content. However, most people legitimately fear their brand story may not be 'baked enough' when taking it to the market. And while this can be a reasonable concern, you must remember that brand storytelling is never-ending. The cycle of building your brand narrative at every customer touchpoint and through each transformative moment of the brand is arduous and continuous. You must get into the habit of designing for good. You must not think like a communicator but instead, like a designer. And you must act like one too.

> 'Design... is simply magic. It is an utter enigma, a mysterious no-man's-land where only the brave (and the brilliant) dare tread.'

In their book *Designing for Growth: A design thinking tool kit for managers*, authors Jeanne Liedtka, Tim Ogilvie and Rachel Brozenske democratize design from an exclusive innovative solutions plan reserved primarily and historically for creatives by proposing the idea that while many of us may not have extraordinary capability for aesthetics and visualization when building a product, all of us can learn to think like designers to deliver a better product than originally intended.

For a time at Microsoft, I was part of the Shared Service Engineering (SSE) Studio team which combined UX designers and storytellers as part of a broader group. This put me in close proximity to these often shy, enigmatic creatures we call designers. And I couldn't have been any happier.

I was elated about the idea of eventually getting to know these savants of user experience a little bit better and already had set a plan in motion not to miss this life opportunity. Every day, I would get up and walk past their visually chaotic – yet fascinating – mood boards, randomized sticky notes and mobile whiteboards filled with wondrous and complicated sketches. And each day, my curious mind would go into overdrive at the sheer sight of these concepts.

I will not confirm or deny that my relentless inquisitiveness about these designers and their designs may have been the very reason I pretended to crave a cookie or two from the snack bar that stood conveniently next to their workspace. But I will affirm that the advantageous adjacency inevitably and eventually invited conversation between us, and this is how, in due course of time, I met Gregory.

Gregory was your typical UX designer: a great communicator and story-teller, while at the same time highly analytical and endowed with engineering logic. Visual and strategic but also driven by empathy and creativity, he was veritably a *sensei* of his art.

On the outside, Gregory seemed like one of the most collected individuals I had ever met. He possessed a Yoda-like demeanour that made my daily meditation approach look frazzled and out of control. I later learned that my assumption was far from the truth. And it was the very essence of UX design that made him maniacal and somewhat obsessed with everything around him.

'It's how you look at things,' he once commented during one of our early unofficial morning meetups. 'As a designer, you're never satisfied because you're constantly looking at ways to improve something, anything, you come in contact with. So, your mind never rests. Most people will walk into a meeting room and simply find a chair to sit on. Designers will walk into the same room, look at the chair and the mind automatically begins to sketch ways in which the chair can be upgraded to provide a better experience to the user. Can it be made bigger? Softer? More usable in any way?'

Sounds impossibly wearisome, if you ask me. But also, absolutely necessary in our quest to put the customer at the heart of our stories.

The magic in brand story begins with getting maniacal, like Greg, about how the story can consistently provide an optimal experience to those who come in contact with it, but especially your audience. And this can only be done by applying the four core components of user experience, namely: usability, usefulness, emotional impact and meaningfulness.

I know what you may be thinking. Isn't this what we've already been doing so far with design thinking principles? To some extent, yes. But there is so much more that can be done with a story to elevate it in a way that it gets past being good to become exceptionally enchanting. There are colour and typography. There are pictures and space and texture. There are so many ways that we can sprinkle this magic to ensure our brand story is easy to consume, easy to apply and hard to forget.

A UX-designed story is filled with anticipation on how the user will interact with it in order to bring the structure elements (story mission, character, plot, conclusion, universal truth) to life in a meaningful way. The digital age has changed the landscape for everything marketing, enabling platforms, solutions and customer demands for something beyond words penned as a narrative. Latest trends in digital marketing lean towards artificial intelligence, chatbots, video and mixed reality integration. This tells us that customers are not just seeking, but insisting on, immersive experiences as they come in contact with the brand and on every touchpoint of the customer journey. As consumers, we know very well what this looks like.

I travel a lot for both business and leisure and find this to be a fertile breeding ground for all types of brand stories. As mentioned before, as consumers, everywhere we go, we're subconsciously weaving a narrative of the brands we come in contact with, based on the experiences they provide intentionally or unintentionally. I once took a ridiculously early morning flight from Seattle to Dallas on one of my favourite airlines: Alaska Airlines. Compared to other carriers, I have come to appreciate Alaska's devotion to their commitment of keeping a caring spirit with customers. On this particular morning, we departed from Sea-Tac airport shortly after 5 am and, like many other passengers, I quickly rested my head and closed my eyes in hopes of finishing my interrupted sleep from the short-lived evening before. But it wasn't too soon after I began to doze off that the captain came on the public address system to disrupt my slumber. 'I know it's very early, folks, and I'm truly sorry to interrupt your nap, but I would be remiss if I don't share with you the majestic sight of Mount Rainier as the sun rises above it. If you're seated on the left side of the Airbus, I highly recommend you open your window to take in this moment.'

Sure enough, I was seated on the left side and wasted no time in popping open the small aperture to display the certainly monumental sight. And there it was. Glistening with overloads of fresh snow flurries, all 14,000 feet of stratovolcanic eminence came at me in 3D like a pointed missile, surrounded by remarkable blended luminosity of purples, blues and pinks. The vision was so clear from my vantage point that I could contemplate every ridge, big and small, surrounding this giant pyramid, and I was stunned at the grandeur of it all. I've been lucky to see beautiful sunrises and sunsets in some dazzling places, from Swaziland and Israel to Iceland. But this, this was something I had never experienced before. Hanging 30,000 feet in the air, the sun had not yet caught up with our altitude and with every passing nanosecond, I observed the fast rotation of our blue planet as the sun raced to meet to us.

I was as thankful for as I was stupefied by the experience. Beyond that, I appreciated being woken up in the name of not missing this exclusive moment because an Alaska Airlines pilot cared enough to make sure I didn't. He obviously could have taken in the sights all by himself, but was mindful about the rarity of this occasion and generous enough to share it.

My gratefulness immediately showed when I posted one of the dozens of photos I captured on social media, tagging it, of course, with Alaska Airlines' hashtag #iFlyAlaska. It's also valid to mention that the only audible expressions coming from all of us on that aeroplane were gasps, not sighs (not one person complained at having been nudged to attest such experience).

This is brand storytelling at its finest. It is clear that Alaska Airlines has set rules to turn their mission ('caring for our customers, our communities, our environment, and each other') into an immersive user experience, giving their content meaning and leveraging practical, not theoretical, considerations to make the story come alive.

With this in mind, I'd like to share four magic effects (or tricks) that can rev up your brand story into action and make it as enchanting and unforgettable as my Mount Rainier twinkle.

Magic trick 1: Don't just define your story setting. Find it

While character, plot and conclusion are necessary to building a basic story, a magical element in storytelling is defining the time and place where the story takes place. However, most storytelling guidance will tell you that setting is only the geographic location and instance that influences the narrative, without considering the remarkable potential that exists in deliberately finding moments and locations that drive user interaction far and wide through every part of the customer journey, where the story can come alive like my Mount Rainier moment.

Finding the setting in the story is all about exploring the many landscapes and ways the story can unfold, based on the changing market, evolving customer and emerging technologies. It's what Rex Hartson and Pardha Pyla in *The UX Book* like to call 'the changing concept of interaction' or the acknowledgement that to users, interaction with a product (in this case, the brand story) is purposeful and they get to decide what that purpose might be after all.

In the context of storytelling, the story is the product and while we may spend time crafting the narrative based on what we believe will land best with our audiences, at the time of delivery the audience will be the one to determine how they want to interact with it and the purpose it has in their individual user experience. Therefore, it behoves the storyteller to find as many backdrops and moods as possible where the story can land.

In business, this can best be done by exploring internal disciplines, culture activation efforts, product or services launches and any other business growth endeavours where customers organically find themselves and the story can be told from. Finding the story setting is having a deep and empathetic understanding about where the customer is, where they are going and when, and crafting the setting around them instead of begging them to meet your story in an established setting they may not be able to relate to. It's what makes the story useful in the user experience approach or what makes it click in the customer's mind once they've learned the theory behind it.

Remember, the usefulness of a product is determined by the user. Therefore, the more places you are able to deliver the story, the better chance your story has to magically make its way into your customer's heart.

Let's take my Alaska Airlines experience as an example of how this particular brand not only defines but finds the setting to deliver a spellbinding narrative. At a high level and based on their brand mission, we know that their brand story centres on customers and the environment (these are the main characters) and that caring is their universal truth. By default, we understand that their story takes place within the air transportation industry during a time when air travel is internationally accepted as a standard means of commuting (market setting). But their commitment to make their mission and story come alive compels them to carefully map out every clock time, calendar time, seasonal time and geographical location in which their brand story has a chance to develop. In other words, they don't just institute a 'once upon a time' for their brand story but everything is calculated to live out the brand story given every opportunity they get. The call from one of its narrators (the pilot) to 'look at the mountain' at a specific moment in time while the audience was physically within reach served as the perfect reminder of what the brand stands for: caring for people and the environment.

Can you see how defining and finding the setting differ? Finding the setting is a continuous approach to making your brand story come alive in as many places and moments as it has the chance to. It is a business strategy to tell the story over and over to multiple audiences in many places and on every occasion possible.

Aside from external environments, I called out internal disciplines as another dynamic setting where the story can and should take place.

Earlier in the book, I mentioned that the brand story won't be told the same way from a salesperson's perspective and from a customer service representative's perspective. And it shouldn't. Each 'narrator' is telling the story from their own space and perception, and the audience is experiencing the brand story from many angles throughout their journey and touchpoints with the brand. This should be considered as part of the delivery strategy by using the converging ideas techniques listed in Chapter 2 and also intention-ally mapping out the different settings within the business where the story is going to be told from.

In the next chapter, we will dive deeper into this concept by learning how to use storytelling as the blueprint of an integrated marketing plan. But for now, I just want you to recognize that internal disciplines are one of the best places to find a story setting.

Magic trick 2: Visual elements are not a nice-to-have; they are a must-have

Now more than ever, the visual identity of a brand story, such as logo, colour, typography, photography and symbols, is critical to how audiences holistically interpret the brand story. Gone are the days when a brand logo or slogan could tell a separate story from its mission and overall business approach without confusing the audience. Digital technologies and plat-forms have spawned the unification of brand storytelling and customers expect stories to be congruent and consolidated on and offline. No, the customer will never stop methodically weaving every part of the brand story every time they come in contact with it, be it through an email, the product or a person who works for the brand. Considering the cognitive processes (or how our individual brains process visual communication) is another enthralling way that brands can design a powerful story. Therefore, take time to explore each of these elements and ask yourself: do they individually and holistically tell my brand story? If a customer comes in contact with my brand logo, symbol, tweet, are they able to identify the story's underlying universal truth? If the answer is no or you are not sure, it's time to re-evaluate each of these elements and strategically incorporate them as part of your story.

Consider the psychological and physiological effects of colour. We live in a world of colour and can appreciate how colour impacts our experiences and influences thoughts. Studies reveal that certain colours can help us remember information, while others can increase our blood pressure. Both of these are simple examples of the undeniable effects this visual element can have.

Match it with a compelling narrative, and you have a powerful storytell-ing force in your hands.

I had the pleasure of sitting through a storytelling session hosted at Microsoft and led by Disney Animation Studios film producer Don Hahn, who is credited with *Beauty And The Beast* and *The Lion King*. While there were many takeaways from his talk, the one that I found most compelling and also practical was how Disney uses colour to guide the audience through the storytelling experience to evoke emotion. They are so deliberate in integrating this magic ingredient as part of their story deliverable that every one of their films is displayed frame by frame to showcase the colour schemes and relationship between them. '…Throughout most of the narrative we use cool colours, but look here,' Hahn explained, and during his talk he pointed to the scene in *The Lion King* where Simba the Lion King fights Scar (his uncle and usurper of the throne). Warm colours are consistently shown in these frames to arouse the audience's mood and stimulate emotion.

If our goal as storytellers is to evoke the right emotions from our audience and we understand that the user experience is subjective, it makes sense to deliberately take as much control of the experience as possible by integrating these visual elements of story that are sure to drive a psychological effect.

Typography is another story element most people tend to take for granted. But as a visual representation of language, type form and anatomy are also an integral part of how the brand story is told. Everything from the type size to the case can impact the effects of the brand story. Just like colour and the rest of the visual elements, typography should be strategically interspersed as part of the story architecture.

In brand storytelling, you will choose which form is best to deliver your stories based on the research you've conducted in the empathy phase of design thinking, always thinking about how these elements will best land with your intended audience. Will your story be a video, a blog, an article? That will completely depend on what your audience wants, but in every case, if it is in written form, you should consider typography as an important element of the story.

> *Typography is the detail and the presentation of a story. It represents the voice of an atmosphere, or historical setting of some kind. It can do a lot of things.*
>
> Cyrus Highsmith

For written-form narrative, typography is the 'first impression' the story makes and the consequence of this, just as with any first impression, is that it defines the success of keeping the audience's attention through the rest of the story.

Another important effect that typography will have on your readers will be comprehension. The Gestalt theory, introduced in the 1920s by a group of psychologists, is a theory that concentrates on human senses and proposes that the mind perceives objects not individually but as part of a bigger idea. Gestalt is a German word for 'shape' or 'form' and the theory believes that the human brain is holistic, therefore it tends to group objects (in the case of written storytelling, shapes and words) to draw a clearer conclusion of the whole story. This means that even before your audience has finished reading the story, how you choose to display it in written form will guide their decision on whether they want to continue reading it or not.

Once again, this goes back to the components of user experience. Visual elements like colour, typography and photography help generate the emotional responses you seek in order to make the story meaningful to the user.

When I was designing stories about digital transformation, we learned that our audience still found value and expected us to deliver written technical stories (particularly white papers and case studies) because to them, this content was fundamentally used as a how-to manual within their own space.

However, through testing, we also learned that our design audience wanted and enjoyed personal stories (blogs) about engineers in the company who were exposed to the daunting task, tension and challenges driving the digital transformation for Microsoft. Through even more empathetic research, we also found that these personal accounts were most compelling and relatable to the audience when told from a first-person point of view.

This new way of telling stories was something we had not done before (in the engineering space), and as we began experimenting with these new designs, we resorted to the traditional branded stock photos to complement our initial stories, soon realizing that these general images were anything but complementary and actually served as counter-effective when visually served.

It wasn't much longer after some of these written stories flopped that we went back to the drawing board and decided to take photos of those actual people to dress up the story. I know this sounds like a logical thing to do from a storytelling standpoint, but for an engineering organization where developers typically don't tell stories and are anything but willing to be showcased as main characters of them, it didn't initially seem sensible.

I share this story with you because when it comes to brand storytelling, you have to get past the established business norms and perhaps do something that may seem counterintuitive in order to effectively integrate the visual elements the story deserves. Make it a rule to explore every creative avenue of visual components in your storytelling and watch your brand narrative spark with magic!

Magic trick 3: Shape your brand assets to help you tell the story

The set of unique elements that make up your brand, such as its logo, typeface, slogans, voice and tone, is undoubtedly another crucial way your customers come to know your brand story. It's important to evaluate the current perception these assets have in the market and whether there is any opportunity to modernize how the brand shows up to tell the story in the most compelling way. It is not enough to revamp a brand mission, define the brand universal truth, craft the story structure, map out the settings and apply visual elements to it. If the brand identity itself is not 'living out' the story in the market, you will have a hard time landing the story with your audiences. To shape your brand assets means to strategically frame these elements so that, aligned to the story, the customer will feel an emotional association to your brand. Many organizations may want to call this a 'rebrand'. I wouldn't necessarily think of it this way. Shaping your brand assets does not constitute a fundamental change of brand elements, but instead, it is a thoughtful shift of how already-existing assets can be successfully integrated as part of your new narrative.

A good example of this is the how MasterCard leveraged their emotive 'Priceless' marketing tagline that has served them successfully for the past 20 years. This brand asset eventually became the theme of their brand story. In recognition of the changing markets, MasterCard chose to shape their long-standing slogan by taking their Priceless tagline from a storytelling theme into a call to action that they recently called 'storymaking'.

The new MasterCard campaigns are now focused on how the brand is turning Priceless into categories such as 'priceless surprises', which gives customers unexpected experiences, and 'priceless causes', which generate donations to chosen charities. Essentially, this original marketing catch phrase evolved into the brand mission to create a new set of customer immersive experiences – and stories.

Think about existing assets your brand has today and how well they may align to the brand and brand story mission you're designing. If you look intently, you might find a vault of immeasurably enchanting treasures that you might be able to sprinkle from different places onto your brand narrative to help elevate the story in the market.

There are plenty of ways to think about how existing brand elements can complement the brand story. Or even the other way around. Remember the design template in Chapter 1? There's a reason you listed the brand attributes that early into the process. A magical story will take what already exists and seek to naturally blend the personality of the brand into the narrative. If the story feels too far away from established brand assets, it may not be reflective of the brand. Keep in mind that the brand story serves to showcase the brand's mission, values and behaviours, so it should never feel disconnected from the brand's core assets.

A good way to ensure you're keeping honest and staying aligned to your brand assets as you develop the story is by asking yourself at many points during the design process: 'Does this storyline *look and feel* like the brand?' In other words, if you were to test that story concept in the market without manifesting the brand name, would your stakeholders still be able to recognize it and link it back to your brand?

I consider myself a foodie... of the worst kind. My husband is a private chef and so I have the privilege of feasting on glorious organic and delectable seasonal dishes – almost on a daily basis. Yes, it's OK to be jealous.

This is both a blessing and a curse, because it has become almost impossible for me to find outside eateries that can even aspire to match my husband's culinary gift to satisfy my very entitled palate. On occasion, we will find a great restaurant that offers the gastronomic experience we're looking for and, as a result, we become very loyal customers.

A trendy new restaurant opened up on the east side of Kirkland, Washington, a quaint little town located a few miles north of Seattle. Sure enough, we made it a point to go and try it out. As we entered the venue, my husband quickly noticed that there was a familiar *feel* to the place. As we were seated to our table and the server came to take our drink orders, my husband couldn't help himself and asked if this restaurant had any connection to another one we tend to frequent on the west side. Neither the restaurant name nor even the menu had any resemblance to the other eatery, but sure enough, the server confirmed that it was the same owners and even the server himself took turns to work at the other restaurant. What gave it away was the way the tables were set, the bakery stand in the corner, the visual clues that we could have been 'there' once before.

What a flawless example of how brand assets evoke feelings, just as the story does. And in their own way, *tell* the brand story. If you take time to creatively blend these elements, you will see your brand story thrive.

Magic trick 4: Keep your conclusion inconclusive

Oxymoronic, right? Not really. The best stories are made of conclusions that are semi-ambiguous in nature. In other words, they let the audience draw their own conclusion. This is not to be confused with the story theme. We have already established that the theme of the story is the brand mission. As previously noted, the story theme should be conspicuously played out through every part of the narrative, leaving no room for interpretation. But an entrancing story is one that gifts the audience with the power to deduct their own learnings. It doesn't put a threshold on what should be felt or cultivated from its universal truth. Think of the best storytelling in Hollywood – movies that have simply left you stupefied and forced you to engage in discussion with fellow moviegoers about their ending. Most recently, Marvel Comics has distinguished itself as an irresistible and creative storytelling force by leaving stories inconclusive and allowing the audience to use their imagination on what may or may not have happened. Inconclusive conclusions also tell your audience that your story is 'not finished yet', meaning you continue to move forward and evolve as a brand and there is much more that they should be anticipating in the future. How can you best do this? By not forcing the story lessons every time you tell the brand story through obvious mention of your universal truth. In other words, keep a little mystery as part of your brand story and let your audience methodically unwrap its universal truth as a magnificent favour.

A brand that has done a great job at riddling narrative is Airbnb. Their mission: to make people around the world feel like they could 'belong anywhere'. Their universal truth is belonging, but instead of directly talking about how their services make people feel like they belong, they collect visual travel stories from customers all over the world and categorize them by experiences such as 'escaping the crowds' and 'big city living'. The stories are inconclusive in that they don't directly speak of belonging per se, but the user-generated content clearly showcases this feeling time and time again through raw and untouched narrative from satisfied customers.

As you may be starting to appreciate, storytelling is a verb. A perpetual scheming of bringing elements, techniques and rules together to keep your audience connected, excited and inspired about the brand through narrative. But once we've determined the best way to structure the brand story, how can we practically integrate it as part of the marketing mix?

The next chapter will show how to build an integrated marketing plan with brand story.

4

IMC Reimagined

Building an integrated marketing plan with story

- Reimagining the brand story message
- Incorporating brand storytelling into your IMC plan

As professional brand strategists and communicators, we understand the value and results of crafting a well-rounded integrated marketing plan. But perhaps we haven't realized that this unification approach should centre around the brand story for unequivocal success. If we are able to secure the brand narrative first, it becomes a lot easier to consistently tell the story across multiple channels, through different tools, activities and processes.

Yet most brands continue to struggle to do this, and that is because traditionally, we've been thinking about the brand story from a static character perspective: the brand mission is written once, the story is crafted once and the character is developed once, if indeed the story and character have been established at all. Most brands have spent time and resources defining their brand elements, which make up the attributes of the story character, but have forgotten that storytelling is a verb. Meaning, the process of telling your brand story is never-ending and the story must continue to unfold from different angles, different places and from a modern narrative approach. Storytelling is an active business model where brand elements continue to evolve along with the brand's own diversification in the marketplace.

Allowing the brand character to evolve, to grow and transform within the brand story is the most compelling part of integrated marketing because it enables an authentic flow of the marketing plan to find its natural and distinctive competitive edge. Have you ever tried launching an integrated marketing campaign that just feels unnaturally rigid? Elements of the campaign appear as square pegs trying to fit into round holes and every person involved in the process is clearly frustrated with it? What's worse, the elements of the marketing plan seem disconnected and distant from one another. This is because they lack application of the storytelling 'glue' to it, which is what brings the message together, and inescapably makes it an integrated plan.

Conversely, some brands will launch an individual flashy marketing campaign, without incorporating the brand story, and it inevitably becomes short-lived. I've seen it one too many times: a brand spends an exuberant amount of funds and resources on one strategic and brilliant campaign. It lands well. It produces immediate results, only to be instantaneously replaced by the next best ad from a competitor. Or worse, they have now set such high standards in the marketplace that they find themselves having to 'up their own ante' and compete against themselves to deliver a more extravagant advert than its precursor. As a result, brands find themselves trapped in a vicious and strenuous cycle of upscaling their marketing campaigns (often with receding budgets), while their customers are also spinning their wheels between feeling inconsistently inspired by these ads but soon forgetting exactly why they truly love the brand.

I'm in no way trying to diminish the potential effectiveness of a single, well-crafted marketing ad or campaign. There certainly is value and importance in these individual go-to-market strategies. But as mentioned before, newer generations are seeking continuity from a brand. They are no longer impressed by one or two inspirational segments showcasing how grandiose the brand may be or what it can offer. Furthermore, we must consider that these stand-alone campaigns also run the risk of lurching so far from the brand's established mission and story that they have the potential of facing strong backlash from their audiences.

Introducing storytelling to an integrated marketing plan looks a bit different from one-off minute campaigns because story takes on an internal approach first, before going to market.

A basic integrated marketing plan consists of five elemental steps:

1 Crafting the message
2 Setting your goals
3 Identifying your target audience
4 Selecting the channels
5 Measuring success

Incorporating brand storytelling into your IMC plan

Notice that the first step in the plan is always determining the marketing and communication message we are looking to land with our audiences. Incorporating brand storytelling into this process is an intentional step to empathetically aggregate the brand theme and story as part of the overall message in order to adequately and consistently establish the brand narrative your customers have come to know and love over time. It's what British advertising tycoon David Ogilvy called the Big Idea, or 'stepping back' and looking at what makes an idea (or in this case, a brand story) big. Ogilvy strongly believed that open-ended and intuitive thinking infallibly led to transforming the language of a brand message, because this 'no assumptions' approach helps make an emotional connection with customers that resonates, is meaningful and can universally be communicated across all media platforms. Sound familiar?

> You will never win fame and fortune unless you invent big ideas. It takes a big idea to attract the attention of consumers and get them to buy your product. Unless your advertising contains a big idea, it will pass like a ship in the night.
>
> David Ogilvy

Ogilvy's Big Idea is what I call that universal truth in brand storytelling. Imagine how many ships have passed in our own brand's port because we've discounted this right-brain judgement approach when strategizing marketing plans! The Big Idea is about saying 'yes, and?' instead of 'no, but' as you craft your brand message. It allows the brand message to find unexpected paths and perhaps even set a different course from the one originally thought of, even if at first it makes no sense.

An example of this is brands tackling social issues as part of their message and brand story today. I conducted a four-month non-obvious trend report using Rohit Bhargava's Haystack curation method to showcase this new phenomenon in marketing: the relationship between brands and social justice. As brands take on a more 'humanized' approach to marketing for more effective consumer connections to emotionally appellant generations (Millennials and Gen Z), brands are faced with the inevitable question: do they have a voice and should they use it?

From an integrated marketing plan standpoint, it would make no sense for traditional marketers to immediately consider this rising trend as part of their brand message. It's way too risky. And it feels uncomfortably unneces-sary. As it did when thinking about going out to market on social media channels at the turn of the millennium, or using email in the early 1990s.

But storytelling and the Big Idea force us to think with a growth mindset because embodying the brand story in every marketing plan message inevi-tably makes us reflect on how pervasively the brand core values are being showcased in every message. When incorporating storytelling into an integrated marketing plan, we indubitably have to ask ourselves: does this message truly reflect the overall brand story?

As mentioned before, the smart customer is looking to emotionally con-nect with the brand and wants to be reminded on a daily basis why they love the brand so much. Why they chose it to be their friend or make it part of their everyday life. A lack of consistency in marketing efforts or a message that is too far-fetched from the brand mission can do more harm to a brand than if no marketing was done at all.

It's the same psychology we use in our personal relationships. Ever have a friend, or better yet a frenemy, who once posed as a friend that always threw mixed or inconsistent messages at you and you couldn't quite figure out what they were about, or decide if you should really be friends at all?

I was in my early adolescent years when I met Angela.* She lived in the same apartment complex as I did, and thanks to no computers, internet or video games readily available for entertainment, I was blessed to spend my summers outside inventing all kinds of games and getting into occasional mischief with other neighbourhood kids, and this included Angela.

Angela was pretty. Not girl-next-door pretty, more like Scarlett Johansson pretty. I can't remember exactly how we met, but I do remember we became inseparable from the moment we did. But it wasn't too soon after I lovingly asked her to become one of my 'BFFs' (that was a thing back then, you know? I mean it really solidified the friendship for eternity and beyond) that I became the unfortunate recipient of her inconsistent messaging. Some days, we would lie on the grass, observing the big blue Florida sky parade cumulonimbus clouds packed with daily afternoon thunderstorms, and together fantasized about future boyfriends and wedding days. Other days, she would randomly tell a 'joke' in ways that left me completely confused about the fortitude of our friendship.

*Some names and identifying details have been changed to protect the privacy of individuals.

'You know that saying, "I got your back"?' my rivalrous companion would suddenly utter. 'Well I got your back... *wayyyyy* back' and then she would burst into some Machiavellian laughter straight out of a bad horror movie. I'd laugh right back to partake in the unwelcome humour, but deep down inside I was sincerely puzzled by it, and this left an unsettling feeling in my stomach. Thinking back, I should have been more in tune with my gut feeling, since a few years later she went on a (very sad) full-frontal attack to steal my boyfriends. Oh, Angela.

While the effects of dissonant brand storytelling may not be as melodramatic as my awful experience with Angela the Backstabbing Monster, there is something to be said about the perplexity consumers go through when they meet a conflicting message from a brand. As I delved deeper into my non-obvious trend report research on brands tackling social issues, I came across that very thing that happens when an incongruous message is delivered by a brand.

In early 2019, razor-maker Gillette got into an unfavourable situation when they decided to align their main brand slogan, 'The Best a Man Can Get', to the demonstrative #MeToo movement against sexual assault and harassment, which had begun on social media just two years earlier. The brand decided to create a two-minute video chastising what they called 'Toxic Masculinity' through depicting a series of traditional boy and male behaviours that intertwine with sexism and that were ultimately considered socially unacceptable. Perhaps noble in itself, and almost heroic in trying to address sexism in today's climate. The ad's tragic failure, though, was not the message in and of itself but the fact that, historically, Gillette's brand story had been rooted in sexist paradigms in attempts to appeal to their main audience: men. Therefore, this unannounced shift in brand message direction did not reflect their established brand values and was met with immediate scepticism about the brand's authenticity and true intentions for this message.

We know well that brands exist to make money. Customers know this too. But because the market and the consumer keep evolving, we also know that past bottom-line-only marketing tactics are no longer effective. When the integrated marketing communications (IMC) concept was first introduced in 1989, it aimed at achieving consistency through the multiple communications and marketing channels. Today, that approach is elevated by going beyond identifying a brand voice, tone and style and aggregating its story.

Building an integrated marketing plan with storytelling is about getting away from the disparate 'ad-to-ad' or 'message-to-message' traditional marketing mentality and positioning the brand theme and universal truth as the foundation of relationship-building inside and outside of the organization. IMC with story is then a fundamental operational shift in the brand's culture and way of doing business.

If these words sound somewhat familiar, it is because they are. They resemble the many ways experts have tried to define the cloud-first revolution or *digital transformation*. While some definitions have been a bit fantastical and others too convoluted to make sense, almost every one of them acknowledges that an essential part of the digital age disruption involves a definitive and introspective look at the way every organization is operating to find innovative and agile ways to stay afloat in the market and industry.

Large or small, your brand is either considering the inevitable adventure of embarking on the digital transformation journey or has already begun. And no matter where in the journey your organization may find itself, there is no better moment to integrate storytelling as the fabric of the brand's modernization efforts. It is, after all, the one tool able to evoke emotion in a time when most business functions will be digitized and automated. So, I'd like to invite you to rethink the basic IMC plan steps, by introducing a storytelling twist.

Let's take a look at how storytelling can help us build a winning integrated marketing plan in the digital age. I want to call this IMC Reimagined.

Reimagining the brand message

By now you should have a clear idea of what your brand story theme and universal truth (the feeling it is evoking by meeting a specific human need) are. When you begin to craft your integrated marketing plan with storytelling, instead of deciding on a specific message you want to land just one time with external stakeholders, leverage your brand's universal truth to help spread the message within the organization first, one internal stakeholder at a time. Remember that good storytelling is about evoking emotion. By crafting the story and delivering it internally first, you are driving a concerted effort to instil your brand story as part of the culture so that your internal audience feels, lives and breathes the story and, consequently, it is authentically told in the market. This is done by creating a set of assets for storytelling. Ideally, the marketing discipline in the organization will own this process and dedicate time and resources to building a hub of storytelling assets that every part of the organization can have access to. Think of it as brand storytelling guidelines. The same way the company's logo and brand elements are made available for all to use, the brand story elements and guidelines should be shared. Building an integrated marketing plan with storytelling begins with ensuring that everyone in the organization not only knows the story but is also able to tell it from their individual working space. While every discipline will certainly tell the story differently, and should, the underlying message (theme) should stay consistent throughout, along with tone, voice and other assets. You can think of this step as an internal marketing campaign that never ends. It is part of the cultural and digital transformation your brand needs to go through and it's a long-term investment, but one that yields favourable results. Part of crafting the message is also enabling other stakeholders to tell your brand story. Partners, board of directors, investors, all should also be closely acquainted with your brand story as well as equipped to tell it. Later in the book, I share specific steps on how to best leverage employees as storytellers, but the first step is ensuring that the brand message is known and understood. This is primarily done by the creation and sharing of storytelling resources and assets.

Assets should include everything from simple walking decks on the overall story, to more intricate instructions on how the universal truth plays out throughout each discipline, product and region. A good checklist of storytelling assets looks like this:

- Main story deck (this is your brand mission in story form)
- Storytelling guidelines (how, when and where to tell the story)
- Storytelling elements (character, plot and conclusion definition)
- Storytelling techniques (how to tell the story)
- Storytelling resources (available training and materials)

Reimagining your brand's message means designing every detail of the brand story and teaching it to everyone who should be telling it. Creating a hub of storytelling collateral is the best way to ensure that the story is unified across the company and that there are no disconnected or diverging stories along the customer journey. It also provides a firm foundation to deliver future ads, campaigns and marketing programs. When the brand story becomes the organization's North Star, every part of the organization will intuitively shape internal and external communications around the story's universal truth. The brand story will become a steady reminder to all stakeholders and an affirmation to every customer who comes in contact with it in the market of why the brand exists.

After establishing a robust brand storytelling engine, you can confidently take the story to market in as many ways and on as many channels as you see fit. As long as each marketing campaign and communication ties back to your brand's universal truth, you greatly diminish the chances of entering the vicious cycle of creating detached adverts or stories that confuse customers. Even if you dare dabble on the risky side with a particular campaign, content will not seem foreign to your audience because you have probed it against your brand's universal truth and it is evoking the same feeling every time.

Resetting your goals

The main goal of storytelling is to evoke the right set of emotions. We learned in the design thinking process that testing the story prototypes enables you to understand how the story is landing with your intended audience. Ultimately, we want to inspire our customers into action, but the first goal is to spark feeling. Everything else is secondary and will come naturally as a result of a successful story. Once again, storytelling begins with your internal stakeholders. They are your first audience and the ones who will turn into 'believers' of the brand's universal truth before anyone else does. Getting your audience to feel the desired emotions is primordial to the integrated marketing plan.

While goals should be SMART (Specific, Measurable, Achievable, Relevant, Time-bound), most importantly they should be shared. In traditional IMC plans, goals are often established and met by marketing departments for marketing departments, and if lucky, the communications departments will join in the effort too. But to drive a truly unified approach in brand storytelling, the reimagined IMC goals should not only be communicated, but shared among as many internal disciplines as possible, if not all.

An example of an IMC Reimagined shared goal across the organization would be: *By 30 January 2024, all employees will be able to incorporate the newly crafted brand story as part of their individual growth plan.*

Remember that the integration of the brand story fundamentally shifts the IMC plan to start with telling the story internally first, so that it becomes the blueprint of how employees do business, advantageously creating advocacy as a result. Once these goals have been shared and employees are individually made responsible to deliver on them within their particular discipline, it will be much easier to drive an external campaign.

Identifying your design (not just target) audience

We have learned that empathy is the main driver of storytelling. In the design thinking process, storytelling begins with empathizing with the audience. This means understanding them from a deeper angle than the conventional marketing persona. When introducing storytelling to an integrated marketing plan, a considerable amount of time should be spent studying the target audience from a design perspective. Remember that driving empathy with storytelling means understanding which customer needs are being fulfilled by the brand and which feelings the brand story is evoking from them. As mentioned in Chapter 1, the more research conducted on your audience the better. Do not underestimate the power of psychographic and ethnographic insights that help you understand your audience's emotions so that you can continue to design your story around it.

In IMC Reimagined, we take a distinctive approach to the brand story by beginning with finding insights to understand if it is awakening the desired emotions in employees, partners, vendors and other internal stakeholders. As you are already learning, this is a key component to brand storytelling as it becomes the fundamental blueprint to how the story will eventually be told in the market.

By now, you have built your brand storytelling engine, along with resources and materials internal audiences can tap into and leverage in their own space. You have also re-established your goals to ensure that these are shared among internal stakeholders, and now you are seeking to understand how the story landed with your internal audience first, before launching it in the market to external ones.

The best way to do this is to gather immediate feedback from internal stakeholders as soon as you deliver the brand story concepts you've created.

Because storytelling starts with an inside-out approach, every communication channel within the organization should be explored to deliver the brand story concepts you've designed in a way that stakeholders can best consume them. Part of the digital transformation journey entails implementation of digital communication tools and applications that facilitate connection and social interaction in the company. As you think of your strategy for creating the storytelling hub and sharing it with stakeholders, you should also be thinking of which channels should be used to tell the story. Because cultural transformation can take time, you may want to consider combining traditional communication channels (such as email) with more modern social tools such as Slack or Yammer. Since the main goals of brand storytelling are consumption and engagement, the best bet is to leverage every channel available to help drive your brand story message. As with any integrated marketing campaign, print media and other physical assets should be considered as part of the plan. Leverage posters and TV screens around the office to continually remind internal audiences about your brand story. The more top-of-mind the brand story is to your stakeholders, the more engrained it will become as part of the culture and operational strategy.

After you've delivered the brand story to your internal customer base, find ways to see how it landed. It's important to know if stakeholders not only understand but believe in the newly crafted brand mission and brand story. How does this story look from where they stand? How does it play out in their particular geography of the company? Is the brand story simple to understand? Is it useful in their space? Does it evoke the right set of emotions from them? Don't be afraid to ask these questions over and over of your internal audience. Remember that brand storytelling is a verb and you should never stop designing it, so that it stays relevant in the market. The only way to stay relevant is to keep crafting the story your customers (internal and external) want to hear. And you will not know what that is, unless you consistently ask them. Make it a practice to get insights from your audience every time and you will soon see positive results in your brand storytelling.

You can then follow the same process for external audiences. This time, it should be easier since you've already had practice with internal ones.

It's also important to consider that both internal and external audiences are usually hybrid. A design audience approach acknowledges the differences between all stakeholders and empathetically seeks to tell an inclusive story that effectively reaches many audiences while at the same time crafting individually relevant stories for each of the particular audiences.

For Microsoft, their global external audience varies anywhere from gamers (often younger audiences) to tech developers and IT professionals implementing cloud services at the enterprise level. Clearly the Microsoft brand story is not going to, and should not, look the same to the breadth of their customer base. Therefore, it largely benefited Microsoft to reimagine their target audience and turn them into design audiences. This made it possible for the brand to personalize their universal truth and exclusively appeal to each particular audience. In other words, Microsoft took its established mission and universal truth ('to empower every person and organization on the planet to achieve more') and empathetically set out to tell individual stories for each of their products and consequently their diverse audiences. While all stories centre on the same theme of empowerment, empowerment shows up completely differently to the young gamer compared to how the seasoned IT professional sees it.

Turning your target audience into a design target audience by listening and gathering feedback, and creating personalized stories per audience cohort, enables you to epitomize the overall brand story and effectively deliver it to your hybrid audiences.

Measuring success

Just like resetting your goals to make them shareable among internal stakeholders under IMC Reimagined, measuring success looks at ways those cross-functional groups can also celebrate shared success. This means that not only will your internal audiences have a few shared goals they're collectively working towards when launching a unified marketing and communications campaign, but they will also have shared metrics that measure the campaign's success as you go out to tell the brand story.

Because the main goal of storytelling is to evoke emotion, metrics should be short and simple: consumption and engagement will probably be the top ones to consider. Your brand story has now become a catalyst to culture activation, as it is serving to articulate the brand values, align strategies and processes, and connect people internally. Isn't this beyond your wildest imagination of what brand storytelling could do for your organization?

For this reason, it is important that the story is communicated often and through all possible channels to your newly formed design internal audience and that feedback is collected just as often to understand how the story is landing. This is why creating feedback-loop channels and systems and establishing insight tools prior to landing the story is extremely important.

Microsoft leverages both internal and external tools to gather feedback from their audiences even as the stories are being crafted (not yet fully created), and are sure to openly and vulnerably ask their audiences about their opinion during the process. For example, for external audiences, Core Services Engineering set up private LinkedIn groups where storytellers could share projects they were currently working on and insider IT professionals who wanted to participate were welcome to review and provide feedback as the stories were being designed.

Again, storytelling is empathetic in its essence, so you will be able to empathize with your audience only if you know and understand how they feel about your brand story. Get creative in your insight-gathering approach. There are countless tools to use today, both internal and external, that will benefit your organization in many ways. The more insight for success measurement gathered, the better your chances of landing a successful brand story.

Later, as the story begins to take on a life of its own within the organization, consider adding more robust success metrics and implementing additional goals through programs such as story ambassadors and internal influencers to help cement your brand storytelling blueprint. There is more on this in Chapter 9.

Once the story has landed effectively internally, you can set specific goals to take the story to market through regular targeted campaigns and ads. Don't forget to establish your baseline (before and after storytelling) to measure how impactful this approach has become for your organization.

Building an integrated marketing plan with storytelling is really about learning to foster empathy from the inside out to fundamentally shift the way your brand story is crafted and told. It's an introspective observation that seeks to understand the customer's experience when it comes in contact with the brand story. It's about crafting a message that is 'for your audience, not to your audience' as my dear friend and colleague Storyteller and former Distinguished Engineer at Microsoft, James Whittaker, is always careful to point out. This means that we don't just build a story, think it's good and launch it, as we would in a traditional IMC plan. Crafting a story *for* your audience means you are considering them every step of the way. You are attentively listening to how they are reacting to the story being told and are diligently going back to refine it, refresh it, replace it, or whatever it takes to ensure it evokes the right emotions from your audience. IMC Reimagined is an empathetic approach to marketing. And isn't empathy the best way to make customers, both internal and external, feel accepted, valued and safe in the brand space?

> Empathy is a key component to designing a successful brand story because it stimulates us to consider the audience during every step of the story design process.

In the next chapter, we will take a deeper look at this compassionate skillset that compels us to reconsider who the main characters are in our brand story.

5

The brand story hero

Put your customers at the heart of your brand story

- Non-obvious trends in customer-centricity
- Steps to unveiling your brand story hero

I was only a child when I had the sheer good fortune of meeting Wonder Woman for the first time. Just like you would imagine her, this warrior princess of the Amazons was everything you would ever hope she would be. She wasn't only gifted with great abilities and demi-god superpowers, but her beauty was infallible and radiant. I couldn't stop looking at her. She was the very definition of beautiful. I was mesmerized by her graceful allure that displayed courage, passion, integrity, confidence and selflessness all at once. In a sea of people, I was one of three lucky kids who were able to get close enough to touch her. Her courageous, yet noble gaze found me and she singled me and the other two kids out of a massive crowd, reaching out her hand and motioning me to come closer. I couldn't believe it! Without taking my eyes off hers, I quickly moved through the mob, extending my short limb as far as I could towards her and eventually putting my small-framed grip into hers. Her skin was softer than it looked. It was soft as silk. And her long, flowy hair smelled like spring flowers. Boy, was I lucky to be in such close proximity to this divine creature. I mean, she was truly, truly wonderful. It made sense why people called her Wonder Woman when her real name was Mom.

What is it about heroes that we love so much? If any character can spark a myriad of emotions in a story, it is the story's hero. Is it their impeccable character traits? Is it that we see a little bit of us in them, or hope to?

Whatever it is, the hero in the story really is the most inspiring character of them all, even if they aren't the main character of the story. Heroes bring us hope, they fight the bad guys, they transcend every obstacle, including themselves, for the greater good. I dare say this is why we want them to win. Because if they win, we all win.

For many years, 'winning' for a corporation meant nothing more than beating out the competition, gaining market share and adding to that bottom line. But as we've been learning, newer generations conjoined with modern technologies and infiltrating competition have pressed organizations to rethink their social value beyond economic impact and challenge themselves to contribute to the greater good.

During my research phase for brands tackling social issues trends, I found a striking theory: brands are evolving into heroes because customers are peremptorily asking them to.

As mentioned before, for this project I used Rohit Bhargava's Haystack method for trend curation. The Haystack method follows five steps (gathering, aggregating, elevating, naming and proving) to help find and compile stories and ideas to further elevate them into trends.

During the aggregation process of this trend report, I began to look at ideas based on how brands can change the world and the human needs and behaviours that influence those ideas. The information I compiled was based on the same demographics throughout each non-obvious trend.

- Millennials and Gen Z, high school education level or higher, income <$25K per year
- Top global brands (Fortune 500)
- Diverse industries and sectors across the world

I gathered information from various online sources, including scholarly articles, news articles, industry articles, blogs, brand websites, research articles and surveys, and these helped me find correlations between different ideas, all mapping back to the same notion that brands have begun to use the 'Hero's Journey' archetype when writing their story.

Non-obvious trends in customer-centricity

I believe it suitable to share my findings with you so that it's easier to accept how this inclination came to pass. These ideas are a result of a large-scale analysis of already-existing obvious marketing trends that attempt to find the unobvious ones with the goal of making new relevant predictions for brands in the market.

Idea #1. Corporate social responsibility today means more than just 'being green'

Influencing behaviour: Newer generations (Millennials and Gen Z) expect brands to have purpose. In years past, the term *corporate social responsibility* insinuated that organizations entertain the idea of elemental awareness for social good. This meant, at the basic level, that they needed to be conscious of the effect their organization had in society and how they should extend some contribution to social good by aiming at carbon footprint neutrality or partnering with non-profit organizations for greater impact. Today, brands are urged to do more than giving back to social causes through affiliations. They're confronted with insistence from consumers to actually drive activism, have a social issue stance and even craft their products and services with philanthropic considerations at the design stage. This concept is interesting because it's creating an opportunity for brands to leverage social good works as a product marketing strategy.

Idea #2. Brands are friends

Influencing behaviour: Customers no longer appreciate brands as a provider of consumer goods and services, but instead they romanticize them as a direct reflection of themselves. Marketing Account Manager for Digital Surgeons, Lauren Fagan, made an assertive observation on this rising tendency when she pointed out that 'companies have the potential to create amazing bonds and solidify lifelong loyalty if they invest in their consumers like you would your friends'. Fagan couldn't be more on point. The emotional connection consumers are seeking with brands is entrenched in relationship-building, and this association has mellowed from buyer–seller to consumer–friend. For that reason, consumers are critically examining which brands they want to 'become friends with' as part of the consideration stage in the purchase journey. This permutation in customer experience is building pressure for brands to further assess whether their behaviour and position in the market are attractive enough to be considered 'friend material'.

Idea #3. Brands must establish and openly share their core values as part of their story

Influencing behaviour: Because consumers see brands as a potential friend, or an extension of themselves, they seek to have full discernment on a contending brand and their core values. Establishing corporate mandates along with ethical norms for your brand and openly sharing them with your audiences is no longer a 'value add' to your business strategy, but an indispensable requirement. Remember that clients are, more often than not, 'courting' many brands at once. There are continuous assessments being made by your audience on how the brand shows up, not in the market but in society. So the most advantageous way to capture and keep your customer's attention is by investing time and resources in instituting and promoting a clear code of ethics, code of conduct and core values that conspicuously delineate what the brand stands for on every front. We're seeing more and more how leading brands are riding this trend as they leverage their 'About Us' webpage real estate to offer open-source access to their company's mandates. They're also weaving their brand core values into their brand story and taking every opportunity to showcase them in marketing campaigns.

Idea #4. Buying from a brand now means supporting a cause

Influencing behaviour: Today's savvy customer is hyper-engaged in social activism and their effort towards driving change includes intentional spending or buying with purpose. Modern consumers are also educated, tech natives, creative, environmentally conscious and never afraid to leverage these idiosyncrasies when making a purchasing decision. Big on 'experiences over things', Millennial buying power is predicted to reach 1 trillion by 2020, while Gen Z, currently accounting for $123 billion in direct spending, is projected to become the largest generation of consumers by this same date. With this in mind, brands must recognize that contemporary spending is closely attached to relationship-building and social activism, for which reason a company's products and services must tell the brand story, grounded on empathy, the brand's core values and a demonstrated desire to be an inclusive friend.

Idea #5. The new buyer is now belief-driven

Influencing behaviour: Closely related to idea #4, but, in essence, preceding it to set its foundation, is the idea that there is an increasing shift in belief-driven spending spanning generations, including older ones. The 2018 Earned Brand report by global communications firm Edelman found that 65 per cent of consumers worldwide are making belief-driven purchases and what's more thought-provoking is that according to this analysis, when consumers feel unrepresented by government, they are looking to brands to 'provide a large-scale moral compass – and rewarding those that do'. This takes a brand's social stance to a whole new level of activism where their Hero's Journey brand story just encountered a significant plot twist.

Idea #6. Companies that do not take a social stance may lose competitive edge

Influencing behaviour: As brand storytelling becomes a prevailing force in driving marketing strategies, and given today's influencing behaviours, it's becoming more and more clear that companies choosing to stay neutral on social and political issues, instead of proactively weaving a social activism angle into their brand story, will sooner rather than later be feeling the negative effects of their decision by losing market share. Associate professor of marketing at Drexel University, Daniel Korschun, in his article published by *Fast Company*, showed research findings on the potential costs for companies choosing to stay silent. An example given in his report was rival US-based rideshare companies Lyft and Uber's approach to President Trump's 2017 immigration executive orders. 'Lyft reacted by publicly opposing the order and pledging US $1 million to the American Civil Liberties Union. Uber was more equivocal,' noted Korschun. As a result, Lyft's response to the issue was generally seen as favourable by consumers, while some customers called for others to boycott Uber altogether. This is another compelling reason as to why you should proactively and continuously design your brand story in a way that keeps your business relevant and competitive in the marketplace.

Idea #7. Innovation is now attached to positive world change

Influencing behaviour: Up until now, we've seen the common-sense reasons for why brands are feeling compelled to take on the 'Hero's Journey' approach in their brand story, starring themselves. New buyer model, consumer expectations and the ever-changing competitive-edge landscape are among several opportunities seemingly driving the brand to 'put on a cape and go save the world' in some form or fashion. Through the analysis process and while uncovering ideas, I slightly touched on brands also having to re-evaluate how their products and services fit into the storytelling strategy through keeping social impact top-of-mind at the early stages of their product-making. But taking it a step further, Founder and CEO of Good Business, Giles Gibbons, in his scholarly article 'The Social Value of Brands', points out that brands can do more than comply with society's expectations: they can be agents of change by becoming social innovators. This is where, instead of making a consideration at the product or service design phase to evaluate where and how already-created products and services can contribute to the greater good, brands can make a shift in the usability, accessibility and desirability of the service or product to purposefully lead that positive impact, essentially redefining innovation.

Idea #8. Brands must be careful when taking a social stance

Influencing behaviour: To conclude, the last idea that transpired from my research comes with the overstated warning that socially conscious brand stories can be a double-edged sword. The Head of Business Development at Neuro-Insight cited Gillette's 'Toxic Masculinity' ad as a prime example of how a strong emotional response to an advert can trigger the human memory's encoding (the process that turns an item of interest into a construct that can be stored within the brain), effectively impacting the subject's future behaviour, including purchase decision-making. This means that if a brand does decide to craft their brand story, taking into account all of the preceding ideas, they must also take time to consider the risks associated with this game plan. While good brand storytelling aims at evoking emotion, if the emotion sparked turns out to be a negative one, it may not be an easy task to regain the customer's trust and loyalty, once lost. Brands should then create a business continuity plan that can authentically address any mishaps or shortcomings in storytelling. But don't fret. Remember brand storytelling follows the design thinking process. And the last step is to test your story concepts over and over to see what works (and what doesn't). If you're using this approach to go to market, you will have the opportunity to quickly recover and go back to the storyboard with controllable damage done and increased opportunity to polish the narrative. 'Fail fast' never looked so good!

I hope these unobvious trend ideas provided good context as to why you may feel the brand should without a doubt be the hero in the brand story. I mean, so far in this modern allegory, the customer has been the imperious almost-antagonist character demanding change from the brand, or else. And here you are, along with your organization, making heroic efforts, moving heaven and earth and reading books like this to meet those demands. And the title of this chapter is making the *customer* the hero of the brand story?

Counterintuitive, I know.

But everything you've read so far about brand storytelling has stretched traditional practice and encouraged creative and nonsensical thought. Storytelling is an art as much as it is a science and if you decide to make it part of your business blueprint, it can potentially transform everything about your brand, from your brand mission, to its culture, to how you operate your business. That is, if you take time to meticulously define the characters in your story in a way that will enable this transformation.

In Chapter 1, I mentioned that you must strategically define the characters in your story, and that leading brands like Disney and Nike always make the customer the hero in their brand story. I also gave the example of brands like Microsoft that went from a product-focused business to a customer-centric approach in their brand story, essentially becoming the 'Robin to Batman', and this shift in business model resulted in phenomenal success for the company in the market. This isn't a surprise to anyone. It is no secret that brands putting their customer at the heart of their business (and story) will always win. But according to a 2018 report by the CMO Council, only 14 per cent of marketers believe that their company is customer-centric, and 11 per cent think their customers agree with that characterization.

Making the customer the hero of the brand story is easier said than done, because our rationale and intrinsic desire are to broadcast and showcase how good our company's products and services are. In our minds, these are clearly the heroes of the story. Without the product or service, there *is no brand story*. So, while we can logically understand *why* the customer should be the hero, it is difficult to see how we can make them one.

But hang in there. It's not as tough as you think. If you've been following the steps laid out in Chapter 4, you've probably done a lot of the groundwork for the most difficult steps already. We'll get to that very soon. But first, let's take a look at the elementary and easiest step in making your customer the hero in your story.

Are you ready?

Steps to unveiling your brand story hero

This really couldn't be any simpler. The first step in making your customer the hero in your story is... literally making them the hero in your story:

- Read your brand mission.
- Read it again.
- Analyse it.
- See if the customer shows up, if they show up at all. See how they show up. Where they show up. Do they show up as a hero at all?
- See if the story is about your product's new awesome features or if it centres on how your products and services make your customer better, enabling them to win.

If your customer's win is not the central part of your brand story, revise it as many times as possible until it is crystal clear to you and everyone around you that your brand exists to make a positive impact on your customer.

Remember that rewriting your brand mission is the beginning of a cultural activation and transformational process your company will undergo. Therefore, after you've revised your brand mission and carefully designed your story, the real work of building a customer-centric brand culture begins. Like everything in brand storytelling, introducing your new hero is a domestic endeavour driven by empathy and evangelized by your internal stakeholders once they buy in.

The IMC Reimagined plan I shared in Chapter 4 laid out foundational steps on how your newly crafted brand story should be shared and diffused first internally and later externally to your audiences. Within the first part of that process is where you have the best opportunity to unveil the customer as your brand hero. The next five steps are both poetic and operational in principle, because each presents a utopic business strategy founded on brand storytelling that can actually be carried out.

Make empathy and inclusion key pillars of your business

After I implemented design thinking steps in my storytelling line of work, people began to get curious about prototyping stories and asked me to share more. It wasn't too long before I was travelling the world and sharing insights on this process. But after a couple of years of telling the same story about storytelling, I realized there was more to it and needed to find out what that was.

At the end of every of year, in the last couple of weeks in December, I take a few days to self-calibrate. I assess my personal brand performance over the past 365 days and critically take a look at areas where I need to do better as a wife, mom, sister, worker, friend, all the things that make up who I am. This is a gruelling and unforgiving process that for the past few years has allowed me to improve and evolve my personal brand, as well as my brand message. What else can be said or done better? How else can it be said or done better?

In December 2018 I had the fortuitous opportunity to visit Machu Picchu for the first time as an extension of a business trip. I invited my best friend of over 25 years to join me in this whimsical bucket-list adventure. For four gruelling days we hiked the treacherous classic Inca Trail, exploring roughly 25 miles of steep, narrow paths deep into the Peruvian countryside and climbing high into the Andean mountains while exposing ourselves to the ruthless elements of nature....

Just kidding. We took the train. But the lazy alternative was just as heart-stopping and awe-inspiring. And it came at the perfect time for my self-deprecating end-of-year process. I really did envision myself coming out of this enigmatic wonder of the world with a newfound sense of individual purpose and personal brand messaging for the year to come. I've always thought of Machu Picchu as a spiritual conundrum of some sort. How could I not? This 'Lost City of the Incas' is one of the most renowned sacred places in the word. Our tour guide even felt inspired at one point to start chanting prayers in Quechua (the native indigenous language). Imagine witnessing these marvellously harmonious invocations coming from a local, in Andean language, and with a dramatic landscape of ancient giant walls and terraces made up of quartz serving as the backdrop. I'm telling you, the universe was certainly conspiring for me to reach nirvana. I was close, very close.

Until a sudden downpour erupted, and my almost-moment, along with my hopeful heart, were both covered with pluvial disappointment – and an unflattering provincial poncho. So much for soul awakening. I was ready for my Pisco Sour now.

Of course, Machu Picchu was an unparalleled and unforgettable life experience. And thanks to my remarkably overindulgent tour guide, I was even able to take a selfie with a llama as I had always envisioned (my bucket list is very precise). But to my personal dismay, I didn't find the spiritual enlightenment I had been desperately searching for... or so I thought.

On a random night shortly after New Year's Eve a few days after the trip, I was suddenly awakened by an urgent brain download. It's as if ideas had been floating around my head for days but my internal *Internet of Things* had to first find its patterns and arrange the data to make them ready for download. In layman's terms, I just needed some sleep to let my brain gather ideas.

'Storytelling 2.0' is the first thing I typed in my phone notes that night. Frantically and almost afraid these concepts would soon disappear from my head, I kept typing away.

Here are the actual chicken scratch notes I took on my phone on 3 January 2019 at 2:43 am PST:

Storytelling 2.0

The reason people share their stories is to evoke empathy.

Steps to becoming empathetic:

Authenticity → Pure → Refined (refining gold process, flux?)

The beginning of empathy is not authenticity but measuring your level of authenticity and refining your brand, brand attributes, brand story until it achieves its purest form (gold refining process)

Peaceable, meaning *inclined to peace*, is more likely to describe people and groups of people, whereas *peaceful*, meaning *undisturbed by turmoil or disagreement*, is more likely to apply to events and situations.

Peace → quiet → shut up (listen)

You go from listening to learning their language

Gentle

Our brains see masses of people but only focus on a few to empathize with (ie end of world movies). Lesson: you were made to empathize with your close network and create a domino effect. Lesson: find the story you want to focus on

Hand exercise

Will Smith and Sophia

Why storytelling works: it focuses on 1 character

After successfully capturing the initial brain dump, I was satisfied and exhausted, so I went right back to sleep. I spent the next few days mulling over this content to 'double click' on what Storytelling 2.0 really meant. As the initial notes manifested, storytelling is all about empathy and inclusion. I mean, of course it is. That's all we've been talking about this entire time.

But here is where it gets a step deeper: it's not just about *crafting* your story with these concepts but about making them *operational pillars* in your business.

Empathy and inclusion should not just be an idyllic part of your brand story, but the very infrastructure of it. As you set out to rewrite your mission and craft your brand story to make your customer the hero, you should also challenge the operational status quo and charter. On what foundations do your customer service, communications, finance, operations, sales and marketing business functions operate? Does each of these disciplines have the habit of consistently asking 'is this inclusive and empathetic to our customer' every single time a new product is being designed, or a new system is created or new customer response is given?

The brand story serves to instil your company's core values and mission to stakeholders, but also to reposition your brand internally and externally to them. Making your customer the hero in your brand story is about incorporating inclusion and empathy as part of your company's core values. List them as such. You don't have to give them big, convoluted, forgettable descriptions. Simply add them as part of your brand's fundamental beliefs, begin using them in your everyday language, and watch magic happen.

Pull in the customer chair

When Satya Nadella invited employees to join him in the arduous journey of turning Microsoft into a customer-centric, learn-it-all, empathetic and inclusive culture, one of the first things he asked employees to do was to ensure the customer became a part of every conversation and meeting they had. Some employees began a 'pull in the customer chair' movement, where a physical chair was brought into the meeting room to represent the customer. Some real geeks got really creative and actually decorated the 'customer chair' to make a bigger point. I must admit, I wanted to sit in one of those chairs. They looked really good. This practice may have seemed superfluous at the time, but you wouldn't believe how effective it became when having business conversations. Being keenly aware that our customer was 'sitting' right there next to us inherently changed the conversations, and eventually the brand narrative.

In order to triumphantly make your customer the hero in your brand story, your internal stakeholders need to get to know the customer intimately. Pull in the customer chair. Make the customer's presence known to everyone in the company by sharing customer insights, enabling direct interaction between the customer and internal audiences whenever possible and ensuring individual employee priorities tie back to customer success goals every time. Functional groups should have at least one or two business goals that reflect a customer-centric business model. If it doesn't, it will not be top-of-mind for your employees and they will potentially get really busy doing other things that perhaps are not directly impacting customers at all.

Making your customer the hero in your brand story is also about introducing the hero to your audiences and letting them get closely acquainted with it.

Give them green eggs and ham

I don't hold the title of salesperson and you probably don't either. But one could argue that no matter where we sit in a company and under whatever function, we're all nothing but salespeople trying to sell the brand value to internal and external audiences every day.

Because of this, if you've worked for a corporation long enough or have ventured to become a freelancer or entrepreneur, at one point or another in your career you've come in contact with some 'salesy' type of soft skill professional training you have been highly recommended to take.

Stage presence, confidence, resilience, passion, strong communication skills, enthusiasm. These are all but a small number of competencies we're required to exert today in order to effectively bring value to the brand and tell the brand story. By all means, we must gain all the knowledge on how to be all of this right now. Our bottom line depends on it.

My first training of this type was led by a top, award-winning VP of sales in a smaller privately owned company I had just joined. Yes, he was the quintessential sales exemplar: striking bright smile, extremely charismatic and good looking, over six feet tall and rocked a pinstripe suit as if they were invented solely for his fancy. He was the type of salesman you knew was a salesman and was going to sell you something, but you didn't care. You were going to buy whatever he was going to sell you because you just couldn't help yourself. There's a saying in Spanish that refers to these types of people. They are people who 'te venden tierra en el desierto' (they sell you sand in the desert... and you buy it!).

I was curiously hesitant about the training he was going to give. Whatever personal development ancient wisdom that had been stealthily reserved for the few and elite for centuries past, he was willing to offer it freely and I was ready to take it all in and take it all to heart. I expected nothing less than the never-told secrets of the gifted rich and famous. A Tony Robbins-type life-altering session that would have *me* growing six feet tall and rocking a pinstripe suit in no time.

But much to my anticlimactic surprise, on the day of the training he walked into the packed room, fashionably late and uncharacteristically almost unnoticed. As he made his way to the front, he began to pass out a copy of Dr Seuss' *Green Eggs and Ham* to every one of us.

Stunned and clearly confused, attendees began to look around the room in hopes of catching a clue on what was happening, and what would happen next. With a quiet sigh as if to modestly grab the room's attention, this commanding Master of Commerce took on a grandfatherly persona, opened the book and began to read from it.

Some people quickly responded to his abstract instructions by following along with his reading. Others, like me, were still looking around, hoping this was some ludicrous but brilliant introduction to his *sensei* ways and that soon he would bring out the master sword of sales and demonstrate how to manoeuvre it to make the kill.

He's going somewhere with this, I elucidated. *Stay alert. The moment of reckoning will soon happen.*

But it never did. Within a few minutes, he finished the reading, extracted his face from the printed work, scouted the room with no show of concern for audience approval, and matter-of-factly concluded 'this is the best and only sales strategy you will ever need', before walking out.

It took me years to 'get it'. But when I finally did, I realized how brilliantly right he was. Dr Seuss' green eggs and ham story is about persistence. It's about telling the story consistently over and over until every potential customer is impelled to try your product or service.

Making your customer the hero in your brand story is about literally naming them the hero as you write the story, weaving inclusion and empathy into it, introducing the hero to your audiences and never letting them forget it.

It is your job as storyteller to proclaim the customer as the hero in your brand story so persistently that when your audiences consume it, they love it, Sam-I-Am!

6

If story is magic, vulnerability is the magic wand

- What is vulnerability in storytelling?
- Waving the magic wand

We love authenticity. We crave it. We preach it. We require it as a main ingredient in relationships, leadership and business approach. But when it comes to strategically applying this bona fide attribute to our everyday business practice, and even more, making it a pillar in our brand story, most of us don't know exactly where or even how to begin. This is because deep down inside, we know too well that authenticity is a direct by-product of vulnerability, and vulnerability is, well, *that which we don't speak of*.

I was once invited to co-present with another influencer woman in tech at a summit for Hispanics. Our topic was 'Storytelling for personal branding'. We divided and conquered, and I was to speak first about the *why* in telling your personal story to effectively build your brand while my counterpart would share the *how*.

I had delivered a version of this talk many times before, but as any good storyteller will do (*hint, hint*), I took the time to research my audience in order to design the presentation exclusively for this cohort. This can't be very hard, I thought. I'm Hispanic. I *am* the audience.

From a socio-cultural standpoint, the Hispanic culture places high value on dignity and pride. It is typically group-oriented, hierarchical in relationships and deeply emotional in communication style. As a people, we enjoy telling good stories and have a built-in animated mechanism (this is a nice way of saying we make uncalculated scary hand movements when talking) that helps us bring stories to life in beautiful and colourful ways. In fact, when presenting to this particular audience, I decided I would jokingly *de-emphasize* how storytelling needs to be emotional, because that's pretty much a 'given' for our origin group.

But during my research, I found it bitterly enlightening that it is those very traits of honour and decency that make us Hispanics very terrible story-tellers – when it comes to telling 'raw' stories about ourselves. I thought individually about every member of my extended family and came to the sad conclusion that I had no idea who my relatives are or what their individual stories were about.

Growing up in Venezuela, I spent countless Sunday afternoons at my grandmother's house surrounded by many aunts, uncles and cousins. All of us would take turns to sit around a long, dark cherry wooden table with mis-matched chairs to eat our matriarch's fish soup and tell delightful fictional stories, cultural legends and myths. But not once did any of these family members talk about their own life journey, their successes or, better yet, their personal struggles. Never did they pass down anecdotes or riddles of true disenchantment and frustrating defeat to new generations. Except for one decrepit photo of my great-grandmother on my father's side, I have no idea what my progenitors beyond grandparents looked like, who they were as individuals or what motivated them to migrate from once place to the other, eventually landing them in the small Latin American country of *Little Venezia*. Thanks to DNA technology, I know that I'm 36 per cent Portuguese, 20 per cent Native American and the rest a bottomless mix of European and African heritage. But when and how did my Portuguese great-great-great-grandfather meet my Native American great-great-great-grand-mother and fall in love? Did they have a salaciously illicit Pocahontas-style romance? Sadly, neither I nor my future generations will ever know. Why? Because in my culture, we consider it rude and disrespectful to our ancestors to expose them in any way that could make them appear anything but successful and ideal. In other words, they can't appear *human*.

'This is why we love *telenovelas*,' I elucidated to the Hispanic summit audience when delivering my personal brand storytelling portion. 'Because all of this melodrama is actually happening in our own households, but we're not really allowed to talk about it.'

While I may not know specifically how your culture or cohort feels about vulnerability, I know all of us constitutionally associate this word with weakness.

The word *vulnerability* is derived from the Latin *vulenrare* which means 'to wound'. Defencelessness and incapability of withstanding an attack immediately come to mind as synonyms of this concept. No wonder we generally cringe at the thought of being perceived as vulnerable – or telling vulnerable stories. Nobody wants to be associated with being defenceless and fragile.

But isn't it also true that we are easily enthralled by those very stories of unshielded abandon? That we find it exceptionally inspiring when someone decides to courageously expose themselves in the most uncertain of ways? We praise those who take a risk to openly welcome judgement and criticism while we sit back as spectators thanking our lucky stars that it isn't us standing there, emotionally naked on a main stage. The juxtaposition of vulnerability is truly a perplexing notion, and one that we must examine further because of what it represents to storytelling.

In her book *Daring Greatly: How the courage to be vulnerable transforms the way we live, love, parent, and lead*, storyteller and University of Houston research professor Brené Brown sharply explains her own feelings regarding this antithesis, and dare I say she is accurately speaking for all of us:

'I want to experience your vulnerability but I don't want to be vulnerable.

'Vulnerability is courage in you and inadequacy in me.

'I'm drawn to your vulnerability but repelled by mine.'

Brown goes on to further explain that while 'we associate vulnerability with emotions we want to avoid… we often lose sight of the fact that vulnerability is also the birthplace of joy, belonging, creativity, authenticity, and love'.

And aren't all those things the universal truths we want our stories to behold?

Vulnerability in storytelling

When it comes to brand storytelling, vulnerability is quite the opposite of powerlessness. It is a mighty force that bursts open emotional awareness. If story is magic, vulnerability is the *magic wand* that unleashes genuine connection with our audiences. As a storyteller, you must boldly grab this powerful incantation instrument and dive deep into the notion of being courageously real when telling your brand story, freeing yourself from the fixed mindset of having to hide your brand's flaws and deficiencies and embracing those transformational moments that led up to where the brand may find itself today.

When Microsoft decided to share their digital transformation stories from an emotional angle, vulnerability became their best tool. I was assigned to do a story on *operationalizing the cloud*, featuring a veteran cloud engineer as the main character. As he and I ventured deeper into delivering a genuine narrative, I could see the story painstakingly becoming more and more vulnerable at its core and was glad our protagonist was not only up to the daunting task of being virtuously forthright about his personal experiences, but proactively decided to lead the charge in telling these exposed tales.

'The learnings, pitfalls and compromises of operations in our expedition to the cloud' blog became an instant hit with our IT professional audience when it was finally published as engineers trekking along their own digital transformation journey tuned into the message that big corporations like Microsoft did not necessarily enjoy smooth sailing on their way to cloud computing, and like any other company, big and small, young and old, the company experienced some bumps and bruises along the way. Microsoft's willingness to share the operational susceptibilities and lessons learned as it pioneered moving data from on-premises to the cloud so that others could learn from their mistakes was so well received that the story evolved into a six-part series and contributed to record-breaking visits to its website.

Vulnerability in storytelling works because it poignantly reminds us of our humanity. It encourages us to move away from the orator-to-audience point of view and begs us to meet the crowd eye to eye. It is precisely there where we have the best opportunity to empathize with one another and, as you already know, empathy is the beginning of great storytelling.

Waving the magic wand

But it's important to recognize that incorporating vulnerability as an ingredient in your brand narrative is easier said than done. Unlike in *Harry Potter*, this 'magic wand' doesn't find you. You have to go find *it* and this is why I want to offer a few tips and tricks that can help you track this energy source and make you bolder in telling your story as authentically as possible.

See your brand as a human

Once upon a time, your brand was born.

It was given a name and a mission, and it set out to live that very purpose.

The brand grew in size and wisdom.

It made friends and foes along the way.

It hopes to one day achieve all its goals and soon live happily ever after.

Your brand is not only being perceived as a human by your customer or being bestowed with human attributes by your chief marketing officer, it can also be considered as a human entity, and for all intents and purposes, should be. When you see your brand as a human instead of as a corporation, you are more likely to accept its imperfections, becoming more forgiving of its past mistakes and shortcomings and also recognizing that embracing these natural 'human errors' along with the tales of these previous misfortunes can be the most innovative way to reach your audience.

It is those stories of failure that inspire the most, because they appeal to the arduous endeavour it took to reach success: humility, resiliency, persistence, hard lessons learned. Remember, *brands are potential friends* to your customer. As the sidekick in your brand story, vulnerability provides a rich opportunity to create a valuable space for your brand character to shine by way of courageously putting aside past pretences and welcoming transparency with narratives that showcase the trials and tribulations your company has experienced thus far in its quest to deliver a great customer experience. This is an effective tactic in positioning your brand as an agent of strength and nobility in its own space and creating closeness to your audience throughout the brand narrative.

Both Starbucks and Apple corporations experienced their fair share of challenges when CEOs Howard Schultz and Steve Jobs, respectively, both left the companies for a period of time but then eventually came back to help turn them around from their struggling condition. Upon these undeniable stories of downfall and in due course triumph, the brands astutely leveraged their provocative chronicles and purposively shared the axioms cultivated to help elevate their brand story. And elevate they did.

Seeing your brand as human is giving your brand permission to show up as vulnerable and, by extension, yourself as a storyteller to tell the brand story from its most authentic and raw origin.

Adopt this practice of veritably and literally *humanizing the brand* and watch your brand narrative teem with spellbinding motion, swiftly enchanting those who come in contact with it.

Set boundaries

OK, I know being vulnerable in your story may sound whimsical and almost too romantic for your liking. The reality is that it's a frightening idea and you're probably second-guessing this notion as a business model. It's almost as scary as it was when your marketing team had to consider opening a Facebook page or Instagram account for your company (*smile*).

Just like any evolved communication strategy, as you whip out your magic storytelling wand you ought to plan for the unexpected and create rules and guidelines to help keep the magic powers somewhat under control. Storytellers are creative journalists who seek to find the best stories to connect with their audience. So far, we've been learning that the best stories are emotional, inspirational and authentic in nature – the very synonyms of vulnerability. But undoubtedly there is a risk we take in coming in from this exposed angle and, like any other business risk-taking, it should be a calculated one.

Remember the midnight enlightenment data dump I shared with you in Chapter 5?

Authenticity → Pure → Refined (refining gold process, flux?)

Being successfully authentic in your brand story requires a smart strategy of refining your vulnerability. You will spend time testing your story prototypes and analysing your audience's reaction to the narrative when you deliver it, but before you go to market and if you decide to be vulnerable with your story, you should also define what vulnerability means to your brand and brand story, the degree of vulnerability you are willing to convey and what is completely out of reach for every storyteller of your brand story.

These boundaries should be a part of your business PR and communications design from the outset and every member of your storytelling task force should contribute to it in some way. Just as you plan for a potential social media crisis, an intention to win by being vulnerable in your brand story should be accompanied by methodically identifying the key messages you want to share as a brand and explicitly pinpointing those stories you are not willing to disclose or acknowledge as part of the narrative. In addition, just as you would for a marketing campaign launch, it is recommended to set systems and processes in place to help you monitor customer engagement, sentiment and overall impact once you've decided to test your vulnerable stories.

A good trick is to test these stories with a smaller audience first. If you have global customers, for example, a smaller region or country can serve as a suitable audience for monitoring impact. At a larger scale, introducing vulnerability in your brand story can be done in a positive and proactive way if properly embedding it as a part of your storytelling toolkit when sharing the brand story with your internal audience first.

As you have already learned, storytelling is more than just telling stories; it is a blueprint for effectively connecting with internal and external audiences. If you choose vulnerability as one of your storytelling pillars, your audiences, especially internal ones, will begin to embrace this notion and leverage it to create magic in their own space. *Expelliarmus!*

Bring reinforcement

Just as empathy can be fostered as a soft skill, vulnerability can be instilled as a cultural and leadership trait of your brand merely by designating your company employees as brand story ambassadors. Notice I am not calling them advocates, because this is not so much about promulgation of the narrative as it is about *representation* of it.

It would be futile for the brand to tell stories that appear courageously open if, at the core, those background characters that contribute to that very story are nowhere to be found in the core message. The example I shared of the cloud engineer who jumped at the chance of candidly confessing his personal struggles during a revolutionary time at Microsoft is a great illustration of how vulnerable behaviour is enforced at the brand storytelling level.

Highlighting individual stories of people who are deep down in the trenches, making things happen, delivering the customer experience head on for your company, is the best way to emphasize the brand's willingness to be open, authentic and genuine with its narrative.

Quite frankly, I daresay that while there is still a place for executives and company leads to continue telling stories of success on behalf of the brand from a PR perspective, it is the viewpoint of the singular brand envoy (the customer service representative, the floor sales associate) that will resonate best when vulnerable stories are told.

Reinforcing the behaviour of vulnerability is about deliberately introducing those supporting characters so that your audience can better understand what it takes for the brand to help the customer win. If your customer is the hero and your brand the sidekick, these secondary characters are strategically being woven into the narrative to uncover *how* the sidekick (your brand) champions the hero (your customer) in the tale. Your employees are your best asset when it comes to showing up as genuine and open in your brand narrative, because they are able to naturally expose the angle of the everyday struggles, organically showcasing what it takes to create and deliver the service or product your customer comes to love.

To effectively bring reinforcement, your brand should create a platform where employees feel free to openly share their personal stories from wherever they may find themselves within the organization. In addition, the company should offer storytelling as a soft skill training to employees and encourage them to ditch the PowerPoint presentation for a personal narrative at the next quarterly or monthly business review.

Microsoft's Chief Storyteller Steve Clayton has taken this task seriously. It's been five years in the making, but today the company offers digital and in-person storytelling courses as part of employees' individual professional growth, a social teams network for storytellers to share personal stories and find community support, and a monthly virtual meeting to provide updates on the brand's storytelling efforts. There is more on training your internal stakeholders in Chapter 12.

Becoming vulnerable in your brand storytelling goes beyond crafting a vulnerable story. It is a true intention from business leads and storytellers in the company to instigate multiple and inclusive angles to the brand story from those who continuously contribute to it.

SCAMPER it

One of the greatest practical and useful exercises in my storytelling practice has also proven to be the one that makes my stories most vulnerable. The SCAMPER technique (Figure 6.1) is a productivity tool created by the late advertising executive Alex Faickney Osborn as part of his list of unconventional ways to think up (brainstorm) new ideas and solutions to create or improve a product.

This mnemonic acts as a 'story prompt' to help further develop or improve the story arc in a more inclusive and authentic way. In storytelling, I have been able to successfully employ this mechanism to uncover new angles of the story I may have not initially considered. At its core, this acronym facilitates conversation with other storytellers and contributors to the brand story about character, plot and conclusion possibilities left unexplored in the beginning.

Granted, if you're really following the design thinking approach to craft your stories, you have probably already spent a good amount of time brainstorming ideas for story concepts. But let me remind you that design

FIGURE 6.1   SCAMPER brainstorming model

thinking is a perpetual cycle and there is no straight path to designing your brand narrative. At this juncture, if you realize the value of authentic and vulnerable storytelling and truly desire to take hold of the magic wand, I invite you to bring your already-crafted storyline to this place of vulnerable ideation and SCAMPER the *magic out of it* by taking the following steps.

Substitute

Ask yourself, what elements of the story can and should I substitute in order to probe a new angle? If, for example, you were to substitute one piece of the story plot for another, what would happen then? How would it change the original storyline and conclusion? Being vulnerable in your storytelling means exploring every and all aspects of the brand narrative, including those transformational and unforeseen plot twists the brand has experienced to better understand how else it can make an impact with the intended audience.

Take a moment to substitute each of the three basic elements of the story (character, plot and conclusion) just for kicks, and see what else comes of this action.

Combine

I'm always asked if 'it's allowed' to combine different storytelling techniques. Is it OK to tell a *Hero's Journey* type story along with a *Mountain* one? Who said it's *not* OK? *You* are the storyteller here and it is you who knows what will resonate best with your audience. Through this particular prompt, you can feel free to blend storytelling techniques you've learned up until now to see what else can happen in the story and how. You can also combine story delivery forms, such as telling the story in both written *and* visual forms. The beauty of being vulnerable in storytelling is that by engaging in this very practice you are potentially discovering your own new techniques and ways to tell stories.

Adapt

This cue calls on us to revisit the purpose of the brand story. Again.
Preposterous! Are you asking we start all over?
Ah, much like its name serves as an invitation to identify a hypothetical new aspiration for the brand narrative, it also acts as a much-needed admonition that our story is never fully baked, that there is always going to be an opportunity to revisit every facet of it many times over and that we should be adaptable to that idea.
This vulnerable suggestion proposes the question: How can you adapt your brand story to serve another purpose or meet another business objective? Could it be that beyond the primary commission of emotionally transferring information and activating culture with stakeholders, the brand story also has the potential to achieve other industry goals? You will never know until you take the time to explore these possibilities.

Modify

How could you change the way the story currently looks and feels? In Chapter 3 I talked about the importance of dressing up your story structure with visual elements. In this step, you get to play with any and all conceivable ways the story can be cognitively understood. Invite your brand ambassadors to offer avant-garde building blocks to the brand story and put them to the test. You may be pleasantly surprised at the results.

Put to another use

Speaking of putting things somewhere... whatever happened to those unused storytelling ideas left behind from your past brainstorming sessions? Is there a chance you can bring them back at this point in your storytelling journey and implement them to get a fresh perspective? This phase invites you to take a step back and insert design concepts you may not have considered at the very beginning to potentially create new narrative theories today.

Eliminate

If you were to completely eradicate a character in the story, what would happen? What if you took out a visual element or simplified the whole story for a lighter version? What if you eliminated the conclusion completely? Another way to make your story vulnerable is to play with the idea of taking it apart or 'dismantling' it to conceivably let some elements shine brighter thanks to the absence of the one you chose to cancel out.

Reverse

Lastly, what if you swapped characters in the story? What if, for a moment, the customer was now a supporting character and the company employees the heroes? Reversing roles or sequences of events in your story will map out new ways to unfold the story and bring more awareness of the significance of each component in the story.

Vulnerability in storytelling is about intentionally poking holes in the allegory to unabashedly expose new vantage points and angles. I hope you make time to play with this exercise and that it helps you unearth wonderful and cutting-edge alternatives for your brand narrative you hadn't yet contemplated.

Stay flexible

It is dutiful to continue to remind you that the design thinking approach is never a fail-proof model for brand storytelling. Instead, it is a creative and innovative scheme derived from those willing to build up their emotional intelligence and embrace a growth mindset in order to achieve a different outcome for the brand and its constituents.

Becoming vulnerable in brand storytelling unquestionably puts the brand in a delicate and somewhat uncertain position and therefore necessitates a malleable adoption of the process. Once you have created parameters for operational efficacy and risk mitigation, inclusively invited ambassadors to share the story from their personal angles and SCAMPERed new ways to tell the story, make a conscious effort to free yourself from the need to be in complete control of the storyline and let it bountifully flow from its many valuable sources.

The reality is that as a storyteller you are not the *Keeper of the Realm* but instead the *Head Palace Scribe*. So, fight the innate temptation to make yourself responsible for the brand reputation in the market when the story is being tested. Branding is about promoting the distinctive core values, products, services, attributes and symbols that differentiate your brand from others in the market. Brand storytelling is using stories to emotionally convey the same message with the added bonus of creating long-lasting, trusted connections with your audiences. This is a consistent and never-ending effort that you commit to, in spite of and unrelated to any other outside contributing factors that will be ever present.

Staying flexible in your vulnerable stories is about acknowledging that while you endeavour to set the tone of the brand narrative in the long term through ingenious strategies, there will always be other circumstances and determinants that influence the brand perception in the market as a whole. As a storyteller, it is your duty to carefully design the brand story, create and deliver a functional and integrated marketing communication plan and splash it with a bit of vulnerability to spread the magic in a certain direction. After that, you should sit back, relax and let the story take form.

If you're wondering what happened with my Hispanic audience when I suggested the notion of being vulnerable in 'Storytelling for personal branding', they first winced at the idea, as I expected, but later they came to the understanding that in today's connected world, where voices are being heard and amplified, it is not only a privilege for our community, but our responsibility to boldly share our stories of losses and wins so that future generations can learn from them and hopefully do much better than us. Indeed, vulnerable storytelling is a genuine opportunity to leave others a better way than we found them when we started work, by imparting wisdom from lived experiences. This serves both at the personal and corporate brand levels.

If you decide to be vulnerable in your storytelling, you will be pleasantly surprised at the immediate response you get from your audience. The emotional reaction might be so powerful that you may begin to feel the effects of 'manipulation with story'. This is where you have to take a step back and ask yourself: Why am I doing this? And where do I draw the line?

The next chapter, in my estimation, is one of the most critical in brand storytelling, and storytelling in general, because it explores the ethical norms of the storytelling craft... which have yet to be written.

7

Ethics in storytelling

When to use your secret weapon

- The importance of ethics in storytelling
- Learning ethical perspectives

I remember the first time I 'discovered' the true power of storytelling as a narrator, rather than a spectator – and that was an entirely different revelation to storytelling. I was invited to deliver the keynote at a women-led social enterprise summit in Ifrane, Morocco and was to speak about how to effectively scale your business through the sharing of your brand story on social channels, something this particular audience had yet to explore or even consider.

I couldn't have been more terrified and yet delighted at the same time. Though I had been on the public stage delivering similar talks for a few years now, this opportunity and platform sang a unique tune, one that I was nervously unfamiliar with. Perhaps it was the fact that this was no ordinary assembly. This audience comprised savvy women entrepreneurs from the Middle East and Africa whose for-profit artisan businesses existed primarily to benefit their marginalized communities. If your mind didn't explode a little, please read that again.

Or maybe it was my preoccupation with what I would need to wear on 'social night' where we were asked to showcase cultural wardrobes representing the region we came from (do I wear a cowgirl hat or a Venezuelan *Liqui Liqui*?). It could also have been that my extended family was going through a rough patch at the time and in hopes of finding a bit of distraction for both of us, I decided to bring my mother along at the very last minute, not really measuring the implications of it all.

Either way, I had 'all the feels' about this trip and *imposter syndrome* was unapologetically lurking outside my hotel window the very night we arrived. Other than being a woman, I felt I had nothing more in common with this congregation of altruistic heroines who didn't seem to worry much about not having an espresso machine within acceptable distance.

As a trained orator, I had learned the fundamental inner workings of 'taking the audience through an unforgettable journey' and understood the basic idea of transferring information through an emotional lens. These 'communication hacks' had effectively positioned me to get in front of hundreds of professionals and deliver a speech, any speech, with astuteness and confidence. I hate to brag, but I was getting pretty good at this craft – and sort of *instafamous*. In fact, my international public speaking calendar began to fill so fast in the months prior to Morocco that I soon found myself sprinting in and out of countries like a runaway convict, flirting with time zone differences, changing wardrobes in airport bathrooms, and begging Lady Luck to let me make my (very tight) flight connections because I had but a few hours to get to my next speaking engagement. Happy to report, Lady Luck has yet to fail me – though my luggage will tell an entirely different story.

When I accepted the invitation for this particular event, I knew I had to pay extra attention to my narrative delivery. My message to this special audience had to be beyond poignant. It had to stir hearts, encode 'feel good' memories, do all the magic that storytelling does and then some, so they could effectively remember what I was going to teach them about... digitizing your business with social media?

Enter the secret weapon: my mother.

As often happens to me, and not because I'm always jetlagged, I woke up in the middle of the night with a grand idea. I was to deliver my speech as scripted, but right in the middle of it, I would interrupt myself and invite my incredibly beautiful and talented mother (did I mention she's Wonder Woman?) to the stage so she could tell her own success story of... telling your business story. In the African culture, motherhood is highly honoured, and mothers are regarded as sacred contributors to society. As matriarchs, they have a sound voice and much wisdom to impart, so everyone pays great attention when someone's mother speaks.

Trying to convince my audience to learn and use digital channels to scale their business in a region commonly teeming with technological challenges, such as unreliable or no network connectivity, was going to be nearly impossible. Unless, of course, my surprise guest would show up in her invisible plane, reel them in with her invisible *lasso of truth* and pave the way for me.

Unempathetic side note: if you invite someone to travel with you, they owe you and you can cash in immediately, especially if it's a relative.

And so it went. I stood before my distinguished audience, delivered half of my speech on why you should leverage social media to share your brand story and bam! The next slide had only one word – INTERRUPT! – and then I stopped talking for a few seconds. That was it. Wonder Woman's invisible plane was about to land.

With amusement, I watched the audience's eyes quickly widen with shock, shortly followed by the wrinkling of brows as they tried to fore-shadow what would come next.

Oh, but they couldn't predict my next move if they tried! Except for the driver who picked us up at the airport, no one had learned that my mother had joined me on this trip. The decision to bring her along had been made just a few hours before the flight, leaving me no time to announce her to event organizers, who were also stupefied.

'I figured, why stand here and talk about the importance of sharing your brand story' – I finally broke my premeditated silence, figuratively drawing my weapon as my mom, obeying her cue, got up from the confused audience and swiftly made her way on to the stage to join me – 'when I can have some-one very special to me testify about how this very notion has benefited her in many ways. Ladies and gentlemen, please welcome to the stage, my mother!'

Applause and shouts instantly erupted as the women enthusiastically jumped out of their chairs acclaiming my Amazonian progenitor who, with much passion and poise, went on to tell her own narrative, favourably cementing my less-than-compelling message into their hearts and minds. My work here was done. I had once again made the audience dance to the beat of my storytelling alchemy regardless of their initial tune, and dancing they were. Literally. That was a sight to see.

And the rest is 'lived happily ever after' history.

After the on-stage adrenaline wore off and I satisfactorily watched imposter syndrome quietly back away from my hotel room window, I noticed another reality-check creature creeping through the crevasses. It was ethics in storytelling. My mind suddenly flooded with questions that seemed to have no definitive answer. *Had I used my mother to manipulate my audi-ence? Possibly. Was that wrong? I'm not sure. Am I hungry or jetlagged? Maybe both.*

The importance of ethics in storytelling

I don't know about you, but when I witnessed first-hand the sheer para-mountcy of emotional control driven by storytelling and understood *I* was the person behind the wheel, a moment of ethical reckoning happened. Remember that, at the very beginning of this book, I mentioned I'd gone on a quest to ask several storytellers in different disciplines 'what is *not* story-telling?' and one of them cautioned that 'it is not manipulation'? It's because they too had had a moment of reckoning and now I clearly understood where they were coming from and just how mercenary stories can be.

As marketing professionals, communicators, or just as humans, we must recognize the unscrupulous depths the art and science of storytelling can reach if ever left unchecked, and the fatal results a narrative's secret weapons can yield if drawn at the wrong place, wrong time or with the wrong audience.

Just as in marketing, moral distinctions, particular principles and maxims ought to govern storytelling efforts, with the goal of carefully examining dilemmas that may arise from using this contrived approach. This is why I feel it necessary to share with you a few practical perspectives that can help tackle potential ethical issues as you begin to construct your own brand storytelling strategies.

But it is fitting to first understand what ethics is not, so that we are clear on how and why we ought to act in precarious situations we may find ourselves in.

Ethics is not:

- **Feelings**. While feelings can help guide some ethical choices by making us feel 'good' or 'bad' about them, feelings can be ever-changing and fleeting and do not provide a grounded foundation for making ethical choices.

- **Religious beliefs or societal laws**. Both religious beliefs and governmental laws may generally advocate high ethical standards, but they are not all-encompassing and can also differ depending on cultural norms or geographic locations.

- **Cultural accepted norms**. Some cultures may have high ethical standards, and some may not. In addition, cultural norms change from time to time and do not provide a consistent set of values. Think of ancient societies like Rome, for example, and what was 'permissible' back then versus now. You may argue that the way they behaved towards one another was not too ethical compared to some cultural standards today.

Merriam-Webster defines ethics as a *set of moral principles*. In essence, a guiding philosophy that enables us individually and collectively to make choices and react to situations.

Ethical perspectives

When considering ethical issues in brand storytelling, it is important to understand the various angles or perspectives that ethical issues encompass. Marketing professor at the University of Notre Dame and co-author of *Ethical Marketing* Patrick Murphy makes a compelling call to marketers and communicators when thinking about socially responsible marketing and the ethical foundations of relationship marketing. In his book, Murphy points out that there are several perspectives to contemplate when making ethical decisions for marketing at different levels, namely the personal, organization, industry, societal and, lastly, stakeholder levels.

From a storytelling platform, I would like us to explore each of these viewpoints in more depth since, as we have been learning, while storytelling can be used a marketing tool, it's a much more complex approach to engagement and communication with stakeholders, and therefore it begs for a more profound examination when being considered for implementation. Let's take a look at how.

Organization (or brand)

In general, reasoning about ethical decisions within brand storytelling is dictated by the brand's core values, business goals and executive leadership. Just as with any new business growth hacking or transformational process, it is the top leadership team that will ultimately decide which stories to tell about what and when, and these may not necessarily align with your individual set of norms or code of conduct. As a storyteller, you are called to design stories that display the heart of the brand, successfully engage internal and external audiences and win potential customers over through an empathetic and emotional connection. But how far your brand is willing to take this practice and which secret weapons it intends to use to successfully land the story will surely depend on the expectations of leadership, and for this reason, as agents of the organization, brand storytellers must check their story design efforts against these intentions and standards earlier in the process rather than later. The best way to minimize ethical dilemmas when crafting brand stories is to establish storytelling ethical values from the get-go and proactively engage in conversations with as many leading internal stakeholders as possible during the conceptual (ideation) phase of storytelling. Remember that storytelling is the emotional transfer of information, and in our quest to evoke people's feelings, we may find ourselves in ambiguous terrain where the path is not so clear. Understanding the criteria for evaluating actions to ethically awaken our audience's emotions is something we ought to always consider.

Following are some questions that may help facilitate storytelling ethics conversations with your leadership and serve as a continuous checkpoint before story concepts are developed and tested in the market. (If you happen to currently serve at the executive level within your organization, these questions can help as a barometer to gauge how closely modern and innovative concepts for business growth align to the company's ethical norms and business code of conduct.)

- Does this story affirm the company's core values?
- Does this story foster trust with each and every stakeholder?
- Does this story help build relationships?
- Does this story showcase diverse and inclusive behaviours?
- Does this story honour the company's commitments and promises to its customers?

In the race to tell a good story, I've seen many brands step off their core value platforms and land disparate narratives that, at the very least, leave customers frustrated and confused because the stories are not reflective of the brand's values; at the highest level, they can show up as inauthentic and distrusting, resulting in quite the opposite effect the brand sought to achieve.

Conversations about ethics in storytelling with your leadership are indispensable to you as a storyteller and to the brand. These discussions will help provide direction, even if the pathway is not completely clear, and give you confidence to continue exploring uncharted territories in the land of tales.

Industry

The marketing and communication industries, as well as whichever industry your company serves (in my case, tech), will generally have a set code of ethics, and these can vary greatly depending on industry type, geographic location and legal regulations and policy. I recommend you take time to familiarize yourself with each of these to best understand the set of expectations and norms required of you as a professional and storyteller. More on this a bit later in the chapter as we compile these expectations and norms into a code of conduct template.

Societal

In addition to organizational, individual and industry standards, Murphy points out in his book that the role of marketing ethics can be seen as critical to both social order and justice, and I believe this applies to every aspect of conducting business, including storytelling. Audiences need to feel that stories are open and transparent, just like purchase transactions, and that as noted in Chapter 5, they are the hero in the story, not the victim in any way. In addition, as we've already seen, the desire of new generations to befriend the brand comes as a direct result of the societal impact the brand is making, or not. Therefore, both the organization and the individual ought to consider whether their set of norms includes a societal aspect.

Stakeholder

Ethics in storytelling needs also to consider any group or individual affected by the story being told. As professionals, we understand that there are various levels of stakeholders we serve. Within the storytelling context, we've been primarily talking about internal and external stakeholders (internal being employees, partners, investors, vendors, shareholders, board of directors, and external being existing and potential customers). There are also indirect stakeholders that do not have a formal relationship with the brand but are still affected or impacted in some way by the brand story. When thinking about incorporating your stakeholders in ethical norms for storytelling, keep in mind that you and your brand will find it challenging to balance the concerns of all stakeholders, and sometimes the best course of action will not be a 'win–win' situation for all but rather a minimization of harm done to the groups involved.

Personal

While, as a part of the organization, you are asked to understand and adhere to its set of ethical norms, as an individual it is also essential that you build your personal set of guiding principles (if you have not already done so) to help you navigate the enigmatic circumstances you will often encounter as a professional in the ever-changing digital landscape. Even more so, a personal code of conduct is especially important to have as a storyteller because, as you already know, good storytelling comes from the heart. If you're not explicitly passionate about the stories you're telling, if you don't truly believe in the story, you will not be able to tell it with conviction, and your audience will immediately sniff it out as fake.

When in Morocco I found myself in a foreign predicament, and the questions that arose from my decisions and courses of action would have been easier to answer had I dedicated the time to create a document that established personal core values and moral obligations to myself and others. But we live and we learn, and thanks to this experience, and a course on marketing ethics I took while working towards my Master's degree, I was able to design a personal code of ethics that today I use as my North Star when conducting business. I can honestly say that this has been one of the best decisions I have ever made as a marketer and storyteller, because it empowers me to do my work from a very authentic place and reduces ambiguity around how I want to live my life and tell stories in general.

I really believe this can benefit you as well, so I've created a template framework to help guide you in writing your own.

PERSONAL CODE OF ETHICS

Preamble

The preamble is the introductory section where you share the purpose of your personal code of ethics. Essentially, you're giving the code of ethics a mission and explaining why it is important to you. Typically, this section will be about half a page to a page long and answers the questions: Why did you create this document? What is your primary mission in life? How will you use it in your life and career?

For me particularly, it was very important to mention that these principles were not only a guide for my business conduct but for life conduct in general. I made sure to mention that I have many jobs and I am many things, such as a wife, mother, daughter, sister, friend, coach, thought leader, storyteller and marketer in the technology industry, and these guidelines would help me to leave an impactful legacy in all of these aspects.

Foundations

In this section, you set out to share the foundations of your code of ethics based on at least three frameworks: moral, societal and professional. This section is typically the hardest to write, because it begs you to think through your own life-guiding principles, possibly challenging those stances that have influenced you since birth: family, culture, society, business. I will briefly break down each section to make it easier, but do take time to expand each unit as this is the meat of your document and should be about 2–3 pages long.

Moral

Here you can share your personal beliefs and values (not society's or those of your place of business), even though they might seem similar or intertwine. Common moral values usually include:

- Always tell the truth
- Have courage
- Keep your promises
- Do not cheat
- Treat others as you want to be treated
- Do not judge
- Be dependable
- Have integrity

In my code of ethics, I do a little deep dive on where I base my values, namely my religious beliefs and specific non-consequential ethical theories I have read about. It might benefit you to read some theories and better understand which ethical theories you set your values on. I will provide some extra reading suggestions at the end of this chapter regarding theories.

Societal

In this section, you can further explore philosophical ideas for social contract where you agree to abide by the set of established and understood principles with your stakeholders. This simply means that you are willing to align to society's rules and thrive in a shared societal environment, not only because you choose to align, but because you are grounding your choice on those personal ethical behaviours you first listed in the moral section. For example, under social contract, you may agree not to physically harm another person because society's laws prohibit it, but you also choose this behaviour because you have agreed with yourself that you will respect and honour others.

Professional

In addition to the moral and societal frameworks, if you work for a corporation or even if you have your own business, chances are that the brand as a stand-alone has established a code of conduct for employees and internal stakeholders. As a member of that workforce, it is your duty to understand and make the choice to align to them. In some instances, you may find that the corporation's ethical principles do not necessarily align to your personal ones. This is where it's very important that you take a step back and reflect on whether you are willing to be a part of the company or not. In addition, there may also be specific industry standards that you need to be aware of and agree to. In the United States, we have a few marketing associations that help regulate standards for the marketing industry. I suggest you look into some of these in your own location and learn more about the ethical principles established for the industry.

Statement of professional values

Here is where you can add a bulleted list explaining your key values specifically to your customers, taking into consideration industry and brand standards. Here's an example of one of mine:

> Honouring every customer and stakeholder by considering the impact every communication or ad will have on them as individuals as well as respecting their wishes as consumers in every situation.

Provisions of conduct

In this final section you will detail the actual behaviours you want to exert in bulleted form. While, prior to this, you were looking at an established set of guidelines, this piece serves to meticulously map out *how* you plan to abide by them. A real example for me is:

> A continuous attitude of gratitude towards all customers and stakeholders. No arrogant or ego-driven demeanour. A selfless approach to be the 'sidekick' of the story and placing the customer or stakeholder as the hero of the narrative in every communication and marketing plan.

Looking back at my Morocco story, and measuring the reasoning behind the decision-making to bring my mother on stage against this set of values, I can genuinely share that though I didn't have this code of ethics written up in this specific way at the time, I've always tried to hold myself against these general ethical standards.

Had I used my mother to manipulate my audience? Not at all. My heart was centred around authentically delivering my message in a way this distinct audience would best understand it. My mother had much more in common with these women, including age demographic and an entrepreneurial history, than I did, with the added bonus that she was, well, Wonder Woman. Good to note, she stole the show so well that I lost her for a few hours after the speech as she made her way through the crowd and even a local TV network who sought to interview her.

A good set of personal value norms will not only service you individually as you build your brand storytelling muscle, but also your organization as it ensures you're crafting the most authentic stories. In the best-case scenario, both your personal standards and the organization's will align. In the worst, they may not, and as an individual you have the right and responsibility to decide whether you want to tell stories for a company whose set of values does not align with yours.

You've probably figured out by now that ethics in storytelling is founded on empathy – the key that unlocks human emotion, vulnerability – the magic wand that reveals the magic of story, and inclusion – the topic we will talk about in the next chapter: Immersive storytelling.

8

Immersive storytelling

Exploring the story experience

- What is immersive storytelling?
- Leveraging immersive storytelling trends

A relatively new term has been born within the storytelling field. The first time I heard it was back in 2017 when I was invited to participate in a storytelling-focused hack: an ultra-condensed, hyper-creative event designed to encourage employees to turn their passion projects into reality.

Only a handful of storytellers, myself included, were fortunate enough to be selected to join Lance Weiler, founding member and Director of the Columbia University School of the Arts' Digital Storytelling Lab, along with his colleagues, to learn about and put into practice this cutting-edge technique that converges media and technology to bring about solution-driven tales of augmented reality.

A filmmaker and entrepreneur, Weiler has been disrupting the entertainment industry for over 20 years in the United States and abroad, and for the next couple of days he was about to teach us the ropes of this applied science in what would become one of the most eye-opening storytelling experiences I had ever been a part of.

On the first day of this World Café, as he dubbed it, we spent time understanding the fundamental topic at hand: young gang members in southside Chicago were using code language on social media to incite rival gangs to meet for violent, and sometimes deadly, altercations. Authorities had become aware of this precarious situation but were unable to find or track any communication patterns to proactively engage and diffuse, since the covert terminology seemed to be in continuous evolution.

The initial table conversations were structured, and it soon became apparent to all participants that we had been intentionally selected to contribute owing to the collective diversity of intelligence in the room. The conversations took place in three rounds, each framed around a question and then building into the next, until the clock interrupted our impassioned workflow and we begrudgingly had to put our pencils down in anticipation of the next day.

The next morning, the team all unintentionally showed up about a half hour earlier than call time. Our hunger for learning was evident. While Weiler had led the session the day before, this time he sat back and observed as one of his colleagues, a renowned gaming guru, took charge and began to explain the day's mission: we were to divide into smaller teams and create a cardboard game prototype that would help bridge communication gaps between two individual parties (or players).

What does this have to do with gang members in southside Chicago? My negative self suddenly crept up. From the puzzled looks on my teammates' faces, I deduced that they too were doubting the reasoning behind this whole experiment. But there was no time for pondering. We had only a few minutes to receive our orders and get to work, and I for once was ready to win this thing, even if it wasn't an *official* competition.

What came next was a series of jam-packed spring-like activities ranging from 22 to 45 minutes where, during every round, we were given a specific set of instructions and materials to evolve our game prototype. Aside from the tight deadlines, that really doesn't seem like a hard thing to do, right?

Wrong. The plot twist (pun intended) was that after every round, each team had to rotate and build upon another team's prototype. In other words, our 'final product' would never come from our original idea. Instead, we would cooperatively evolve someone else's concept.

You're kidding, right? Cross-group collaboration will never get me a trophy. My dark side was getting the better of me.

By the fourth and final round, our group was unquestionably mentally drained. The demand to creatively evolve something founded on someone else's original design proved to be more challenging than initially anticipated, and we were clearly running out of ideas. Thirty out of the last 45 minutes had already passed during the last assignment and my team had accomplished next to nothing. Some team members resorted to fastidiously playing with Play-Doh, while others indulged themselves in the assorted afternoon refreshments and yet others repetitiously reviewed the sticky notes left by the last team in futile attempts to gain new insights into the undertaking that sat in front of us. I nervously paced back and forth, acutely aware of the ticking clock.

The task at hand was to mature a simple communication strategy showcasing two participants. After a lot of silence and useless mini brainstorming sessions, the lightbulb finally went off: we would elevate the game to make it an interactive message of love versus hate. Below are the game rules.

Game name: Love vs Hate

Number of Players: 6

Game Objects and Roles: Player 1 (Messenger) must successfully convey the message of LOVE to Player 2 in a specific time. Player 2 (Collector) must collect all LOVE objects into a bucket to win. Players 4–6 (Distractors) distract and confuse Players 1 and 2 with HATE and DISTRACTION objects so that they do not communicate effectively.

Game Contents: LOVE, HATE, DISTRACTION figurines made of Play-Doh, collection bucket, hourglass, blindfolds, board.

Game Assembly and Setup: Game board between players. Collection bucket at Collector's end. LOVE objects at Messenger's end. HATE and DISTRACTION objects evenly distributed on both sides of board.

Game play

Coin toss for Players 1 (Messenger) and 2 (Collector), rest of players are Distractors.

Players 1 and 2 are blindfolded.

Clock Begins: set to 1 minute.

Turn Sequence: On minute 1, Player 1 takes a LOVE object and tries to place it on Player 2's side of board for pick-up, while Player 2 searches for it. Distractors will also place other objects, disrupting connection between Players 1 and 2. Once the minute is over, new player sequence begins.

Winning: Players 1 and 2 win against Distractors if they are able to successfully connect and collect LOVE objects into Player 2's bucket.

Voilà! We had completed our task.

With only seconds to spare, we ran back with our game prototype in hand ready to deliver the [winning] model. As you can imagine, we had little time to work out the minor details, such as who would play the Messenger and Collector roles, so when it came time to play, we spontaneously requested volunteers from the audience and very soon realized that this impulsive decision added a special variation to game-playing. While Player 1 was from our team and fundamentally understood the game rules, Player 2 had only just been briefed about what to expect from the Distractors. Our volunteer truly had no idea what was about to happen in the next sequence of events. And the truth is, neither did the rest of us in the room.

Distractors declared an all-out war. They made loud noises. They manipulated objects to increase their similarity in appearance to that of LOVE objects and confuse the players (remember, they were blindfolded, so they had to feel the objects on the board). Some even began removing LOVE objects from the board when it became apparent that the Collector was making some small progress and finding a connection path to the Messenger. I watched in horror and disbelief and a sudden sense of duty to end this unruly behaviour came over me, but it was quickly relinquished as I noticed the room audience was lighting up with emotion in anticipation of what would happen in the next several seconds. Instinctively, I let the game take its course. In the midst of the chaos, Player 1 realized something was off. Too many distractions were happening. Too many things felt out of control. He could 'sense' the Collector's anguish in trying to communicate but not being able to reach each other. As the sand sank faster into the bottom piece of the hourglass, the Messenger did the unexpected: he boldly stretched out his arms and softly grabbed the Collector's hands from the top of the board, gently placing a LOVE object in the centre of her palm. The audience gasped in unison and the room was suspended in a paralysing and deafening silence in the seconds that followed.

That, my dear reader, is *immersive storytelling*.

What is immersive storytelling?

You may not find an official definition of this concept in books or online yet, as it is one of those relatively new digital age terms that have yet to find their place in the digital transformation landscape. But if I had to contribute to this definition, I'd seek to borrow from the self-branding statement of the person I believe to be the godfather of immersive storytelling, Lance Weiler.

Weiler describes himself as a 'storytelling agnostic whose work is not limited by running times, mediums or platforms'.

It's true. Immersive storytelling explores and experiments with many environments, or storyworlds, with the goal of giving people the feeling of 'being there' and, through that feeling, creating an added layer of authenticity and empathy to the story, exponentially increasing its chances of success.

In the game prototyping experience I just shared with you, you only *read* what happened to my team and me. Your exposure to that moment is driven by a singular-faceted event based solely on *my* subjective forbearance of it. Had you been present in that room, your experience as a spectator, team player or even Player 1 or 2 would have provided an entirely different understanding of the occurrence and narrative, though the allegory's elements and universal truth remain the same.

Immersive storytelling takes the audience further than any 2D or 3D experience ever can, enabling a 'theory into practice' approach because it invites the audience's additional human senses to converge into the story.

Therefore, if storytelling is the emotional transfer of information through the introduction of a character, plot and conclusion, immersive storytelling is the emotional transfer of information through the *embodiment of a character in a storyworld*.

But how is this relevant for brand storytelling and how can we begin to apply it in our own space as digital marketers and communicators? I'm glad you asked!

We're already seeing how virtual and augmented reality platforms are rapidly integrating themselves into the customer experience, essentially contributing to the customer's self-indulgent demands of becoming an active character in the brand story. Digital transformation is forcing the traditional narrative structure to emerge from its grassroots design where the audience happily took the passive role of a listener, reader or viewer to become that of a 'lived experience' where narratives incorporate the latest technologies such as 360° video or holograms to invite the audience to experience the story within a particular environment.

Some brands are already harnessing the power of immersive storytelling and winning. In 2017, IKEA launched Place, an augmented reality app that enables customers to preview how furniture pieces can look within a particular floorplan space through the convenient use of their smartphones. This integration marked a significant milestone for the furniture retailer in their digital transformation journey and continues to be a popular differentiator for the brand in the market.

The reality is that it's only a matter of time before this innovative brand storytelling approach completely takes over the traditional written storytelling methods and becomes the norm. The introduction of immersive storytelling may give you the overwhelming feeling that you have yet to catch up with the *old* method... but I say be comforted instead, because you now have the opportunity to consider this leading strategy as part of your future brand storytelling plans.

In Chapter 3, I briefly mentioned how UX-designed stories oblige us to get maniacal about providing an optimal experience to our customers through everything from typography to story setting to visual elements. And now, we should consider environment as an add-on element. As stated earlier, immersive storytelling is about intentionally creating a favourable environment for your audience to zestfully experience the brand story. And while storytelling with design thinking principles continues to faithfully drive the idea of a low-cost, low-effort approach, it would be a disservice to you and your brand not to invest in future communication technologies as part of your digital transformation journey.

Immersive storytelling trends

With that in mind, it's important to carefully analyse relevant market trends that can help you decide which type of technologies can help create the best immersive environments for your brand story. For this, I have created an opportunities chart (Table 8.1). By using this chart, you can fill in relevant trends as well as 'unknowns' within your specific industry, design audience, current technologies and even society that exist in your individual space and can help you uncover ideas for your immersive storytelling consideration process. The more time you spend researching these trends, the more opportunities you can find in your specific landscape.

TABLE 8.1   Opportunities chart

	Current trends	Unknowns
Industry		
Design audience		
Technologies		
Society		

Let's say I were to fill in this chart for a company within the tech industry (as it happens to be my field of work) in my quest to find opportunities for immersive storytelling. My chart would look somewhat like Table 8.2 at a very high level.

TABLE 8.2   Opportunities chart example

	Current trends	Unknowns
Industry	Autonomous things, augmeneted analytics, AI developments, blockchain, empowered edge, smart spaces	How will AI and IoT continue to evolve their own intelligence? What does autonomous things mean to traditional products? How do smart spaces/modern workplaces disrupt working environments as we know them?
Design audience	Smart, cutting-edge, easily bored, wants to get to the point fast, likes 'how-to' stories, enjoys reading	Will they still like reading in the near future? Will 'reading' look different if integrated with mixed reality?
Technologies	Digital channels, cloud computing, latest hardware, holograms, subscription model	How fast will these technologies evolve and need to be adopted by my organization?
Society	Innovations, well-being, social justice, environmentally friendly, connectedness, mindfulness, purpose-driven, emotionally charged	What will society norms look like in the near future and how will they affect social interaction?

By taking time to analyse market and audience trends with this context, you can purposely begin to map out which immersive experiences fit best in your brand storytelling. The following are types of immersive brand storytelling techniques that currently exist (and that may be obsolete, evolved or replaced by the time you finish reading this book).

360° or spherical video

As the name suggests, these video images are captured either through a collection of cameras set up in different places or through a panoramic or omnidirectional camera in order to provide a 360° view for the consumer. As with everything immersive, the upside of using this technique is that it offers more information than the conventional approach, and the more information you're willing to give your audience, the bigger the potential you have to increase trust and loyalty with your stakeholders. This immersive medium adds another layer of authenticity because it displays every possible angle, so there are no 'hidden corners' or 'behind the scenes' scenarios happening in the background, which are usually obscured, but known to the viewer. For storytellers in traditional disciplines such as the entertainment industry, this type of openness can actually signify a nuisance, because most conventional techniques in storytelling draw upon illusion to successfully deliver the stories. However, in brand storytelling, the ultimate goal is to be as authentic and vulnerable as possible, so 360° video may be a good narrative channel to consider. From an immersive angle, this technique gives the audience a decent level of interactivity with the storyworld by providing an option to play with the story content through movement of the frames or clicking of links, if available. Effective ways that a brand can integrate 360° video into their brand storytelling are by using them for:

- company events, keynotes, product announcements;
- customer-specific messages from executive or top leadership;
- advertising.

One downside of this technique is that the stories being told through this medium are still told through the videographer's angle, so the view is limited to the filmmaker's camera's movements. Nevertheless, if a photo is worth a thousand words, how many words is a 360° photo worth? At the very least, dabbling with this inventive technology puts you at the forefront of digital marketing and makes you a thought leader in immersive storytelling. Storytelling never ends and always tests new platforms that appeal to your audience. This one might be one to explore.

Gaming or emergent storytelling

While your mind may go directly to videogames as you read this subtitle, you may be surprised to find that videogames are but a fraction of gaming as a type of immersive storytelling technique, and for brand storytelling purposes, videogames may not apply as a technique at all.

I began this chapter by sharing with you a story about how our extended group of storytellers at Microsoft set out to build a series of evolved board-game prototypes with the goal of solving a real-life societal issue in southside Chicago. Bringing you back to that story, after that extraordinary moment when Player 1 reached out for Player 2's hand, all of us had an acute understanding of what immersive storytelling meant. The *universal feeling* (or emotion activated and unanimously felt by all of us coming in contact with this live-action narrative) was that of *accomplishment*. This elated feeling of triumph happened when the two desperate players finally thought outside the (cardboard) box and were able to successfully communicate with one another. But notice that I label this juncture as the moment of universal truth and not the climatic point of this chronicle. For all of us, the actual turning point happened when Weiler *anticlimactically* broke the atmospheric silence, expediently leveraging our universal truth moment to point out just how visionary we can all become when we endeavour to conquer something specific and how we could conveniently use those newly discovered raw instincts, competencies, imaginative workflows and cross-group collaboration techniques to help him and his team devise a decoding method for authorities to help translate social channel communication between gang members. Because in that game, real lives were at stake.

I'm not a gamer myself, but through this rigorous hackathon exercise I quickly learned a few basic truths about game designing that later served me well when introducing emergent storytelling as a technique in business. These are:

- By design, all games are broken. The challenge is to fix something.

- Game design considers how it will empower the players. Creative power, destructive power, manipulative power are but a few types of powers that players are given for a chance of winning the game.

- 'Gameplay' is a catchall phrase that mysteriously fits into every context of a game conversation, even if it doesn't make sense. Keep reading this gameplay to learn more.

At its best, game storytelling ditches the theoretical allegory of sorts and dives right into the practical schooling of literal character embodiment in the storyworld, exasperating the main character's need to win. Within the brand context, game storytelling engages the audience so deeply into the brand story that the level of empathy towards the company is almost as high as it is with the self. The audience is systematically learning about the brand story from a first-person perspective and naturally discovering by what means they interrelate with it, as opposed to being told by the brand. This direct interaction with the brand mission, core values and universal truth 'speaks for itself' and creates a tremendously powerful bond between the brand and the audience.

At its worst, like in my own game prototype, at any given moment the active character may decide to improvise and disrupt the gameplay sequence, creating an alternative storyboard of universal truths for the brand. Not too bad an outcome, if you ask me, because this can help uncover alternative angles the brand may not have contemplated otherwise.

Effective ways that a brand can integrate game storytelling into their brand storytelling are by using it for:

- Customer-related internal mini hacks: establish the challenge, empower players with your brand story core values, mission and universal truth and let stakeholders creatively hack solutions in game format.

- Gamification reward platform for customers: whether sales, marketing or other incentivized programs, use your brand storyline and elements to create immersive gamification reward experiences for your customers.

- Social advocacy: both internal and external stakeholders can participate in a gamified approach to social amplification of your storytelling content. More on this in the next chapter.

Mixed reality

The very premise of this book is founded on the notion that the integration of the latest digital technologies into every aspect of business (also known as digital transformation) is forcing the blending of the physical world with the digital world (also known as mixed reality or MR), and brands are having to recognize that traditional means of engagement and marketing between organizations and customers are rapidly becoming obsolete.

Digital technologies have significantly raised the bar on what engaging content can look like, and when it comes to brands that seek to be thought leaders in digital marketing, the use of virtual reality (VR) and augmented reality (AR) offers a new realm of opportunities to create compelling and innovative content.

Differentiating itself from emergent storytelling or 360° video, this multilayered approach to story offers exciting new storyworlds to be explored and controlled by active characters. The storyboard is nonlinear, and the design feels almost boundaryless in this story-living model where unique elements come together to create a more dynamic and emotional experience for the audience. At its early stages, this immersive storytelling approach required an even more focused embodiment of character because it necessitated the use of supporting gear (such as vision goggles) to invite the character into the story setting. However, AR has quickly evolved to leveraging mobile device camera views paired up with social media application filters to overlay content into the real world.

At a high level, many brands in many industries have already begun adopting this immersive technique to bring products and services to customers where they are, as opposed to expecting customers to come to them. With AR and mobile technologies, brands are helping customers envision themselves using a particular product or service, and this has proven to be a very lucrative marketing tactic. In 2018 alone, AR advertising brought in $428.3 million in revenue and it's expected to top $2 billion by 2022.

But we've learned that storytelling is beyond a marketing tactic or tool. It is an intentional approach to connect at a deep and emotional level with our stakeholders. So how do we go beyond short-lived marketing gimmicks and integrate this immersive technique into the long-lasting brand storytelling strategy? Effective ways that a brand can integrate mixed reality storytelling into their brand storytelling are by using it for:

- Offering new dimensions for your brand storyworlds: as you define and design the brand story setting, character and plot, think of ways that these environments can creatively pop up on a customer's mobile device through holographic content, for example.
- Weaving user sensory experience scenarios for your products and services into the brand story, not as a marketing campaign.

Live streaming

While broadcasting in real time has been around for a little while longer than 360° video, emergent storytelling and mixed reality, it continues to be a leading immersive storytelling technique that is most compelling against all others because, well, it's real time.

The word 'genuine' often comes to mind when live streaming is used as a platform. The idea that *anything can happen* gives the audience a sense of camaraderie with the storyteller as together they navigate a somewhat ambiguous storyline. Social media influencers have built their empires on this immersive technique simply because of its highly engaging features such as informal direct interaction and unfiltered display. Best of all, it's relatively inexpensive, and most social channels have provided a live streaming vehicle to deliver content to audiences, so that storytellers, once again, can meet customers where they are. Another benefit of live streaming is that your content has the potential to reach audiences way beyond your target as viewers invite others to join in the fun. This immersive storytelling technique can be a real differentiator for your brand in the market if you're primarily looking to establish relationships and increase brand awareness.

Beyond marketing, live streaming can beef up your brand storytelling in multiple ways. Effective ways that a brand can integrate live streaming into their brand storytelling are by using it for:

- Creating a sense of urgency for your brand story: is there a new character, product or plot twist you want to introduce to your audience? Announce a special event to your audience and tell them live. As you continue to evolve your brand and brand story to meet customer demands, using this avenue to vulnerably share your journey with your audience may help you win extra points in the trust and loyalty departments. So many brands today choosing to take a social stance, for example, have failed to show up authentically to their audiences, even if they truly intended to, because their advocacy move was abrupt and offered no context. I imagine that if, prior to launching the provoking, and generally displeasing, Gillette 'Toxic Masculinity' ad I mentioned earlier in the book, a Procter & Gamble storyteller had strategically jumped on a two-minute live stream and introduced the setting and reasoning for this brand's shift in core values and alignment to the #MeToo movement, the response from the public would have been a lot different. Live streaming offers an opportunity to bridge on-the-spot (often seen as more vulnerable and authentic) and already-crafted content, showcasing an ability from your brand to dabble with new technologies in the quest to capture audiences from different angles.

- Giving the audience an 'inside look' at the brand: while a lot of progressive companies have now taken the cue from Apple to live stream their hero product reveal events, a smaller-scale, more mundane approach can invite audiences to experience everyday operations or a Q&A conversation between leaders where they too can engage and immerse themselves in the story. At Microsoft, engineering disciplines offer a monthly webinar to help answer questions around products and services. This has become a very popular and successful storytelling practice, leaning into the brand's universal truth of empowerment, because it not only opens a new door of connectivity between customers and the brand, but enables those customers to learn directly from those individuals who sit at the forefront of the technology.

These are just a few examples and ideas of immersive storytelling techniques that you can begin to explore as you build your brand story. Remember, storytellers (you and I) are in the never-ending quest to evolve the brand story in creative and meaningful ways. As more technologies arise, we'll have more opportunities to discover new ways to share the narrative... and change the gameplay. Consider it a true privilege to be a frontrunner of brand storytelling in this digital age, where everything is curiously unpredictable, and you get to pioneer it for your brand.

FTW!

9

Your best brand storytellers

Employees and influencers

- Building a storytelling army
- Designing the story persona
- Employees and influencers: the good, the bad and the ugly

Both employee advocacy and social influencers have always existed in one way or another as an effective means of promotion for brands, even if not officially and specifically selected by the organization. People are natural storytellers and, as social beings, we innately connect with friends and acquaintances through the interchange of allegory, often about our mundane day-to-day activities, which surely bring us back to our place of work or preferred grocery store (brands we often engage with). It is also no secret that celebrities, journalists and industry experts have consistently influenced purchase decisions simply, and sometimes inadvertently, by sharing their choice of fashion brand or fast food restaurant. But with the decay of traditional marketing and the fast advancement of technology, these two orator forces have risen in an unprecedented way to become today's top digital marketing and storytelling channel: social media.

In the early 2000s, social media began to empower individual users to establish credibility with particular audiences, outside the once fortified walls of traditional marketing and PR. By virtue of authenticity alone (there's that word again), when brands were still wrestling with the idea of investing in such things as a Facebook page or Twitter account because there was no way of tracking return on investment (ROI), an army of savvy *socialpreneurs* (or early social media adopters) began to explore each of these channels and build their reputation with niche audiences, simply by sharing their expertise or showing up 'behind the scenes' of a manicured camera. Celebrities and 'nobodies' alike, choosing to ride this wave, began to enjoy a new and direct medium to approach and connect with their audiences, and this marked the beginning of what today is known as influencer marketing, a $10 billion dollar industry that is leading the way in brand marketing, and consequently, storytelling.

While I recognize that there are several types and levels of brand endorsers in the industry, for the purpose of building your brand story, I'd like to group influencers and employees together under one category: story persona.

In Chapter 3, I briefly touched on UX design principles to reinforce the importance of carefully crafting the brand story so that it can provide an optimal experience to the audience. And that is the key word: experience. The 'emotional transfer of information' is an *experience*. Empathy is an *experience*. Vulnerability is an *experience*. Story is an *experience*. And no matter how well we think we've designed the story, it is how the user *experiences* the narrative that ultimately determines how effectively it will land.

> In UX design, an earnest piece of the design process is defining the *design persona*. Notice that I didn't say the *user persona*, which we know to be a hypothetical representation of the target audience.

Much different from a user or marketing persona, in UX, a design persona is crafted to best understand the relationship (or experience) between the designed product and the user. In other words, design personas give the *product* a hypothetical personality.

I'd like to borrow and also modify this UX concept to serve brand storytelling because, while the story is the final 'product', it is the *storyteller* who makes the story come alive and unlocks the story experience for the audience.

Where would the iPhone be if someone other than Steve Jobs had shared its remarkable tale of origin?

How impactful would the World Wildlife Fund be as a global organization without its A-lister celebrity advocates?

Would National Geographic have as much success and influence on Instagram without the posting of raw, individual journalism allegories shared by those experiencing the 'behind the scenes' while on assignment?

Building a storytelling army

I think you get my point on how pivotal the dependency between stories and storytellers is, but you already know this. Lately, we've seen brands significantly increase their spend on influencer marketing and employee advocacy efforts, with some investing up to 40 per cent of their total marketing budget in influencer marketing alone. Brands are recognizing the paramountcy of granting storyteller duties to the *humans* of the brand instead of the organization as a whole, and this is paying great dividends.

I've personally witnessed global corporations such as Adobe evolve their employee advocacy programs from merely providing curated brand content for employees to share to decisively equipping their employees to embody the brand story and weave it into their own personal tales, intentionally activating them as brand story ambassadors. And the results are fascinating.

Any other author would share this instance in case study form, but in the true fashion of storytelling, I asked Jose Camacho, Social Media and Employee Advocacy Program Manager for Adobe, and also a personal friend, to give his exclusive account of how employee storytelling developed at one of the world's most prominent multinational software companies.

HOW ADOBE'S SOCIAL AMBASSADOR PROGRAM EVOLVED FROM TRANSACTIONAL EMPLOYEE CONTENT PUBLISHING TO A ROBUST COMMUNITY OF BRAND CHAMPIONS WITH STORYTELLING

My name is Jose-Andres Camacho. I am a Social Media Enablement Strategist at Adobe, responsible for scaling, mobilizing and leading the brand's Social Ambassador Program by working cross-collaboratively with global teams to help equip employees to learn and tell the Adobe brand story and evangelize it by passionately sharing it on social channels, organically consuming our products and enthusiastically participating in our corporate social impact efforts.

When I started the role in June 2018, I knew very little of employee advocacy or storytelling and how both are being leveraged by businesses for competitive advantage in various industries today. Although I was aware of overall employee advocacy tactics, never had I seen it sourced to the scale chartered by my newly assigned team at Adobe.

Our immediate goal was to get at least 50 per cent of our enterprise-wide employee base of plus 20,000 to not only learn, but love our brand story so much that it would instinctively propel them to generously share it with their individual audiences on a regular basis. I will be honest. I did not fully grasp how brazen a goal this was. At the time we had around 700 users on our employee advocacy program, some of whom were not even considered active. But shoot for the stars, you'll at least land on the moon, right? I had much to learn – very swiftly.

As I began my research, the Head of Employee Advocacy and I instantly began to uncover a number of innovative opportunities to implement as part of our wider strategy to scale the program in a healthy way (I'll explain what this means later on).

Our first step was to get the right tools in place for scaling. From the very beginning, a key partner in our employee advocacy efforts was our technology partner, EveryoneSocial. EveryoneSocial is an employee advocacy and social selling platform that helps companies diffuse their brand story and story assets, such as news, articles, video and documents, for employee curation and sharing.

We needed to measure active users as a baseline for benchmarking. So, we defined an 'active user' as someone who had logged into the tool at least once in the past 30 days. Then we established goals.

Naturally, with a tool like EveryoneSocial, there are a variety of metrics you can employ to track success. For us at Adobe, we determined that the two biggest key performance indicators (KPIs) were the number of users in general and the percentage of active users, since our primary goal was to scale quality storytellers. In addition, we also implemented secondary performance metrics to help us understand the efficacy of the program as a whole. Our KPIs looked like this:

- Percentage of active users
  - User logged in within the past 30 days
  - Goals
    - 50% of employee base
    - 30–35% of users reaching best-in-class ranking per EveryoneSocial tool criteria

- Social channel metrics
  - Reach
  - Engagement
  - Lead generation (visits to Adobe.com domain)

We also tracked the number of suspended users as part of our strategy to keep people active by implementing a 'purge' initiative where, semi-annually, we would reach out to inactive users, encouraging them to log back into the tool within 10 business days to signal to us their commitment to keep their accounts instated, otherwise to let those 10 business days pass and we would give their licence to another user.

Then we laid out the storytelling strategy.

One of the major draws to our program was the ability for employees to use EveryoneSocial as a personal social media content aggregator tool. We understood that our new storytellers had individual motivations for sharing stories and that though the overall brand story was the same, it could be broken down into mini-stories (always leading back to our universal truth) and distributed in categories through different storylines for personalized sharing. So, we created eight storytelling streams varying in topics from 'Adobe news' to 'Digital Experience', 'Creativity' and 'Leadership'. Every day, users would log into EveryoneSocial and find the latest articles, blogs, videos and tweets to engage with and share to their own social network. They could also schedule any of these story pieces to be shared at the best time for their audience within specific channels such as LinkedIn and Twitter. Users had a variety of social channels to choose from, including Facebook, Xing and WeChat, and in case they had a hard time adding their own 'spin' to the story arcs, we included generic, pre-written social copy to ease the burden of coming up with tweet-worthy verbiage.

It was important for our users to be emotionally connected to these stories, rather than seeing them as typical brand marketing content, so we spent a lot of time carefully curating each piece of content and ensuring that every one of them represented the Adobe brand values and mission the best way possible, every time.

Then, it was time to scale.

At first, we started with a smaller group of early adopters to have an opportunity to observe and gain insights into our working model. As the program gained traction, we began to strategically reach out to some Adobe internal teams and invite them to partner and pilot our program within their discipline, not only to help build buzz and activity on social media but to ladder-up to the wider organization goals, where appropriate.

For example, one team we piloted was a group of about 160 talent acquisition team members where we implemented targeted goals, including but not limited to:

- Talent team would share at least one social post per week.
- Adobe hashtag use to increase by a minimum of 15% year over year on LinkedIn, Instagram and Twitter channels.
- Follower count for Adobe social accounts to grow by 15% year over year.

Within just five months, the pilot tracked so well that our team was asked to expand and roll out to the entire employee experience organization.

Pro-tip: If you have a 'Sports Marketing Program' or similar function within your company that partners with local concert venues, stadiums and arenas, ask about how your Employee Advocacy Program can partner with them. This partnership comes in handy when they have unused tickets to local games, events, concerts and so on which you can leverage as Program incentives. We managed to make an arrangement with our respective Sports Marketing Program manager to prioritize our advocacy program team for any outstanding event tickets so that we could award them to exceptional Social Ambassador champions. This turned out to be a great call, especially when we agreed to become hyper-creative and tune into gamification for added impact.

One way we encouraged a healthy sense of competition among colleagues was by leveraging EveryoneSocial's gamification features, the leaderboards. These performance-ranking boards play a key role in motivating teams towards sharing and engagement metrics. For example, if we wanted to encourage users to post more engaging content, we would award more points to content that resulted in a certain number of engagements by their audience instead of the amount of actual content itself.

The leaderboards also enabled us to target specific geo-location campaigns. For example, in the summer of 2019 we received four free tickets to an upcoming DJ Khalid concert at Oracle Arena. Because we had recently onboarded a cohort of around 350 interns, most of whom were from the Bay Area, we decided to run an impromptu contest with all Bay Area interns. The contest would run for five days and the top four interns who shared the most stories would win the Khalid tickets.

The results were bewildering. In our five-day contest, we saw:

interns);

- +593% in Adobe stories shared to social media from this cohort alone;

- +14% engagement within the five-day period.

More recently, we had an opportunity to give away 20 free tickets to a San Francisco Giants vs Chicago Cubs baseball game to a group of fortunate social ambassadors. Using EveryoneSocial's reporting and analytics features, we pulled data to find top-performing Bay Area social ambassadors in terms of engagements during the month prior and without warning reached out to them to surprise them and let them know they had won.

These 'surprise and delight' experiences have become extremely valuable for us in terms of building energy and positive relationships in and outside our Social Ambassador Program versus the expected awards users are already aiming for as part of gamification. Through this experiment, we also began to appreciate the importance of imparting the brand story outside of digital walls.

As our program began to build demand among business units and organizations across Adobe, we saw an opportunity to think bigger. Because of this, our team began to shift its focus to elevating brand storytelling skills among the Social Ambassador Program. We did this in several ways. First, we launched the 2019 Employee Advocacy Learning Series of webinars in January 2019. This series of educational webinars included topics like:

- 'Optimizing Your Social Media Presence: How to Save Time and Bring Together the Content You Love', which focused on enablement around high-value behaviours like creating personal streams on EveryoneSocial where users can create feeds that automatically pull in content from sources like RSS Feeds, Google keywords, #hashtags and @Twitter handles.

- 'How to Optimize Your LinkedIn Profile (and what to post)', which helped users put their best foot forward on LinkedIn in terms of publishing frequency, tips, direction on where to find Adobe-branded cover images and other best practices.

The series' goals were twofold:

- Educate our users (and wider employee base) on high-value behaviours because we found that users who created personal streams shared six times more content over those who did not.

- Drive awareness to the Adobe Social Ambassador Program and keep our enablement resources top-of-mind.

Also, in conjunction with our learning initiatives, we introduced fun and rewarding networking events to create a deeper sense of community and buy-in.

Today, Adobe's Social Ambassador Program has progressed from being simply a transactional content-creation approach for employees to a healthy community of brand storytellers, and the numbers speak for themselves. Beyond numbers, the brand enjoys an equipped and increasing group of employees who regularly and resourcefully share the Adobe story, have a distinct social presence, regularly use our products and get involved in our corporate social impact efforts.

When I first arrived at Adobe, our original mission was to help Adobe employees and partners show their support for Adobe online, discover relevant content shared by fellow employees and stay up to date with industry news. While that was an appropriate charter for our team at the time, it has since evolved to a robust brand storytelling function, one that tears down organizational silos and works cross-collaboratively with other teams globally.

Looking to the future of employee advocacy and brand storytelling, I see organizations championing internal influencers and company leaders to have a truly unique and powerful influence on digital channels by moving away from merely regurgitating curated content and empowering employees to tap true thought leadership via user-generated content (USG) and other forms of digital expression, enabled by the brand and resulting in a true sense of community and culture engagement between brand storytellers, both digitally and physically.

So there you have it. There is no question that humans telling the humanized brand story works. But if every brand begins to tune into employee advocacy and influencer marketing practices, won't brand storytelling eventually get diluted and, like everything else, become obsolete? I began this chapter by acknowledging that employee advocacy and influencer marketing have always existed, even when there was no official title for these marketing 'techniques'. They existed organically because, as humans, we naturally seek to engage authentically with others, and they will continue to exist years from now for that very reason.

Side note: I would be remiss if I didn't make a clear distinction between employee advocacy and influencer marketing, before plopping them together into the story persona. So, I drew a quick table showcasing each technique's most valuable attributes, types, trends and statistics (Table 9.1).

TABLE 9.1 Employee advocacy and influencer marketing statistics

	What is it?	Types	Trends & Statistics
Employee Advocacy	Recruiting and incentivizing employees to share their support for the brand, brand products and culture to help raise positive awareness about the brand	Early adopter, champion, internal brand influencer	• Brand messages reached 561% further when shared by employees vs the same messages shared via official brand social channels • Employee advocacy programs with at least 1,000 active participants can generate $1.9M in advertising value • 65% of brands reported increased brand recognition after implementing an employee advocacy program • Leads developed through employee social marketing convert 7x more frequently than other leads
Influencer Marketing	Recruiting and incentivizing people who have built a reputation for their particular talent or expertise in a topic and have gained a follower audience because of it	Celebrities, industry experts, content creators, micro and nano influencers	• In 2019, 320 new influencer marketing focused platforms and agencies entered the market • Businesses who understand influencer marketing can gain up to $18 in earned media value for every dollar they spend • 69.4% of influencers chose to be influencers so they could earn revenue • 70% of teenage YouTube subscribers say they relate to YouTube creators more than traditional celebrities

While there are clear differences between the two, from a brand storytelling perspective, both serve to tell the brand story efficaciously in what may be the most authentic and relatable manner to the audience. I encourage you to research which storytellers work best for your particular brand and brand strategy, but will call out that nano and micro influencers are becoming more prominent in the influencer space because they tend to be more zealous towards the niche audience they have come to organically amass as a result of their personal efforts. For that reason, if you were to ask me, I would say your best brand storytellers are employees and micro influencers. Both are authentically and emotionally tied to the brand story – and not interested in 'selling' to their audience.

But not everything in story is a fairy tale. Some brands are still struggling with getting the best ROI from influencer marketing or employee advocacy campaigns, if any at all. So how can we maximize our resource investment efforts when selecting the best storytellers to go and tell our carefully crafted brand story? By carefully defining the story persona, of course. And this can be done in five easy steps.

Designing the story persona

Step 1. Evaluate your brand story characteristics

In Chapters 2 and 3, we learned about the many brand story elements, such as the universal truth, structure, colour, typography and other attributes, that make the story come to life. As you get ready to match these attributes with the story persona (or chosen storyteller), it is wise to review these characteristics one more time and cross-reference them against each type of orator contender to understand highest level of suitability. A few questions to consider during this evaluation process are:

- Does this [influencer or employee] best reflect and represent the brand story?
- Who is this [influencer or employee] as a character in the brand story?
- Does this [influencer or employee] seem more like an intruder or a natural addition to the brand story?

Choosing and crafting your brand persona begins with evaluating which personalities can best complement those attributes you have carefully given your brand story. There is nothing more disappointing than to see a brand put extraordinary efforts into the meticulous design of their brand story, only to have it fail miserably because they didn't take time to also craft the story persona.

Step 2. List your audience motivations

I know well that you have already defined your audience and reflected on which emotions you seek to evoke from them through your brand story. But throughout the book, I keep iterating that the audience is in continuous transformation. By the time you read this chapter, the very motivations that were true for your audience a few months or weeks ago may be completely different. Therefore, as you decide how your story personas will look, sound and approach the audience, it makes sense to revisit the list of factors that keep your audience inspired and engaged to help define those persona traits. When listing your audience's motivations, consider the following:

- If you have a hybrid audience, will one story persona suffice, or will you need more than one? In the case of Microsoft, I have mentioned before that their audience expands across a multitude of industries and cohorts. For that reason, they craft different stories, all tying back to the brand mission and universal truth, so they design several story personas to appeal to their diverse audience base.

- Does the story persona attract your audience? Let's remove the brand story from the equation for a second. If the story persona alone were to show up in front of your audience, would they be wooed by it? Would they want to learn more about the brand because of it?

Whether an influencer or employee, every storyteller contracted to tell your brand story should observe the attributes and personality you give the story persona designed by you and your team, because it considers your audience's motivations and desires. In other words, it is customer-centric in essence – it keeps your customer (not the storyteller) at the centre of the story.

Step 3. Explore the story persona affordances

In UX, there is a term used to describe the offering and value a product provides the user, based on the user's perception of it. This is called an affordance. In *The UX Book: Process and guidelines for ensuring a quality user experience*, author Rex H Harston explains than an affordance can be seen as the physical relationship the user has with the product.

There are four types of affordances in design, namely cognitive, physical, sensory and functional, and I will once again tailor this notion to brand storytelling to help you design the best story persona (Table 9.2).

TABLE 9.2   Types of design affordances

Affordance Type	Description	Example
Cognitive Affordance	Story persona behaviour that helps the audience identify and foreshadow something specific about the brand story	A catch phrase that an influencer or employee will always say before introducing a part or all of the brand story to their audience
Physical Affordance	A story element that the story persona leverages to physically engage the audience	A call to action, a stage prop or visual element during storytelling
Sensory Affordance	Elements the story persona uses to engage the senses of the audience	Is the persona's tone audible enough? Their presence noticeable enough?
Functional Affordance	Attributes the story persona has that serve to successfully drive the brand story mission	How does the story persona effectively evoke the emotions from the audience?

With this in mind, think about whether and how the personality guidelines you attribute to the story persona consider these affordances.

Step 4. Explore the emotional job the story persona delivers

This wouldn't be a storytelling book if it didn't mention the word emotion repeatedly and in every chapter.

The story persona is in essence the face of the brand story. Everyone who comes in contact with the story persona, whether in an influencer or employee form, will make judgements on the brand based on how implicitly they deliver the brand story. For this reason, it's vital that you determine the emotional elements the story persona has and plays and how these are translating the brand story. A few things to consider when exploring the emotional job of the story persona are:

- Does the persona awaken the same emotions from the audience as the brand story does? If you were to hire a social influencer, for example, that is known to be extremely sarcastic in his tone and manner but your brand story's mission is to evoke a sense of benevolence, this may come across as conflicting to your audience. When designing your brand persona, ensure that as a stand-alone it speaks to the brand's universal truth through its own core elements.

- Does the persona set the mood for the brand story? Emotions, moods and feelings are all part of the brand storytelling experience. How your story persona shows up will create the setting for the story in and of itself and it's good to consider how effective this setting is.

Step 5. Give your persona an identity

Alas! This is the culminating and most fun part of crafting your story persona. After you've studiously taken time to revisit your brand story characteristics, audience motivations, affordances and emotional value, it's now time to begin crafting your story persona just as you would a marketing persona or other types of fictional representation characters. As a marketer, I know you're a guru at creating personas, but given this niche character, I still want to offer some tips that you may find useful:

- Give as many personality attributes to your story persona as possible:
  - Example: My story persona is a neighbour, friend and hero to all XYZ Company stakeholders. While modern and tech-savvy, her physical attributes blend well with XYZ's humble beginnings, so she does not take away from the nostalgic charm and experience that the brand's origin story proudly provides the audience. The story persona gives comfort and an emotional experience through thoughtful and immersive sensory and physical experiences, and she knows well the audience's motivations and seeks to meet them every time. My story persona is always smiling and delighting audiences with her welcoming and authentic presence.
- Share this characteristic definition with your potential storytellers:
  - Influencers, top leaders in the organization, regular employees, celebrities and anyone else who has been granted the official storyteller task for your brand story should recognize the key attributes your story persona possesses and embody them within their own disposition. But

please do not get me wrong. The story persona serves only as a guiding light to show how the story can best be told, not as a dictated and inflexible approach to storytelling. Remember that the story persona enables the relationship between the brand story and the audience, and it is clear that every storyteller will manifest the brand story to the best of their ability within their own context, as they should. Nevertheless, as with everything branding, it serves the brand best to establish norms and guidelines to keep the path of the brand story headed in its best direction.

- Revisit the story persona attributes periodically:
  - If you've learned nothing else from this book at all, please remember the *one* thing I have been stressing from the very beginning: storytelling is a verb. Part of the continued design thinking process is prototyping and testing concepts, and this includes your story persona and its attributes. The brand, brand story and brand stakeholders are all continuously evolving, so the attributes you bestow on the story persona may be irrelevant very soon. Thankfully, your audience will be honest enough to indicate whether the story persona is still evoking the right set of emotions when delivering the story. Continue to listen to them, observe and see what warms their heart, as the story gets told in many forms, channels and through many storytellers.

Employees and influencers: The good, the bad and the ugly

Now that you have a North Star for your potential storytellers, let's take a look at the roles each plays in your brand storytelling, as well as the benefits and risks associated with each so that you can maximize the success of your story.

Employees

Unlike influencers, employees are already an integral part of your brand story, so once you've shared your newly crafted story using IMC Reimagined techniques, they will uniformly own it, live it and tell it, right? We wish.

In Chapter 4, I highlighted how brand storytelling serves as a culture activator and how an integrated marketing and communication approach can furnish strategic resources to help invigorate this key group of storytellers to authentically live and breathe the brand story. But as we apply the concept of story personas, how can this tactic properly commission internal storytellers – C-suite leaders and customer service representatives alike – to wondrously permeate the brand tale to their individual audiences in the most magical way? By probing the possibilities.

Most brands I've come in contact with understand the importance of designing the brand story (this is why you're reading this book) but have an exceptionally trying time when having to operationally bridge the gap between the intersectionality that employees at every level and discipline of the organization bring to the brand story. Therefore, they sadly end up succumbing to the safe, unoriginal and often fruitless content-curation employee advocacy model that some third-party tool offers, leaving the most important part of brand storytelling on the table: story personification.

Don't commit brand story suicide. You and your team have been working very hard to design a stunning story for your stakeholders and, as a final strategy step, it is critical to look at the primary storytellers and the roles they play in the organization so that you can best empower them to impart the story.

The chart shown in Table 9.3 illustrates the differing storytelling roles that employees of the organization can play as they take on the story persona, and the related pros and cons that can affect your storytelling strategy. This scenario assumes that your brand has decided to implement storytelling as a blueprint for business growth, and that leaders are not only supportive, but also helping drive the strategy.

Remember that this chart only showcases a general idea of how employees of the organization may play a part as they envelop the story persona, so you can take a more targeted employee advocacy approach and increase your chances of triumphantly landing the brand story internally. By no means is this a concrete idea and, in the spirit of design thinking, it's once again essential to remain flexible when integrating storytelling strategies. I encourage you to use this chart as a template and take time to plug in your own organization's leadership roles and how they currently play in your storytelling strategy.

Influencers

I won't spend a lot of time explaining the role that influencers can potentially play in your brand story because you already know. But I do want to remind you of a few general pros and cons of leveraging this storyteller force as you continue to strategize the best ways to land the brand story with your audiences:

TABLE 9.3 Employee storyteller role pros and cons

Employee Type	Storyteller Role(s)	Story Persona Pros	Story Persona Cons
Top Management (C-suite level)	• Impart brand story from the top down to internal stakeholders • Funnel and fund storytelling strategies • Equip and keep middle managers accountable for driving storytelling strategies in their discipline	• Already believe in and consistently reinforce the brand story • Influencers and thought leaders within organization • Embody the story persona attributes • Effectively contribute to emotional function of the story • Understand audience motivation at a high level	• Historically, not highly or authentically engaged on social channels • May be disconnected from some design affordances • May push back on brand storytelling efforts if ROI metrics are not clearly defined
Middle Management (division head, regional managers)	• Help diffuse brand story into departments • Allocate dedicated budget to storytelling practices • Decide on and create distinctive narratives focused on audience base • Equip and keep supervisors accountable for properly executing brand story consistency within their departments	• Embrace telling the brand story and story persona attributes • Are micro influencers within organization • Define hybrid audiences • May be more in tune with social media engagement	• May not understand intricacies of storytelling design and continuous evolution approach • May be less concerned with the emotional job of the story and more concerned with the functional affordances in respect to the bottom line

Role			
Supervisory (supervisor, program manager)	• Infuse brand storytelling to employees on a daily basis as part of the brand strategy • Execute on defined storytelling techniques for their particular department • Equip and keep employees accountable for understanding and telling the brand story individually	• Consistently tell the brand story • Are nano influencers within organization • May have an active social media and digital presence • Have close visibility to story trickling down to employees • Understands pain points of storytelling design evolution	• May be more concerned with the emotional job of the story and less concerned with the functional affordances in respect to the bottom line • May be tempted to take a 'behind the scenes', less involved storyteller approach in attempts to help employees shine
Employee	• Tell and personify the brand story to stakeholders within their specific role • Are consistently learning the new or evolved brand storytelling techniques • Capture frontline feedback on brand story from customers	• Social channel early adopters and consumers • Understand audience motivations • Can influence storytelling evolution based on customer feedback • If trained well, can display the story persona identity successfully	• May not be fully equipped to offer all design affordances • Are not necessarily concerned with functional or emotional story persona jobs • Have no say in budget spend
Contracted work force	• Serve as an extension of employee when personifying brand story • Align to brand story strategies as part of work deliverables • Can also capture feedback from customers	• Serve to amplify the brand persona • Can bring an 'outsider perspective' to how effective the emotional and functional story jobs are	• May not consider themselves to be a part of the brand story • Are not concerned with design affordances

- Pros
  - o Significantly helps amplify the brand story and build trust with external audiences
  - o Has massive target audience reach
  - o Can deliver on all story persona affordances
- Cons
  - o May not be a true fan of the brand story and may run the risk of showing up as inauthentic
  - o May be very costly
  - o Is short-lived

Crafting your story persona and deliberately endowing certain groups with brand storyteller powers is a sure-fire way to see your tireless story-building efforts come to fruition in the most magical way. Happy designing!

10

Marketing (actually, testing) your brand story

- Defining key assumptions
- Ground rules for testing your story

Congratulations, you did it! You worked tirelessly to craft an enchanting brand story, faithfully placing your customer at the heart of it, delicately sprinkling it with visual elements and immersive techniques and thoughtfully designing a story persona to ensure the tale is told in the most compelling way imaginable. Now you're ready to take it to market.

Unlike a traditional product marketing plan that follows rules such as:

- Define situation analysis (SWOT and current market status)
- Define goals
- Determine KPIs
- Identify target audience
- Define content and channel strategies
- Set marketing budget
- Outline cross-functional team responsibilities (RACI)

taking your brand story to market is less about, well, marketing – and all about *testing* the brand story concepts you created during the prototype phase. If you've been following the design thinking approach to storytelling, you've already spent time empathetically researching your design audience, defining, ideating and prototyping diverse story concepts that tie back to your brand mission and universal truth. And now, it's time to get them out there and see how the audience responds.

In Chapter 2, I briefly touched on how the test phase is somewhat of a soft launch project where you are able to observe and evaluate whether and how the story concepts you designed resonate with your audience the way you intended them to.

Indeed, it can be a bit unnerving to hit the market with story concepts that feel somewhat unfinished. To ease your nerves, I want to offer a pre-testing tool that may serve in measuring the WOW factor of each design concept before getting it out there: the Key Assumptions table. Used in design thinking to critically appraise the value, execution, scale and defensibility capacity of each design concept, this technique leaves nothing to the imagination when it comes to exploring conceivable ways a prototype can flounder.

Defining key assumptions

After designing concepts, the key assumptions table acts as a scorecard by letting you benchmark specific criteria under each capacity (ironically, also called 'test') and against three main experiments, namely thought experiment, 2D/3D and 4D.

Each of these experiments consists of expedited observations captured through quick exercises as follows:

Thought experiment: learned through analysis of existing data (research you conducted at the beginning);

2D/3D: learned through quick dialogue with the market (conversations with stakeholders);

4D: learned through lived experiences (conducting a live trial with a controlled group);

I know what you may be thinking: You want me to test the story *before* I test the story?

More or less. I consider this assumptions table to be more of a quick temperature check to help gauge the design concept's aptitude in the market. Please note that by no means does this process supplant the actual testing phase of a design concept. You will learn later in this chapter than during the testing phase, you and your team will spend a substantial amount of time observing and gathering necessary feedback from your stakeholders to improve your brand story. So, it is not recommended to shortcut this aspect of the design thinking process in any shape or form.

Nevertheless, I have personally found value in using the key assumptions model for vetting my story concepts before they hit the market and I want to share with you how I've used this concept in the past. For this example, I will illustrate a real-life case where I contributed to a city placement project. This particular city was interested in showcasing its distinctive destination attributes through storytelling efforts. I developed a total of four story concepts, one of them called 'The Myth'.

This particular concept focused on the region's rich evolution, history, mythologies and culture. In the interest of protecting the actual story concept, I have slightly modified it, but you will still be able to capture the process flow.

When submitting The Myth story concept to the key assumptions process, I began by analysing how this concept aligned against each criterion under the value, execution, scale and defensibility tests columns. For each criterion under each test, I added a new row providing a description of how The Myth could meet that specific criterion. Then I began to benchmark. Every time the description met a criterion under the value, execution, scale and defensibility capacities, I would place an X in the appropriate box, including any time I had had the chance to conduct a quick experiment to test it. The more boxes marked, the more the story concept's WOW factor.

Table 10.1 shows the results of my key assumptions about The Myth. You will note that there are no 4D boxes marked because I didn't get that far into the project.

As you can see, this particular story concept doesn't really show up strongly when it comes to having a WOW factor. Would I still have chosen to take it to market? Possibly. But only if I followed some rules.

Story concept testing ground rules

In this chapter, I want to offer some story concept testing ground rules that may help you best test your brand story concepts in savvy and delectable ways.

Rule #1. Consistency is brilliancy

Brand strategist Taughnee Stone, in her article 'The psychological reason why brand consistency is so important', says that brand consistency is about

TABLE 10.1 Key assumptions

Key Assumptions

Story Concept Name: The Myth	Thought Experiment (learned through analysis of existing data)	2D/3D (learned through dialog with market)	4D (learned through lived experience)
Value Test			
• Customers want it			
• Customers will pay for it			
• Partners want it			
Appeals to most current tourism trends: eco-tourism, sustainable, historic, solo, small town travel	X	X	
Meets design goal of making customers feel engaged, inspired, refreshed, hopeful and excited	X		
Stakeholders agree this IS fundamentally the region's story	X	X	

Execution Test

- We can produce experience technically — Technical experience is through digital channels — X
- We can acquire customers — Business is already operating. It's a matter of unifying the story. — X
- We can operate business as it grows — Acquiring customers depends on story launch date

Scale Test

- Addressable market is big enough — Aims to reach global market — X
- We can acquire customers affordably — Can be scaled consistently year over year — X
- Revenues exceed costs at scale — Contributes to bottom line goals

Defensibility Test

- We can protect advantage — Risk on advantage: other regions may copy
- Advantage increases as we grow the business — The more the story gets 'out there' the more the business will grow

trust, more than anything. I couldn't agree more. In earlier chapters I gave the example of how Gillette and their 'Toxic Masculinity' ad showed up as a disparate brand storytelling strategy, resulting in irreparable backlash from their target audience. This fluke in storytelling messaging, the opposite of their historic brand values, ended up costing the company significantly in terms of market positioning, and months after this unfortunate market scheme the brand was forced to reduce the price of their shaving products by as much as 20 per cent. Conversely, studies show that brand consistency can generate as much as 23 per cent more revenue for the brand.

Consistency is the name of the game when it comes to launching your story concepts. Everything from your brand mission to your logo, social media channels, marketing assets and more ought to uniformly echo your brand story's universal truth and conjointly evoke the key feelings you defined for your audience early in the design phase. If story concepts call for an overall brand refresh, you may want to consider that as part of your long-term brand story marketing plan. But for the most part, your story concepts have already been guided by the brand mission and core values, so they shouldn't fall too far from the (brand) tree.

Aside from ensuring that brand story concepts are driven by the brand identity and personality, to test your story concepts in the most consistent and advantageous way it makes sense to make your brand's universal truth the ultimate marketing goal. When deciding to go to market, the number one indicator that your story is winning the hearts and minds of your audience will be when the audience's natural emotional response to the story is exactly what you sought to evoke from them from the get-go. Story provokes action. Expect your audience to enthusiastically engage with your brand and storytellers as soon as they have been 'struck' by the story concept.

Also consider making your search engine optimization (SEO) keyword the universal truth for your brand. At Microsoft, the universal truth is empowerment. The brand mission is *to empower every person and organization on the planet to achieve more*. The feeling they want to give their customers (internal and external) is that of empowerment. You will most likely see this word, empowerment, showcased in every mini story, over-arching message, internal and external brand communication and advertisements coming from Microsoft. It's even stamped on the back of the employee badge. You will know you're effectively marketing your brand story concept when that *one thing* you want your brand to be known for is widely recognized as synonymous with your brand by your audience.

Rule #2. Show, don't tell

To best promote your brand story concepts, forget about *most* of the marketing techniques you've come to know thus far. Though some overall marketing plan strategies, such as setting goals and establishing (flexible) metrics, still apply to comprehensively advertise your brand story, overall SEO and lead-generation-driven tactics are not the brand story's objective. Remember that your brand story is not a product, it's actually the brand itself represented in story form. Therefore, the marketing goal for your brand story is to ensure that the brand core values and mission are showcased at their best.

Keep empathy and vulnerability top-of-mind. Don't forget that design thinking begins and ends with empathy. Stay empathetic to your design (target) audience and story personas (storytellers) throughout the launch process by creating feedback-loop systems to capture immediate feedback (more on this a bit later).

Also remember that the best stories are the most vulnerable ones. Fight the urge to clean up or polish the story concepts too much. Prototypes are raw in essence and that is what makes them beautiful.

Outline and openly share your story concepts strategy with internal stakeholders and story personas using the IMC Reimagined plan to create an open communication flow:

- Which story concepts will you go to market with first?
- Which marketing channels will you use?
- Who will share these stories?
- Who and how will your brand engage with your audience?

Be ready to fail fast. Build a contingency plan. If the story concept fails, how will the brand respond and recover? Are there story concepts in the pipeline or are you ready to modify and relaunch? To make things easy, this plan can mirror your already-existing social media crisis plan for the most part.

Rule #3. You're in it for the long haul

Storytelling is a futuristic brand strategy that solicits present-day activation. Although prototyping and testing cycles will by nature have a fast turnaround time, the actual elapsed time for designing and launching stories until one 'hits' is a prolonged tactic that follows no specific timeline. In short, you're in it for the long haul.

Furthermore, it's important to keep in mind that your brand story also acts as a culture stimulant and trust-building catalyst with internal and external stakeholders. And neither of these is constructed overnight. However, while your story concepts are being tested in the market, you can continue to be highly productive through observing and gathering data for improving the next round of prototypes, as needed. Staying true to the design thinking model, design cycles never really end, so developing a habit of steady research for improvement will serve well throughout the brand story evolution.

A great way to create a dynamic observation system is by putting together a launch management task force comprising internal and external stakeholders who will not only be willing to provide honest feedback once the stories go to market, but also share a different perspective altogether. You will be surprised how many trusted partners, employees and vendors are willing to participate in this exercise. All you have to do is ask. Microsoft offered the opportunity to partners and customers to give constructive criticism on story concepts before or shortly after they hit the market, and they were more than willing to share their opinion because they truly care about the brand and the brand's success. Notwithstanding, this process can only work if there are robust listening tools in place. The most important resource when implementing listening programs is people, not tools, who engage at the human level with those stakeholders investing their time in giving feedback. Consider piloting a closed social network group as a start and see where it goes from there and whether you're able to scale. The more human your observation approach is, the better the assessment you will be able to gather and the more opportunity for improvement you will find.

Rule #4. Go with the character flow

Once the story concept lands, anything can happen. It can go viral. It can flop. It can have impact on an unintended and untargeted audience group. It can be misconstrued or taken out of context on social media, if you choose this as a go-to-market (GTM) channel. Thankfully, you've already prepared a contingency plan for these unwelcome, but plausible, events. So, let's focus on yet another tenable instance that may actually serve the story in a positive manner: character flow.

Great storytellers are flexible in their approach. They're never too attached to an idea and are typically open to the possibility of the story itself or a story character taking on a life of its own and forging a new narrative path. Because you have made the customer the central character in your brand story, there is a good chance that the customer may take the narrative lead at one point or another. How you choose to handle this shift in story plot will speak volumes to your customer base as to how they truly are regarded as the central character.

I picked on Disney as a brand at the beginning of the book because, at heart, I am a sold-out Disney fan. If you know me, you know the nauseating depths of my unhealthy obsession with The Walt Disney Company. I would like to say that my infatuation for *the mouse* began back in my home country of Venezuela, where like any child living outside of the United States, the sheer notion of travelling to America to meet Mickey is a far-reaching preposterous idea. But it wasn't until much later in life, when I was already married with kids and still very much in love with the brand, that my shameless fascination reached its all-time high.

Conveniently, I lived in Florida and *obviously* my family and I were proud Annual Passholders (we paid a hefty chunk of hard-earned cash for year-round admission tickets to the parks). I've lost count of how many times I've visited the parks over the course of 28 years. Quick maths will have me at over 150 times, at a minimum (yes, I'm bragging), but I can tell you that every time I visit, it is a delightful and surprisingly different experience.

It may be because Disney is simply doing what it does: magic. It may also be because I endeavoured to find new experiences (character dining, events and behind-the-scenes tours).

On one particular occasion, I reserved us the *Marceline to Magic Kingdom Tour*, a fascinating three-hour guided walking tour that takes you through the streets of the Magic Kingdom through the eyes and history of Walt Disney himself, offering vaunted secrets of the man himself as well as behind-the-scenes access to the three classic rides he designed: Pirates of the Caribbean, It's A Small World and Haunted Mansion. I won't give it all away in case you want to partake in this in-depth experience one day (highly recommended), but I do want to fast-forward to the moment we walked past the crowds in our VIP line (I'm still bragging) through the notorious garden entrance of the Haunted Mansion ride. As we were getting ready to enter the house, our tour guide made a sudden stop and pointed to the floor.

'Does anyone know what that is?' she asked, in true Disney enchanting fashion.

We directed our gaze to where she pointed and noticed a ring stuck in the cement floor.

'A ring!' yelled the youngest member of our tour cohort.

'Indeed!' the tour guide confirmed.

She then began to explain the history behind the peculiar jewel stuck on the ground:

A few years back, we remodelled the Haunted Mansion entrance. The place where the ring sits now was actually a hole on the ground where an old fence locked in. After we removed the fence (and the lock), we overheard park goers asking where the 'ring' had gone. Patrons had conceived a story about a bride who had died and come back to haunt visitors in the Mansion. This was not at all part of the original storyline for Haunted Mansion. However, we at Disney create and recreate the stories our customers want to hear, so we decided to include this fan-fabricated character into the Haunted Mansion storyline, and as a result placed an actual ring on the floor to help corroborate it.

Now *that*'s true character flow. See why I (and possibly the rest of the world) love Disney so much?

Disney and other winning brands are nimble enough to welcome the natural development of a brand story and story characters. As your story concepts unfold in the market, consider enabling the idea that your customer may thrive on your storyline and carve a new story concept altogether, as long as the stories stay true to the brand's universal truth and mission.

Rule #5. Make it shareable, scalable and available

Your story concepts will take on different shapes, types and forms, and they should. You may choose to test long-form video, immersive storytelling, The Mountain structure or the Hero's Journey. You may test different shades of colour or new typography in visual elements. Whichever way you've chosen to design your story concepts is all part of the innovation you bring to your brand story, but do keep in mind that when they go to market, the stories should be made readily available to your audience, scaled fast and shared by everyone.

AVAILABILITY

Don't make your audience come to you. Go where your audience is. Put the story in front of them and hand it over like a gift, because it is. In today's content-saturated world, the worst thing a brand can do is expect the customer to consume content directly from their website or digital account. Wooing is part of the storytelling approach. You have to invite your audience to join you in the storytelling journey. So, make concessions to show up where your audience lives. If the bulk of your design audience has moved to Instagram, for example, your brand story needs to go there.

Side note: as of 2019, Instagram is now the leading digital channel for influencer marketing.

SCALABILITY

Yes, these story concepts are prototypes, but just as you have planned for possible failure, have you also planned for unexpected blow-out success? If a prototype video story hits, for example, how will you take this concept and adapt it as a permanent piece of your brand story? Do you have the right tools and resources in place to elevate it? Take it global? Localize it?

SHAREABILITY

Aside from making your story concepts available in the channels where your customers are, the concepts should also be easy to share. Use tweetable quotes in your written content, create snip bits of longer-form video, use social channel features such as Instagram stories to break down the content even more. Integrate digital symbols such as emojis, memes and GIF images to bring a different angle to the storyline. In today's hyper-connected world there are many low-cost resources available to quickly evolve a prototype concept. Keep your creative juices flowing!

Rule #6. Stay curious about your audience

Empathy continues to rule every aspect of brand storytelling and can become more pervasive during the testing phase. In your preoccupation to get these stories to market, you may be tempted to disengage empathetically with those at the heart of the story. Yes, you may have put listening tools and systems in place, and even invited some customers to be part of your feedback taskforce. You may also have agreed to stay flexible, should your customer decide to alter the narrative structure in some way, and made efforts to ensure the design concepts are readily available and distributable, but have you created an open space where you have the ability to accurately understand your design audience's thoughts and feelings towards your story concept?

Beyond listening tools, take time to try to see the story from your customer's perspective when the story lands. Be critical of it, as the customer would, and when you receive feedback, find opportunities to gain more insights into why they feel a certain way about the story.

I once resorted to asking 'why' seven times after receiving customer feed-back on a story concept:

Why do you feel this way about the story?

Why?

Why?

Why?

Why?

Why?

Why?

The results were fascinating and enlightening in many ways. I was able to go back to the drawing board with a new sense of direction because I took extra time to understand my customer's experience with the story. I beg you to make it a daily practice to pause for a moment, in the middle of the daily madness, and think about your customer as a human, not a customer. Remember they too struggle, have fears, get tired. This will serve you (and them) well during the testing phase – and long after.

Rule #7. Engage, engage, engage

Have you ever met a very charismatic and inspiring individual, perhaps a public speaker or thought leader, and your first inclination was to try to connect with them on social channels, only to be left vulnerably floating in cyberspace waiting for some kind of acknowledgement or response on their behalf that never came? There's nothing quite as disappointing as this, and so much wrong with it too. But that's another topic to chat about another time. The point I'm trying to make is that brands that do not have a customer engagement strategy in place are driving the exact same unpleasant experi-ence with their audiences, and this disorienting feeling is exponentially exasperated when the failure to connect on behalf of the brand happens *right after* a highly emotional story captures the customer. What an unfortu-nate misstep!

Because storytelling is an emotional experience, if it lands well, at the very least you can expect your audience to want to engage intimately with your brand because *that's* what it set out to do. Good stories awaken the brain in all kinds of beautiful ways and prompt the audience into action. Remember?

I often tell the story of how I make my teenage boys take me out on son-and-mom dates. Being the only female in the house (even my dog Dino is male, as were our deceased pets Ninja the gerbil and Bubbles the goldfish), I am regularly exposed to action and adventure entertainment, movies and TV shows, so I find it fitting to put them through the 'misery' of taking me to the cinema to watch 'chick flicks'. Often these happen to be... you guessed it, Disney movies. I know they secretly love them.

On one occasion, it was my oldest son Alex's turn to take me out. We went to watch the highly anticipated Disney Pixar movie *Coco*. In short summary, the story is about a Mexican boy who believes his life's calling and dream is to play the guitar for a living, but because of a hard family-imposed rule he is simply not allowed to play any music.

The story warmly unfolds in true Disney fashion, and by the finale, every seated person in the theatre, including my teenage son, was drowning in tears (although he'll tell you his were the result of... allergies). As we walked out of the theatre, I could see Alex reflecting on the storyline in silence (he's our shy one), and then his eyes suddenly lit up and a smile overtook his once sombre countenance as he grabbed my arm enthusiastically and said 'Mom! I want to get a guitar!'

The guitar now sits in his closet. But that's not the point. The point is that the Coco story provoked an inevitable desire in my son to do *something*. *Anything*. The story lit him up inside in so many wonderful ways that there was no other way to respond but impetuously.

The hope and goal are that your story concepts triumphantly do the same for your audience, within their own context of course. And when that happens, how will your brand engage back? Are you prepared for the many inspired Alexes to flood your social channels as they react with emotion?

Creating mechanisms and investing resources in customer engagement processes is not a nice-to-have, but a must-have in storytelling. This is customer experience at its finest. You've come so far in this game. It would make no sense for your brand to go through all these efforts in creating and delivering an impassioned narrative experience, only to fail at what it ultimately set out to do: connect with the audience. Be sure to create simple and feasible ways for your audience to engage and stay engaged with your brand at all times.

Also remember that younger audiences desire to build deeper relationships with the brand. They are not interested in quick, convenient and impersonal communication. They expect the brand to invest as much time as they deem necessary, building trust through a connected experience. So, as you set up engagement shop, map out a set of techniques that will deliver quality engagement to your audience and not leave them defencelessly hanging out there.

Rule #8. Recycle and upcycle

So, the concept failed for some reason. Don't fret. The good news is that prototypes by definition are low-cost, low-effort solutions, so unlike a lot of the marketing content you may be used to producing, this content is malleable and easy enough to repurpose.

We first have to consider that there are many external influencing factors that can potentially affect the performance (not the aptitude) of a prototype in the market. Timing, channel, market, distractions, trends, industry news and many more can be culprits. So before you decide to repurpose altogether, do remember that you *are* in the test phase of design thinking and that if during this time you elected to follow some or all the ground rules proposed above, you will have a lot of valuable data to rummage through and help you gain a deeper understanding on where the concept may have gone slightly wrong. Spend some time there, analysing the possibilities. By now you can probably call yourself a storyteller *and* data analyst professional (*smile*) and there's nothing wrong with that, if you ask me. Often, we rush to just get content published for the sake of content, instead of for the sake of our audience. What makes storytelling an innovative approach to communication is the dedication you are putting into creating and launching the stories your customers want, not the stories *you think* your customers want. With that said, after you've spent what you believe to be a considerable amount of time investigating the data and are not finding too many patterns or indicators, it's time to recycle and upcycle.

The possibilities with concepts that are not an immediate success are more than great. Don't forget that the reason the concept became a concept in the first place is because it met all the criteria in the design thinking phase. It was born out of a brainstorming ideation session and passed the prototype phase too. So, these concepts are still quality content, and as author Seth Godin once said, content is 'the only marketing left'.

UPCYCLING

The prototype may be good at its core but perhaps requires a fresh perspective. Take it back as it is to a brainstorming session to see what else can come of it as an idea. SCAMPER the heck out of it or submit it to a Six

Thinking Hats exercise or any other type of approach that compels looking at it from a new angle. This alone may bring infinite possibilities for a new and improved prototype to test.

RECYCLING

It may never come to this, but once you've exhausted upcycling possibilities, you can resort to repurposing the story concept altogether, as you would any other content. Explore ways that it can take new shape or form beyond a storyline. Can it be used as a talking point in a corporate walking-deck presentation? Can it be turned into an internal podcast or newsletter? Get creative about giving your concept a new life. By now, you're also a creative genius!

Testing your story concepts doesn't have to be a tedious or lengthy process. On the contrary, it can be an enjoyable and very insightful step in your storytelling design, if you take the time to put the right parameters and processes in place. You can then watch your stories take their rightful place in the market and benchmark to scale.

11

Benchmarking your brand story

- Main indicators for benchmarking story
- Leveraging existing metrics

If anything could poetically capture benchmarking for storytelling it is a quote by Singaporean political activist and teacher T P Chia. He said: 'We all live at the mercy of our emotions. Our emotions influence and shape our desires, thoughts and behaviours and above all our destiny.'

We've spent most of this book learning about the art of storytelling. However, I did mention that story is both a science and an art, and here's the science.

Great stories stimulate senses, activate feelings and unapologetically exhort the audience to do *something*. *Anything*. But when we pause to ponder about the *real* possibilities of story, what it can *actually* do to *and with* our audiences, I don't know about you, but I get an unsettling and apprehensive feeling of what could actually be at stake. Shall we call this the 'surprise element' in story?

I was once invited to speak about the power of storytelling at a tech conference in Stockholm. As a true storyteller, I'd like to paint a quick picture of the scenario I walked into.

The audience comprised over 200 top IT professionals, developers and decision makers in the industry looking to optimize their businesses by learning innovative solutions to scale during their digital transformation journey. Needless to say, this group was extremely deliberate about how and where they would choose to spend their time to learn new insights.

By definition, 98 per cent of the audience was male (and I truly hope that by the time you read this, that number will have shifted more towards higher female representation in the tech industry, but that's another story). The mood was reasonably impassive. OK, *very* impassive. Not only because this is how 'techies' tend to be in general, but as I quickly learned the night before during the speaker dinner, the Nordic cultures, and especially Swedes, approach life with a certain degree of *lagom*, which translates into 'just the right amount of', meaning a reliable degree of moderation. That's a nice way of saying 'emotionally reserved' if you ask this Latina. And my talk was about letting story awaken *all* your emotions….

I had of course done some research of my audience prior to arriving. But truth be told, during my analysis, I quickly became side tracked (and kind of enamoured) with the mythological idea that this population was primarily Viking by heritage. Seafaring warriors, explorers and raiders are *anything but* lagom in my estimation! Surely I would walk onto the stage, ramble about this and that, and conclude with a victorious raise of a hand while shouting 'Skål!' and watch this rambunctious crowd jump out of their chairs in uproar and cheer me back with gusto. But I learned on speaker dinner night that no such thing would probably happen. This audience was too collected, and somewhat sceptical in general.

The presentation room was cold that morning. Literally and figuratively. I could feel their eyes stare me down with a cool and laid-back brashness while I nervously pretended to check my speaker notes to avoid them. Imposter syndrome sat comfortably on my right shoulder whispering: just get through it and go home, they'll forget about it *and you* soon.

I delivered the same speech I had given dozens of times before and, as usual, ended with the grand finale of an emotive video that typically drives my audience to tears, this time with little hope of it eliciting this reaction. Knowing what effect this video has had on past audiences, I would usually sit back and enjoy watching their physical response become apparent as the story visually unfolds and their emotions begin to awake. But this time, I shyly hid behind the podium to check 'my notes' again, expecting nothing more than a blank stare from them in the end as they scrupulously mentally questioned why I had wasted their valuable time. I could hear their thoughts, too.

As the video came to an end, I walked up to the centre of the room, as I usually do, to leave the audience with a final thought. Imagine my surprise when I finally faced my Scandinavian assembly and saw dozens of them crying hysterically. I mean, hysterically. Emotion had overtaken the room, *lagom* was nowhere to be found, and I think it took imposter syndrome away with it.

Indeed, it was a beautiful thing to experience, but so unexpected that it took me a few days to actually process – and benchmark – what had transpired.

Measuring the impact of storytelling isn't easy work. For one thing, the primary goal of story is to arouse emotion, and unless you can earn the bragging rights of seeing your audience cry like I did with those Swedish men at the tech conference, *every single time* you share your brand story, it will be difficult to quantify success. But it's not impossible; you will just have to get a bit more creative.

Main indicators for benchmarking story

Because story is rooted in feeling, there are no existing mechanisms to help determine precise metrics or KPIs (although some of my Nordic friends will debate that, thanks to AI, emotions may soon be reduced to data and this will become a possibility – stay tuned for Chapter 13 where I talk more about predictions for technology and artificial intelligence). However, there are three main indicators that can help confirm your brand story is headed in the right direction and will ultimately result in contributing to your overall business goals. These are:

- emotion
- reaction
- and lasting action

Ideally, for benchmarking, you will include storytelling as part of your brand awareness effort, which usually doesn't have a solid metric plan but more of a *contribution* recognition of the overall business objectives. For example, we understand that the level of consciousness and emotional response that consumers have to a company is directly tied to their purchasing decision, although there is no definitive metric that can track or confirm this. Look up the definition for 'branding' and you will get anything from 'the promotion of a company' to elements that make a brand recognizable, such as logos and symbols, to my all-time favourite description by *The Branding Journal*, 'the process of giving *meaning* to a specific organization, company, products or services by creating and shaping a brand in consumers' minds'.

Marketers will typically measure brand buzz by tying branding efforts to specific all-up marketing metrics such as earned media, website traffic and social engagement. The logic is simple: the more excited people get about the brand, the more consumer engagement the brand gets. The same can be applied to storytelling, since story is one of the biggest catalysts in brand recognition, if not *the* biggest.

Leveraging existing metrics

To this extent, I'd like to help you simplify this benchmarking process by categorizing your already-existing branding metrics into the indicators I previously mentioned above, and also placing them in order of sequence, meaning that metrics achieved in emotion will lead to metrics achieved in reaction, so on and so forth.

Emotion

You've already learned that the first indicator that your story is performing well is when it successfully captures your audience's heart and stirs up their emotions. But not just *any* emotions, the ones you intend to awaken through your carefully designed story. Taking it all the way back to Chapter 1, this indicator serves to measure your brand story's functionality. It answers the basic question: Did my audience feel _____?

But which metrics determine this? We can easily say 'reach' and 'mention'. The hypothesis here is that as your brand story begins to make its way into the hearts of your stakeholder groups, their emotions will lead them to echo the story, helping amplify it in the most gratifying fashion. Let's take a look at how this can potentially unfold.

We ought to remember that the brand story is always serving two main stakeholder groups (internal and external), each containing a design audience, and within each group these two metrics may look completely different. For this reason, I want to capture how reach and mention serve each stakeholder group when the story lands successfully, through a comparison sheet.

Once your brand story begins to resonate in the hearts of your stakeholders, and most importantly, your design personas, it will also resonate in their minds, and this will ultimately result in an emotional response from them. Former Professor of Psychology and Director of the Swiss Center for

TABLE 11.1 Emotion metrics for stakeholders

Audience	Brand Mentions	Content Reach
Internal stakeholders: owners, employees, partners, vendors, shareholders, investors	Overall brand mentions increase and the brand's universal truth is consistently associated with the brand. Let's say you've determined your brand's universal truth is 'belonging' or to make your audience 'feel like they belong'. You will know your brand story has become top of mind for these stakeholders when they steadily make use of the word *belong* or *belonging* as an extension or description of the brand. For example, you may begin to hear stakeholders say things like: • XYZ is all about belonging • XYZ product makes me feel like I belong • XYZ always equals belonging Mentions are organically made internally and externally as stakeholders freely and naturally begin to share the brand's universal truth as part of the core brand messaging.	The number of people who see your brand story content on internal channels (emails, enterprise social tools, presentation decks) rises because people in this internal stakeholder group are starting to assimilate the brand story into their overall messaging when referring to the brand.
External: consumers, society, government	Media and industry coverage grows and digital channels are picking up on the brand's universal truth and key messaging shared by internal stakeholders. Because of this, they also echo the message. For example, media outlets recognize the feeling the brand is meaning to give customers: • XYZ's products are making people feel like they belong • XYZ stands for belonging	The number of people who see your brand story content on external channels (news articles, social posts, print media, traditional media) increases as the brand gains recognition in the marketplace by the core message it is sharing

Affective Sciences in Geneva, Klaus Rainer Scherer, in his article 'The dynamic architecture of emotion: Evidence for the component process model', observes that our emotions are caused by our thoughts. I hope you're beginning to see the scientific correlation between brand awareness and emotional response: the more consistently you tell the brand story, the more exposure your audience will have to it, the more likely they will think about it and the more chances your story will have to evoke their emotions. It's a simple game of maths. And Brand Marketing 101.

When I began to build my personal brand with storytelling techniques, I wanted to showcase many aspects of who I am as a person, not just a professional, and highlight the numerous things that make me uniquely me. I didn't have the official title of Storyteller yet, but instinctively understood the compelling nature of capturing my audience's attention through the clever use of words. I knew words had power. I just didn't know *how much*.

When I decided to take my newly created brand to digital channels, I set out to leverage valuable real estate that's often wasted, such as LinkedIn's profile headline section, which most people use only to put their current role title on, or the About Me section, taken for granted by many when they simply describe responsibilities within their current role.

I can't quite remember the original profile biography I wrote, but even though it has evolved many times through the years, the core message and key words remain the same today. Here's my current LinkedIn About section:

High standards + high heels always on the next adventure to disrupt something. Dreamer. Strategist. Venezolana. #Storyteller. #Inclusion advocate. Believer. International keynote speaker. Author Brand #Storytelling. Sometimes insomniac. Ice cream = superfood

It wasn't much longer after I had publicly shared some of my very personal descriptors, such as my love for ice cream and fixation with high heels, that I began to receive unexpected messages and mentions from my network (shall we call them 'surprise responses'?) regarding my branding.

'Just passed a shoe store. Saw these and thought of you,' messaged a colleague, along with a photo of a beautiful and colourful pair of stilettos.

'Ben & Jerry just announced a new ice cream flavour, did you see their Twitter post?' would tag someone from my Twitter network to ensure I didn't miss this ice cream opportunity.

People were associating me with the very key words I had purposely used to brand myself with, and it was quickly evident to me that the psychology of branding had been activated. When my network had sporadic mundane encounters with shoes and ice cream, I (or my brand) would automatically pop up in their minds. I had given my audience more 'everyday' to correlate me with, and naturally, mentions began to rise on social channels. Coincidence?

Reach and mention are two metrics that can be used to gauge not only how emotional your audience is getting about your brand but how much it knows about it and its universal truth. I should point out that mentions may be positive or negative, albeit we hope for the positive ones, but I am of the school that *anyone* taking the time to reference your brand at all is a sure indicator that the brand has at the very minimum made an impact on them. Your job is to make sure it's a good one.

When I was managing social media support channels for Microsoft, we encountered many opportunities to tell the brand story in ways we hadn't thought of before. From a customer support perspective, audiences who reached out to us were engaging with our brand because they needed, well, support. It hadn't occurred to us in the discipline that these connection points with customers were in essence brand *mentions* and *reach*. Social support sits under the customer services discipline at Microsoft, not the brand marketing one. In our (siloed) minds, those of us working under this structure were only to engage with our customers in a reactive fashion when customers reached out to us for help, while the job of diffusing inspiring proactive content to audiences belonged to marketing. Our responses tended to be dry and somewhat antisocial, even though we were talking to our customers on social channels and the underlying expectation was that the connection with the brand on those platforms would be less formal.

The funny thing is that our customers were the *same people*... and when they 'talked' to Microsoft, whether on our main or product channel as a response to a deeply moving story or to request assistance on customer support ones, they anticipated the engagement experience to *feel* the same. Some of you would say this is a no-brainer, of course, but at the time, the uncertainties of effectively managing digital channels were as painfully unfamiliar as the notion of using story as pervasive means of connecting with customers.

Truth be told, digital age disruption has forced marketers and communicators out of their comfort zone, and all we've done since the birth of these new technologies is nervously navigate the ambiguous landscape, learn and continue learning from how our customers react through the process.

Understanding customer sentiment is never a bad idea.

It will benefit you to pay close attention to the mentions your brand gets by internal and external stakeholders and treat them like one more engagement opportunity. Your audience is talking to and about you, and these are the most obvious occasions to impart brand values to them through your story. Have you considered taking a stroll by Redditt and Medium to see what your customers are saying about your brand there? While your brand may not be actively present on *every* digital platform, it doesn't mean your customers or potential ones are not. It makes sense to periodically invest time and resources in understanding your brand's influence on secondary channels and perhaps take a moment or two to engage.

I once decided to personally engage with one of our Microsoft customers on Twitter. He made mention of our brand to his network (not to us directly), but we were monitoring channels and I noticed that he was visibly upset about not yet receiving his highly anticipated Windows 10 update after he'd sign up for it months ago. The product rollout was scheduled to download in waves, and he was impatiently frustrated about the length of the process. I recognized this brand mention was a good opportunity to engage. This customer was excited about our new product and looking forward to experiencing it. He was a fan of Microsoft and I realized that though I wasn't going to be able to offer him a solution (he simply had to wait for the product to arrive as scheduled), I could provide an alternative way to make him feel *empowered*. So, I reached out and openly invited him to join our Windows Insider Program, an open worldwide program that allows people to test software before release. The customer was not only delighted that Microsoft proactively reached out to him, but was thrilled to be invited to the program and happily accepted.

Your brand storytelling will undoubtedly spark a new surge in mentions and consequently reach, both earned and owned. It's smart to leverage both to continue inviting reaction from your audience.

Reaction

On 6 February 2007, a woman named Lisa left her place of work, got into her car and drove almost 1,000 miles from the US state of Houston, Texas to Orlando, Florida.

To save travel time to her destination, she wore adult diapers. She was desperate to get to someone, right away. She needed to confront the person she considered to be her romantic rival – the person who had stolen the affection of her lover.

Lisa Marie Nowak was a naval flight officer and NASA astronaut. She was also in love.

This is a true story. And as bewildering as it may seem at first, it honestly becomes a bit mundane in our minds when we learn this broken-hearted individual's emotional state of mind. We've all heard the many outlandish stories about people in love doing, well, outlandish things. Perhaps *you've* done a crazy thing or two in your time, in the glorious name of that thing called love. Experts rank love as one the most powerful human emotions, closely following fear and anger, which psychiatrists have determined are the only two emotions engrained in us to ensure survival.

I want to call out love, because it serves as a great example of the reactive punch that feelings can provoke.

While the love your audience will have for your brand story will be more of a *slow burn* rather than a *rapid fire*, when a brand story manages to unlock and agitate strong feelings, you can expect a sure automatic and unconscious reaction from the audience. And just like we can attach some branding metrics to emotion, we can also apply benchmarking indicators to reaction. For ease of readership, I will leverage the same table format used in Table 11.1 and attribute the reaction metrics to it: this time, engagement and conversions (Table 11.2).

A great way to drive more engagement and conversion with your brand story is to pitch it internally to other disciplines. I will share more later in this chapter, but let's talk about the final and, in my humble opinion, most valuable benchmarking metrics of brand storytelling: lasting action.

Lasting action

Delving deeper into the formidable notion of love as a notable example of how strong feelings can incite action, those of us fortunate to be or to have been in a long-term, caring romantic relationship understand that after the early endorphins and oxytocin effects of being in love wear off, what's left is a strong desire to stay bonded with the person we love in an enduring partnership arrangement. In the same way, once your stakeholders 'fall in love' with your brand, they will intuitively want to keep connected to it. Your younger audiences will finally befriend it, and what follows next is the culmination of everything you sought out to achieve with brand storytelling: positive culture shift and market placement.

If you've ever read a book or article about how culture shift happens in an organization, you already know there are key milestones, one leading to the other, as well as indicators that transformation is happening. A simple plan would look like Figure 11.1.

TABLE 11.2 Reaction metrics for stakeholders

Audience	Engagement	Conversions
Internal stakeholders: owners, employees, partners, vendors, shareholders, investors	As your brand story begins to take effect on this cohort, you can expect this audience to start bonding at a deeper level with the content. The brand's universal truth is not just top of mind, but a catalyst for unification between teams, departments and disciplines through the storyline. Internal stakeholders will not only enthusiastically begin to share, like, and comment on content that tells the brand story, but feel a sense of ownership of it themselves and begin to adapt the stories to their own spaces. Building on the same example as before, you may find, for instance, a finance analyst taking XYZ's universal truth of 'belonging' and start applying it to her financial reporting: 'This is how XYZ is making people feel like the belong' or vice versa when sharing data about business results.	Conversion for this cohort is not much about actual sales (though story can and will contribute to an increase in internal audiences buying or using the brand products), but more about belief.
		This word is often used in faith-driven associations. When someone makes a choice to trust in a certain religious conviction they *convert* into it as a result.
	If you were still hesitant about implementing an employee advocacy program until this point, now would be a great time to start considering implementation. The brand core message is resonating with your audience, they understand what the brand is about and what it stands for and are connected emotionally to it. This is the beginning of your company's culture shift driven by the brand story.	Similarly, when the brand story productively influences this particular audience, an act of faith or 'buy in' is made by them, transforming them from passive to active storytellers. In laymen's terms: your internal stakeholders are no longer a part of the brand contributing to its success, they become *the* brand driving success. This conversion act is a momentous milestone in your culture activation, and no coincidence that it walks hand-in-hand with engagement.
		While you will not be able to directly quantify conversions internally, there will be a palpable shift in culture-driven initiatives. Your internal stakeholders will visibly showcase a renewed sense of passion and respect for the company and its values and will not be shy to evangelize it.

TABLE 11.2 *continued*

Audience	Engagement	Conversions
External: consumers, society, government	Just as you assume a greater response from target audiences when you deliver a targeted marketing campaign, you can expect your external audience to begin engaging more and more with your brand story and content as they respond emotionally. Mentions will turn to likes and shares, and your website traffic may also increase significantly through nothing but organic amplification of your content. When the brand culture is activated by storytelling, external audiences will take immediate notice and even sceptics will become curious about the reactive attention your brand is getting. It's really the same science behind viral posts. By now, we've understood that viral posts at the very core are relatable and emotional so people feel compelled to share them, because in some way, the content 'spoke to them'.	As mentioned before, you may not be able to precisely associate lead generation or conversion to brand storytelling, but when mentions, reach and engagement increase, there will be an inevitable impact to overall conversions. It's recommendable you work with cross-functional teams such as sales and channel marketing before launching your brand story to learn the baseline on current conversions so once the story begins to spread, you can determine how impactful it is becoming (did the conversion rate steadily increase month over month soon after your story landed?) A friendly reminder: you're in it for the long haul so while you may get an immediate reaction from your audience, actual conversion may take a bit longer to quantify.

FIGURE 11.1   General brand culture activation journey

The same occurs with market placement ambitions. Brands striving to position themselves as leaders in the market understand well that there are specific steps the brand needs to take to get there because, in essence, it's also disrupting a culture: an industry one. Brand positioning has become such a crucial contributing factor to the achievement of business goals because, as we keep learning, the digital age has moved aside traditional brand placement efforts, empowering customers instead to make and share their independent assertions of the brand, which has shown itself to be at times more influential in the market than the proclamations of the brand.

After the brand story has captured your audience's hearts, just as you intended, and they react to it, engage with it and convert by it, the imperial consequences of culture movement and thought leadership will be yours to enjoy (Table 11.3).

Similar in many ways to measuring brand equity, the definitive telling that your brand story is doing what it set out to do in the market and with all your stakeholders is when it becomes apparent that your audiences now have an emotional association to the brand and brand story. This ultimately results in consumers choosing to do business with you and not the competition. Remember, 'our emotions influence and shape our... thoughts and behaviours' and there is nothing more emotional than a well-told story.

TABLE 11.3 Lasting action metrics for stakeholders

Audience	Culture	Thought Leadership
Internal stakeholders: owners, employees, partners, vendors, shareholders, investors	Looking at the culture transformation plan in Figure 11.1 (and really, any other iteration), you will notice that these types of core business transformation plans always start with commitment and communication from top leadership. They have to. The beauty about culture activation with storytelling is that *it is* the communication from leadership about the culture they want to have.	At this point and stimulated by culture transformation, your internal stakeholders are *living* the brand story. Through established content hubs (mentioned in Chapter 4), systems and programs such as employee advocacy in place, this audience will not only know and live the brand story, but be wholly equipped to tell it.
	You've worked incessantly to design a brand story that creatively captures and delivers the essence of the brand mission – the very objectives top leadership defined and established for the brand. And unless you took this opportunity to make a full brand refresh (which would also need alignment with leadership), the content you're sharing with your stakeholders is purely the brand's core value…in story form. In essence, you have managed to *emotionally transfer* the brand's mission to your constituents and as a result, you can expect that their reaction to it will propel a lasting outcome.	Because these stakeholders are also professionals in their field and have activated the brand story as part of their individual messaging, they will subsequently begin to get recognized as an authority in their specific field or discipline. Their brand storytelling will evolve them into trusted sources that inspire others and they will inherently be seen as thought leaders.
	Culture activation with brand storytelling happens naturally when stakeholders begin to integrate themselves as part of the allegory because they have understood that they very much *are c part of it*. This is a fundamental change in mindset and behaviour whereby internal stakeholders recognize that the brand story showcases the brand and the brand is its people. No longer is the brand story seen by this audience as an independent approach to connecting with external customers but instead, it is collectively believed to be the blueprint of how business is carried out operationally and communicatively internally. And as a result, culture shift occurs.	

TABLE 11.3   *continued*

Audience	Culture	Thought Leadership
External: consumers, society, government	It is true, culture shift also occurs in industries. The 'tech giants' that once roamed the tech landscape such as IBM, RIM and Motorola, contributed to a set of standards and behaviours in their own time. Today's tech world looks and feels much different thanks to new kids on the block. And the tech culture as a whole will continue to rapidly evolve when the *Robopocalypse* is finally here. To external stakeholders, the shift in your brand's behaviours also causes a shift in their own conduct. As internal stakeholders take ownership of the brand story, the brand's universal truth will permeate and resonate with audiences in a way it can never do from a marketing approach. The message will be shared from internal stakeholders' personal convictions and this external audience will finally customer a part of the brand story, but that they are the *very heart of it*. This will be the greatest legacy your brand story will have in the market.	Concurrent with internal stakeholders becoming thought leaders in the industry, the brand also has great chance of becoming recognized as a thought leader itself. While many brands may still be trying to tie core messaging together, bridge internal communications silos and induce culture shift while navigating the ambiguous digital transformation journey, your company would have evidently demonstrated its innovative ability to modernize itself with a meaningful and unifying narrative, and that will make the company (and you) an expert in your field.

12

Villains and antagonists

The bad guys who want to tear down your brand story

- Why villains and antagonists?
- The bad guy archetype
- Your one and only offensive weapon

What's a story without a villain? Most storytelling experts will tell you that though not every hero necessitates a villain, a *great* story will include an anti-hero or bad guy because these characters instigate conflict – and tension typically tends to make the narrative more exciting.

If your brand story has a hero (your customer) and sidekick (your brand), it makes sense to have an opposing or complementing character actively working to create obstacles and challenges that the hero needs to overcome in order to win. The struggle that villains or antagonists provide in the narrative add an extra layer of empathy from the audience towards the hero and sidekick. The more conflict heroes and sidekicks experience brought on by opposing characters, the more enthralled the audience becomes with foreshadowing the outcome and story ending.

The brand story content can include – but is certainly not limited to – your brand's history, mission, purpose and core values. Sharing bygone accounts to create nostalgia is a great way to entice your audience and can likewise serve as an opportunity to introduce those contending characters that are very much a part of the narrative. What challenges did the brand face in the beginning? Which competitors gained market share in the industry that propelled a complete rebrand or product extension?

Nevertheless, villains and adversaries are not narrowly reserved to condemning the actual storyline. These rival characters can and will be found in the unlikeliest of places, anywhere they might be an opportunity for negative outcome to the brand, brand story and the entire process of storytelling, including its design. Even *you* as a storyteller unknowingly may become an anti-hero to the narrative. So in the interest of landing a well-told account, we must leave nothing to chance when exploring the challenges and obstacles your brand and brand story have and may continue to encounter throughout their life journey.

Why villains and antagonists?

You may be asking yourself why I chose to share insights about villains and bad guys this late in the book. Well, for three simple and obvious reasons:

- If an opposing character had surfaced as a key part of your brand story during the ideation phase, you would have naturally included it already.

- The purpose of bringing these bad guys to light is not to coerce you into including them as part of your brand story (although you may very well do so if you see fit), but to bring awareness to existing opposing forces that may want to tear apart the careful weaving of the narrative you've constructed.

- If, after reading this chapter, you find it necessary to include some of these rivals in your narrative, by all means feel free to do so. The beauty of prototyping stories is that the process never ends.

I grew up scarcely watching television at the time you had to inconveniently take turns with other family members to get up and manually change the channel. Not that there were many channels to choose from. We only had three. And barely two of those had a good transmission signal. Children's programming was sporadic and there wasn't a great selection of age-appropriate movies or shows to choose from, but occasionally one of the local TV networks would announce that a family movie was going to be shown on prime time (8 pm) and this would signal a countdown for my sisters and me to convince our mom to let us stay up late that day and watch.

One of the first motion pictures I had the joy of watching was *Bambi*, the story of a young deer who explores the dangers and fun of life in the forest as he comes of age. I had seen but a few other movies prior to this one, but for some reason, this specific feature left me stunned for days. If you're not familiar with the tale, the movie climaxes with the abrupt killing of the buck's mother by an unseen hunter. Disoriented and alone, the fawn sets out to find solace and new friends. It was the first time I had been stupefied by such a dramatic moment, and also the first time I was exposed to a hidden or 'ghost' villain. Though the frame quickly moves to develop the rest of the plot, my mind stayed fixated on that one scene throughout the movie – and for days after. This villain had changed the course of everything and I couldn't help but wonder how differently the story might have unfolded had this tragic act never occurred.

Villains and antagonists give context to the plot in a way that no other character can do, because they make us see the level of evil or opposition through the eyes of the protagonist. In the case of Bambi, man is the villain, but we know well that, in general, mankind is not all evil.

In the brand storytelling context, villains can range anywhere from competing brands to siloed internal systems and processes that disrupt the brand equity goals and unified brand voice and message. When thinking about your brand story villains and antagonists, it's important to identify the amount of impact and opposition each of these characters affords so that you can decide if they should be given a starring role in the brand narrative, if any role at all.

The choice of *waving the magic wand* to vulnerably share the depth of challenges and obstacles your brand has encountered throughout its life journey is none other than yours to make as the story designer. But there is an unquestionable place for these contesting characters to make a debut within your brand narrative at some point or another, and I believe it benefits you to consider doing so.

To have a little fun, I'd like to categorize these bad guys into several villainous archetype categories, and offer some helpful tips and tricks ('weapon of choice') you can use to help you confront and, hopefully, defuse them. This list can also serve as a determining factor when trying to decide which bad guy best fits into your narrative as the story takes shape and form in the market and expands into mini-stories. Truth be told, all opposing characters fit into your brand tale, but not all may be suitable for your audience.

Fundamentally, it's important to understand the unique differences between villains and antagonists.

The Merriam-Webster dictionary defines a villain as:

a character in a story or play who opposes the hero

a deliberate scoundrel or criminal

one blamed for a particular evil or difficulty

while an antagonist is 'one that contends or opposes another'. In many cases, an antagonist is not necessarily a villain, or even a character. It can be a force that brings conflict and opposition to the protagonist, even within himself.

With that in mind, let's take a look at our brand storytelling list of bad guys. Please note, this is a general catalogue just to give you an idea of some of the characters that may be playing against your brand and brand story. You can certainly have more than these in your own narrative and I truly hope you get creative enough to keep adding to it. The more contention you uncover for your brand story, the more insight you gain about what may be militating against its success.

The bad guys archetypes

The company

Bad guy type: Antagonist

Your company may very well play an enemy to the brand story if its current culture is not entirely aligned to storytelling principles or not yet ready to implement the strategy. While the organization as a whole may recognize the importance of this engagement innovation, the company's core behaviours can oppose the overall notion and indirectly choose against assimilating brand story as a business impact strategy.

LEVEL OF OPPOSITION IMPACT

High. Company culture evolution is an ongoing battle for brands seeking to transform today. Legacy (old timer) internal stakeholders can bring frustrating, palpable resistance to this induced change, especially when the type of adjustment requires an added level of ambiguity, such as prototyping and testing stories during a time when brand transformation already brings its own set of nuances.

DEFENCE WEAPON

Consistency. As you set out to launch your brand narrative to internal stakeholders first, it is vital that they receive a consistent message outlining the how, what, when, where and why of storytelling. This will indicate to stakeholders across the company that storytelling is indeed the way the brand is going in its efforts to modernize communication across the board.

A reimagined integrated marketing approach (explained in Chapter 4) can assist in the swift modernization and assimilation strategy and help brand storytelling integration.

Leadership

Bad guy type: Antagonist

Assuming you began your brand storytelling efforts because you were able to pitch it to top leaders and were given the green light and support from them to start experimenting with storytelling as a strategy, it may be difficult to get full buy-in from peer senior or mid-level leaders across the rest of the organization.

Storytelling naturally induces a culture shift, forcing stakeholders to reflect and think differently about how they are currently engaging and communicating with their audiences. The fact that presently established communication strategies may no longer be as relevant as they once were for the brand is an uncomfortable truth to accept, to say the least, and this can result in adverse reaction.

LEVEL OF OPPOSITION IMPACT

Moderate. Like any disruption, this business plan alteration can be met with some conflicting opinions from frontrunners and influencers in the organization who may not truly understand the capacities of brand storytelling, storytelling in general, or may simply not want to align to these cutting-edge engagement principles.

DEFENCE WEAPON

Top leaders. Leverage top leadership to help communicate and evangelize the new strategy to your internal stakeholders. In essence, they are the ones that ultimately spearhead this effort and you will not only need their agreement and verbal support to establish this ground breaking plan but their commitment to hands-on influence integration.

Don't forget your best storytellers: employees! A well-thought-out employee advocacy program can help in tandem with leadership.

Business functions

Bad guy type: Antagonist and villain

As opposed to the brand and its leaders who may be understandably contending against the brand storytelling approach because this modern method agitates conventional norms, discipline functions can not only be an obstacle to effectively incorporating brand storytelling into the business, but also serve as a direct malefactor when attempting to unify the brand message from every angle of the organization.

LEVEL OF OPPOSITION IMPACT

Depends. Mid-size to large corporations will have a harder time successfully implementing brand storytelling techniques in the various disciplines. For the most part, the majority of business functions act as stand-alone entities, and this siloed model often creates hard-to-bridge gaps within an organization.

If your brand is just starting out or small in size, it will be easier for you to implement brand storytelling as a business goal and bring these disciplines close together. But in general, it's important to keep aware that these organizational models, notwithstanding the size of the brand, traditionally operate under a fixed mindset approach, which is always detrimental to seamless execution of any brand strategy and culture shift activation.

DEFENCE WEAPON

Top leadership. Same weapon as for 'Leadership'. Your leaders are your best ammunition when it comes to tearing down silos in your quest to integrate the story narrative within each and all of these functions. Using the IMC Reimagined idea and encouraged by top leaders, discipline members can tap into a set of brand storytelling resources that will serve individually within their space.

Systems and processes

Bad guy type: Villain

Just as with discipline functions, long-standing as well as newly implemented systems and processes within the organization can play an anti-hero part in your brand story owing to the complex and sometimes disparate functions these perform. Think about a marketing or sales leads tracking or conversion system such as Salesforce, for example. As your sales teams begin to assimilate and even tell the brand story in their own space to their individual audiences, this technology can be simultaneously telling a disparate and contradictory account to those same customers.

Remember that brand storytelling is not just about designing a narrative told from the brand's perspective, but also about 'speaking it' to your audience through the end-to-end experience your customers have at every touchpoint with your brand.

If internal systems and processes that enable customer transactions (both internal and external) do not align to what the brand is saying its mission, core values and behaviours are, your story hero (the customer) will become frustrated and confused.

LEVEL OF OPPOSITION IMPACT

Moderate. There's a reason 'systems and tools' always come high on the list of areas for improvement in most employee surveys: they usually suck. The main complaint we have about them is that they don't 'talk to each other', so how can we expect them to cohesively deliver the brand message to your customer?

It's important to recognize the impact these mechanisms can have on your customer as you tell the brand story and find ways to close the gaps between the promises the brand story is making and what is actually being delivered.

DEFENCE WEAPON

Digital transformation. The good news is that even if your brand has not yet started to integrate digital technology into the business, it will have to do so very soon. This will compel a makeover of most, if not all, systems and processes within all areas of the business. If the business has already started in the digital transformation process, chances are you still have a while to go (all of us do). Therefore, in either case, you have a great opportunity to use the brand story as the North Star for driving customer experience through these modern mechanisms.

Technology

Bad guy type: Antagonist

Technology can be a great ally to your brand story, but if misused, it can also be an opposing influence. If you don't take the time to carefully choose adequate technology to deliver your brand story, your story may not land as intended with your audiences, creating the opposite effect to the one you were aiming for.

Earlier in the book we learned that the story form (video, podcast, immersive), or really, the technology you use to tell the story, is defined at the prototype phase. As you have already learned, any and all elements in storytelling ought to consistently and empathetically consider your design audience above all.

In today's rapidly evolving digital landscape, technology can become obsolete in a matter of months or weeks, making your story seem antiquated if you fail to flexibly recognize and stay on top of this progression.

LEVEL OF OPPOSITION IMPACT

High. In the next chapter I will share additional details about predictions of the impact that the impending and much-anticipated Robopocalypse (machines, AI and automation) will have on brand engagement and communication efforts. But at the very least, your brand should consider moving towards a nimble approach to changes led by technological advances.

Systems, processes, leadership, the company and the brand story can all become victims of today's digital revolution, paralysing efforts at customer engagement if not assimilated and addressed properly.

DEFENCE WEAPON

Empathy and flexibility. Having the privilege of personally experiencing fast-paced evolution, both internal and external, brought on by our own technological advances at Microsoft, I can attest to the importance of staying empathetic and flexible to keep relevant as a brand.

Technology is not a villain so it does not need to be combatted. It is a driving force that instigates reform and the most sensible way to confront it is by adapting to it, embracing its metamorphic powers and continuing to integrate its new offerings into the brand story.

Competitors

Bad guy type: Villain

If your brand story's ultimate goal is to effectively engage your customers and win their loyalty, competing brands fighting to gain market share and 'steal' your customers are your number one brand story villains.

These merciless mischief-makers are out to discredit the message you have meticulously designed and shared. They are ruthless and unsparing in their approach and will go to war with you for the ultimate prize: your brand hero (the customer).

LEVEL OF OPPOSITION IMPACT

State of emergency high. Your competition is out to get your customers and inflict pain on your bottom line through a calculated and utterly destructive attack on your brand story.

Once you go out there to tell your audiences in a very emotional, authentic and perhaps even vulnerable manner what your brand is about, your competitors will waste no time in shamelessly attempting to steal not only your customer, but your brand story content to misuse, forge or even break apart and take it out of context to use it as a weapon against your brand.

DEFENCE WEAPON

Consistency. You've learned that brand storytelling is a long-term indoctrination process, and while competitors will do what they do, if you remain consistent in telling the brand message over and over, your audience will begin to recognize and embrace its universal truth. While you should keep track of your competitors' whereabouts and tactics, it's important not to get distracted in the game of telling stories. Stay focused on steadfastness and pay more attention to your customer's reaction than to that of your competitors. In the end, if you find competitors mounting a full-frontal attack on you, you know you're on the right track to engaging your customer base.

My life and business rule is: love your enemy. If you have none, you're doing it wrong. A great sign that your brand story is resonating in the industry is when your competitors are paying attention.

Storytellers

Bad guy type: Antagonist

In Chapter 9, we took a deep dive into your brand's best storytellers. But, as you know, there are plenty more reciters out there telling your story, officially – and unofficially. Storytellers are the most organic and vivid way your story is told.

Storytellers are individuals who assimilate the story and regurgitate it back with their own spin. It is through them, and the personal flavour they add to the narrative, that accounts come to life in many forms and shapes, independent of the functional and emotional job you gave the narrative.

Though scientists have yet to completely understand the manner by which the human brain retains information, we do know that as we receive information, we incorporate our own lived experiences and biases to assimilate it, so every piece of information we capture is seen through our particular lens.

This cognitive consumption of stories can be both a blessing and a curse, if not planned for.

LEVEL OF OPPOSITION IMPACT

Low. In the last chapter, I shared that brand mentions are indicators that your brand story is resonating with stakeholders and other audiences. If the brand story lands well, you can expect individuals to consume and naturally want to share it, obviously from their own perspective.

All of us love a good story and love to share a good story. It's an actual positive to learn that your brand story is emotional and memorable to your audiences. But it is important to remain mindful of any possibility of distortion of the storyline.

Human tendency is to add on, distort or take away from baseline information. The impact storytellers in general can have on your brand story is that it may get distorted over time, if left unchecked.

DEFENCE WEAPON

Consistency. Once again, while audiences may inherently distort the brand narrative with their own biases and assertions, the best way to keep your brand story intact is by making your brand the only source of truth to the brand story through solidly remaining consistent in the messaging. I know you are beginning to recognize a pattern here: consistency is brilliancy and the strongest weapon your brand has in ensuring that the narrative stays intact. This is why having a well-planned launch strategy for both internal and external stakeholders is crucial when deciding to land the story.

You

Bad guy type: Antagonist

As the story designer, you are the best case of a supporting character evolving into an antagonist of the brand story. You've worked so hard at creating prototypes, testing and redesigning narratives that when one of the stories finally lands, and lands well, it may seem very plausible to stop the design thinking cycle. This logic is not only dangerous but destructive to your brand narrative.

I cannot stress enough how the many forces that play against a compelling account (new technologies, demanding audiences, evolving products and services) force the continued cycle of story prototyping.

You should never get too comfortable with the brand story. It's important to remember that this narrative is always in prototype mode and can and should be continuously modified, evolved and adapted so that it does not become stagnant.

LEVEL OF OPPOSITION IMPACT

Low. The hope is that by learning the principles of UX and design thinking applied to storytelling, you've developed an 'eye' for keeping your story relevant and a taste for continuing the design thinking process. Just like my friend, Gregory, the maniacal UX designer who is never satisfied with his designs, my aspiration for you as a storyteller is that you will continue to iterate the brand story because you will never be fully content with your product.

DEFENCE WEAPON

Prototyping. Periodically continue to submit the storyline through different possible iterations based on benchmarking metrics and overall industry and technology trends. This will ensure minimal impact to the integrity of the brand story.

Society

Bad guy type: Antagonist

As an indirect stakeholder, we've learned that society does play a part in the success of the brand story. In Chapter 5, I spent some time sharing non-obvious trend ideas primarily led by societal behaviours that drive marketing trends.

As with all villains and antagonists, it's essential to acknowledge how any and all behaviours can influence assimilation of the brand story and put a plan in place to contain possible antagonistic responses from extended audiences when the story hits the market. Neglecting to do this can negatively impact on the narrative.

LEVEL OF OPPOSITION IMPACT

Depends. Societal behaviours can truly be unpredictable. Anything can happen at the time you decide to launch your brand story. Independent of your planned efforts, a movement of some sort (eg social justice) could be brewing and the narrative can find itself intertwined in these messages. Misinterpretation of the brand story content is likely to occur, breaking apart the essence of the story.

DEFENCE WEAPON

Social listening. As you learned in Chapter 10, launching your brand story is really testing it. To diminish possible impact to the brand story mandated by societal behaviours, it is recommended to continuously listen for clues as to the stance that members of society may currently have on specific topics and how the brand story could be interpreted if launched during specific times. Though your intent is to reach a design audience, society as an extended stakeholder ought also to be considered when marketing content, because it can influence the overall effectiveness of brand positioning in the market.

Your offensive weapon

All in all, as with any story, the villain or antagonist can only be as strong as its opponent. Otherwise, we couldn't consider them a rival force. With each of these bad guys, I shared specific defence weapons you may use to combat their possible aggression, but did you know that you do hold one *offensive attack* armament that is sure to proactively assail each of these characters, protecting your brand story in the most powerful way?

This weapon is none other than training.

When my 'storytelling with design principles' model began to resonate with other colleagues at Microsoft, I started to receive dozens of requests from teams all over the world asking me to train their specific groups. Even though Microsoft as a company was already leading the way in storytelling efforts, where Chief Storyteller Steve Clayton and his team strategically set out to unify the Microsoft story from the top down through creation of a central hub of guidelines, assets, online training courses, hosting an annual storyteller summit at headquarters open to anyone who wished to learn more, and sharing Microsoft Story deck templates, it was still difficult for anyone who did not consider themselves a storyteller (the rest of the employee base and internal stakeholders) to feel ownership of these incredible resources and apply them in their own space. More so, there was *so* much information available that these stakeholders didn't know where to start.

It may seem obvious that by creating so many resources people will innately self-teach, feel like a storyteller and go out and tell the story. But by now you have learned that storytelling is not just about telling the story. It is an all-encompassing approach to connectedness, business transactions and communication. Therefore, training on storytelling goes way beyond fundamental teaching. It is an act of transmitting the brand story in such a way that your stakeholders feel proprietorship over it and can also see themselves as part of it.

So far, I have lightly touched on training in Chapter 4 as part of the resources your brand should offer in the reimagined integrated marketing plan and in Chapter 6 as an open door for employees to build their vulnerability muscle when telling stories, but was waiting to get to this chapter in order to deep dive into how to best train your stakeholders so they can feel empowered to take ownership of and tell the brand story as the choice weapon of attack against maleficent forces wanting to tear down your story.

As American author, salesman and motivational speaker Zig Ziglar once pointed out, 'There is only one thing worse than training employees and losing them, and that's not training them and keeping them'.

A few tours around the sun as storyteller and hundreds of storytelling training sessions later, I can personally attest to the sheer omnipotence a good storytelling training session can have. Sitting in the trainer seat, I've learned much over the years about what does and doesn't resonate with audiences, and from those learnings I want to offer some practical wisdom so that you can build up your army of storytellers in the most effective manner and hopefully diffuse much of the antagonism and villainous assaults.

Attack mode: training internal stakeholders

Notice that I am purposeful in calling out *internal stakeholders*, not just employees, as your offensive battalion. Everyone that is closely working with or for the brand and committed to the organization at some level or another should be regarded as part of this mighty army that is going to enthusiastically protect the integrity of the brand narrative. Once you have armed them with a set of resources and brand story assets, the training begins. Aside from the regular capacity training best practices you may already know, below are three wisdom training rules you can leverage to successfully accomplish this mission.

Training rule 1. Teach them 'the ways', not just the story

The reason many training sessions fail to produce long-lasting results is that as a common practice and to maximize resources, companies tend to saturate trainees with information. Statistics show that 'after one hour, people retain less than half of the information presented' and 'after one day, people forget more than 70 per cent of what was taught in training'.

The best way to teach anyone is through hands-on practice. Take time to walk your audience through the art of prototyping the brand story. Instead of telling them what the story is, give them the raw materials (brand mission, core values, universal truth) and walk them through a quick session of what it means to be empathetic, guide them as they themselves define the story characters and, on the spot, ideate and prototype the story, later 'testing' it with the same audience in the room.

I have been able to practically train audiences in design thinking steps in as little as one hour. Obviously, I have had much practice at it, but you, as the story designer and master storyteller, have already been intimately acquainted with the design thinking process. Leverage this mastery to teach others. Whether in person or via video, the steps used in a hyper-engaged and creative session are the same:

- Introduce and share the brand story and story mission with your audience.

- If training is in person, I highly recommend that a physical printout is handed out so that trainees can write on and review the story in a palpable manner.

The brand story can be told in many ways, but the most effective way for this training session is a 'meet the company' walking presentation deck that not only provides the narrative but also statistics and milestones as extra content:

1 Introduce and explain the design thinking principles applied to storytelling (Chapter 2) and break down each phase.

2 Empathize. Explain the importance of building empathy as a soft skill.

3 Define. Ask them to define their own audience (who will they be telling this story to?), then give them five minutes to review the materials and identify as many characters in the story as they can. Finally, share the list of characters designed in the story so they can compare.

4 Ideate. Get a volunteer to take the materials and make the story theirs (eg My Brand Story) through inserting their own lived experience with the brand into the main narrative. (If training is on video, you can act the same volunteer scene with the help of other trainers or colleagues to illustrate practical steps.)

5 Prototype. Get another volunteer to share how they intend to tell the story to their particular audience using the assets the brand has created.

6 Testing. After they have defined their own audience, ideated and proto-typed their brand narrative using the resources you provided, get a final volunteer to showcase the final prototype to their audience.

This will prove to be a very fun and dynamic storytelling training session. Teaching your audience how to prototype stories instead of what the story is will give them an invaluable skillset on their way to also becoming a storyteller.

Training rule 2. Explain, don't just make resources available

Just because you've created a great set of storytelling assets and resources does not mean your audience knows how and when to best use them. Take time to walk your stakeholders through all of the assets available: what they are, how they can be used and, most importantly, which they can best lever-age within their own spaces. The power of brand storytelling increases exponentially when your internal stakeholders not only understand the narrative and are able to identify their own audience and take ownership of the story, but can also strategically select the elements of the story that are best suitable to their audiences. This transforms the story into a live source of content that adapts to every internal aspect of the organization. Dumping content and resources in an information hub without giving it context will be a waste of time for you and your stakeholders. Take time to create story-telling guidelines that explain the non-negotiables and negotiables when telling the story. A suggested list is:

- Non-negotiables (no one can deviate from these)
  - My story deck
  - Story mission and universal truth
  - Storytelling elements
- Negotiables (storytellers can pick and choose whether and how to use these, based on their specific audience needs)
  - Storytelling techniques, ways to tell the story
  - Brainstorming session resources

Training rule 3. Train again and again and again

Need I spend time expanding on this rule? *Smile*. This rule is simple: every time the story evolves, your stakeholders will need to be trained.

My wish for you and your brand story is that it will thrive in the most improbable environments and surpass all attempts by malicious forces to discredit it in front of your audiences. Your brand story is a masterful piece of art and should be able to withstand villains, antagonists and any other offensive bad guys....

But, will it survive against the machines?

13

The future of brand storytelling

How AI, machine learning and automation can tell only one side of the story

- Enter: the machines
- The race against the machines
- AI technology trends

As we near the end of this brand storytelling guide, I would be remiss if I didn't acknowledge the very thing that sparked the idea of writing a book on brand storytelling for the digital age: technology – and its rapid advances.

I've mentioned once or twice how lucky I consider myself to be on many counts… and not necessarily because I've never missed a connecting flight to this day. *Knock on wood!*

I'm thankful to have been born in one of the most strikingly beautiful and culturally rich countries in South America: Venezuela. To have had the opportunity to immigrate and build a life in the United States of America, the Land of Opportunities, where hard work and tenacity remain the fabric of forging new chances and innovation, even for those of humble beginnings, like myself. Most importantly, I am richly blessed with people. People in my network. People in my family. People who have become family. Those people have shaped the person I am today and, in some ways, influenced parts – if not all – of this book. Some more than others.

The year was 2015 and, as part of a learning series at Microsoft, I received an invitation to watch a live webcast of a Distinguished Engineer (that's a real title) sharing insights on storytelling. The name of the talk alone was good enough to catch my attention ('The Art of Storytelling'), but it was the fact that this was an *engineer*, albeit distinguished, who was teaching the course that made me look twice. Now, you may not know much about engineers. But if you thought marketing folks like you and me have a hard time with story crafting and telling, you may find solace in the idea that just by you being able to post an Instagram story, these computer scientists deem you a master of digital communications. It became clear why this story-telling talk was filled to capacity, both in the actual room and online. It was by an engineer *to* engineers.

I didn't have much time to google Dr James Whittaker prior to the session. So, without much context, I went in expecting nothing. What came at me through the screen in the 45 minutes that followed was so unexpectedly fascinating that I was left with the impetuous desire to do the exact thing I've been telling you story does: act. But how? My first thought was to send him a short and sweet email, simply thanking this brilliant Master of the Story Art for the illuminating talk. My next thoughts were:

Boring and without consequence.

Everyone else is probably already doing that right now.

He won't even respond.

Did I want him to respond? Of course, I wanted him to respond!

But why do I want him to respond and for what? Who is this person anyway?

I googled.

I shouldn't have googled. That made me even more intimidated and confused as to how exactly I should act, and why. But this data-scientist-turned-oratory-guru and his stories were so compelling that I needed to do something. Anything.

It occurred to me that my colleagues too needed to hear the secrets and importance of evoking stage presence sorcery and the hacks of inflecting your voice when sharing a narrative for deeper impact, among other story-telling incantations. So, without hesitation, I offered James an invitation to share his talk with my colleagues in Florida within the upcoming months, sometime in the Fall. Just so you know, in the States, *nobody ever* turns down a trip to the Sunshine State of Florida. I mean, ever. Especially coming from Seattle.

As expected, he said yes, and all was good in the world. Until months later – and with only a few weeks leading up to the much-anticipated event – to my huge disappointment, James decided to cancel the trip owing to a work conflict.

Disenchanted, but not defeated, I leveraged our second communication (his cancellation notice) to extend yet another invitation to give a future talk. This time the session would be for a more intimate audience (my immediate discipline team during an offsite event in Seattle). I also nonchalantly threw in a request for him to become my storytelling mentor. He accepted the first request, then flat-out rejected the latter. 'I have too many mentees and too little time,' he replied dryly. But life has taught me that 'no' is the beginning of negotiations, so I pressed a bit further. 'How about I just stay in touch with you via email and periodically ask questions on a particular topic, as needed?'

And thus began our beautiful mentor relationship.

In just a few years, Doc James has taught me an innumerable amount of storytelling wisdom and I owe much of my current stage platform to his patient dedication and teachings. I consider one his most important teachings to be the way he has personally and extremely successfully been able to bridge the gap between the left and right hemispheres of the brain, wondrously marrying the insightful and creative with the logical and analytical in order to deliver enchanting tales of data, cloud computing and bathtub Internet of Things (IoT), proving not only to his peers and other highly technical audiences around the world, but also to those of us in marketing and communication disciplines on the other side of the pond, that the mastery of story is a free and attainable gift for all who truly desire to pursue it. In tandem, he taught me the importance of learning code (something I promised him I'd start doing soon) and having a deeper understanding of how technology will continue to evolve to something greater than we can ever envision – and perhaps scarier than we will ever imagine – because that is in essence what makes storytelling an even more pervasive idea for businesses today.

Enter: the machines

I would be lying if I said that I know a good amount about technology because I've worked in the tech industry for a while now. Whereas, from the very start, I could understand the basics of computer science and the products that big tech companies serve and continue to evolve, it wasn't until I became a storyteller within the engineering discipline at Microsoft that I actually had the chance to get my 'hands dirty' with technology. There were three storytellers in total in my immediate group, each of us assigned to two functional areas or business pillars of the company; one of mine included AI and Data (told you I was lucky). Hence my job was to find relevant and exciting stories anywhere in the organization where these categories took place. And exciting I found. After successfully breaking my first story rooted in design thinking principles, I went on with a newfound confidence to unearth remarkable tech tales that had been secretly waiting to be shared with the rest of the world in an empathetic manner. Words, acronyms and ideas such as containerization, intelligent cloud and intelligent edge, which had theoretically been a part of my fundamental knowledge, became tangible models that 'real live' people I was talking to were actually building or contributing to in one way or another. I had the chance to hold in my hand an IoT device the size of a smartphone that was more powerful than a mainframe. I interacted with a very friendly robot roaming the hallways that was kind enough to point me in the right direction when it learned I was lost and trying to find a conference room. The machines were no longer a fable or futuristic fantasy. They were real things cohabitating with me and they looked very different from that clunky, metallic intruder that invaded my living room only a couple of decades ago.

'Does it talk back?'

You better believe it. But that's the wrong question to ask.

According to Doc James, in his *James Whittaker's Little Book of The Future*, the question today is not *if* machines will talk back, rather *what will the machine say?*

Alluding to the supremacy of IoT and how data – fuelled by machine learning (ML for short) and AI capabilities – enable connected 'things' to become more intelligent, Doc James makes a case for a not-so-far-from-now future when the relationship between humans and machines will turn bidirectional, information will be shared between both sides and the machines will never cease to learn human patterns of behaviour in their quest to offer a more personalized customer experience… in record time.

Here's an excerpt:

For example, if a conference room could talk, what would it say?

With that as the guiding question, it's time to brainstorm.

First, a conference room would understand its schedule and know who was attending each meeting. Seems simple enough, right? Those data are, after all, readily available in employee calendar apps.

Collectively, the conference rooms in any building would know each other's schedule and guide any employees with the intent to meet to a free room suitable to their group size, purpose and time requirements.

One could ask a conference room: 'Is everyone here?' The answer is discoverable based on the meeting invitation and recognizing the faces of the people in the room. Furthermore, a missing person might be geo-located using, say, their phone (they are, after all, employees of the company) and their estimated time of arrival could be established.

Predictions of a close integration between humans and futuristic technologies abound. An *MIT Technology Review* article in 2017 revealed the effects every industry will begin experiencing within the next four decades alone. In the next few years, intelligent machines will be able to:

- write high school essays (2026)
- drive trucks (2027)
- work in retail (2031)
- work as a surgeon (2053)
- write a bestselling book (2049)

Wait, did they say *write a book*? You mean... tell stories?

Indeed, they just might.

Through stochastic processes (a mathematical theory of probability) and as we speak, machines are learning to collect key data insights to build algorithms that can mimic not only the way the human brain works (AI) but also the way humans *learn*.

AI capabilities are well positioned to outsmart us in many big ways and in very little time because, unlike humans, the machines are awake and working on finding these pathways 24/7. They don't need to pause and grab a meal or deal with an untimely relationship breakup. They don't spend time doing other 'human' things like going to the gymnasium to maintain their bodies or the cinema to refresh their minds. Their entire job is to get smarter and better at whatever craft they've been created to do. And smarter and better they will get.

But rather than comparing how much more *physically* powerful those ubiquitous, agile, ever-working superbeings might be against our lesser, hungry, tired and needy species, I'd like to point out the true determining factor in genus superiority when it comes to telling stories. It's the place where no robot can ever outdo, outwork or outshine us. A wild and untamed landscape where autonomous human emotions wrestle, reconcile and most times direct us, whether we like it or not: the human heart.

You see, the stories machines might be able to tell may be good on paper. They may be perfectly crafted, grammatically correct and might even have some built-in algorithm where the best choice of vocabulary, punctuation marks and stances will yield a flawless manuscript for market share. Sure, a robot might learn to skilfully put its 'thoughts' or data sets together and come up with a bestselling romance novel after quickly acquiring understanding of the mechanics and formulas it takes to write a top-ranking fiction book.

But will it speak touchingly, with wisdom and empathy towards its human readers, drinking from a fountain of personal lived experiences, possibly rooted in past agonizing heartbreak? Will its eyes well up with tears while it recounts and reflects on personal clandestine moments with that special someone who became the inspiration for and bears striking resemblance to a particular character in the story?

Machines may soon be able to pen stunning accounts of character, plot and conclusion in remarkable storyworlds and even learn to mechanically simulate the emotional transfer factor a great story commands – but only because they've been told to, and not because stories inevitably come as a result of the desires and recesses of their soul or spontaneously birthed from illuminated imagination. Because they possess neither – and they never will.

The race against the machines

For a while I gave a popular storytelling keynote talk entitled 'Empathy: The race against the machines' where I would spend the first few minutes warning audiences about the impending Robopocalypse, later to put them at ease with my personal conclusion that these heartless cyborgs will never own the empathy, vulnerability and ethics required to tell an authentic and emotional allegory. The truth is that this talk was originally intended for those very engineers who are precisely contributing to the cataclysmic digital doomsday. It was to serve them as a poignant reminder of the importance of working on the empathy soft skill on a daily basis, because as 'creators' of these cyborgs, the future would look frightfully dire if they weren't intended to make compassion the cradle of these smart machines. The talk later evolved into that notion of 'Storytelling 2.0', gifted to me by the spiritual significance I felt at Machu Picchu, where empathy rises as the evergreen fabric of not only story, but everything 'human connection' we do to ensure our own survival amid the digital age.

Ironic as it is, empathy was once an enemy to the human race's existence. Experts may not agree on the final number of emotions humans have, but they do agree that our primal ancestors were mostly driven by anger and fear so that they could stay alive. Otherwise, they might have been left behind while feeling bad for, and trying to assist, a neighbour with lesser physical, mental or resources capacities.

But times have changed. And empathy is becoming an increasingly crucial factor not only in our species' survival but in that of our businesses too. How lucky are we to be able to draw from our own feelings and emotions to successfully adapt to the ever-changing elements that threaten us?

'Humanizing the brand', 'connecting at the human level with customers', 'doing H2H (human to human) business' are all slogans you've heard in recent years and will continue to hear more and more as companies persist in making strides along the digital transformation journey through tapping into the inescapable truth that humans have an ingrained desire to stay engaged with one another at the very 'heart' level and even so more now as we face the Robopocalypse.

Try explaining that one to Siri or Alexa.

This is why we don't care as much about perfectly crafted stories; instead we'd rather hear tales of flawed and broken people. Stories sprinkled with a little bit of *defect*, so we, as humans, can intimately relate to those characters... and even the storytellers and story designers behind them.

Then again, that's not to say the up-and-coming highly intellectual android community can't bring value to our brand stories. *Au contraire!* I know that in the last chapter I listed technology as one of the brand story's antagonists. But I did also mention that, matched with human empathy, technology can actually serve as a powerful catalyst to the narrative. And it absolutely should.

If we do it well, our machines will serve to speed up the story design process and ensure they reach our intended audiences faster than we'll be able to creatively think up more ideas.

Most of the android prophecies lean towards the notion that machines will ultimately exist to make our lives better, less cluttered and less busy by taking on routine operational minutiae and nuances. Today, my house is not considered a 'smart home' by any means, but I do live alongside a few AI friends that ease up on annoying house chores such as automated floor and carpet cleaning and small tasks like dimming the lights or ordering pizza through voice command. I'd be surprised if you weren't doing the same. Machines have seemingly made their way into our homes and offices and we have slowly but surely adapted and welcomed their convenient presence.

Given that these AI companions have gracefully infiltrated parts of our everyday lives to bring about a new set of advantages for practical modern living and working, and that machines have already disrupted the marketing and communication industry to enable a more rapid and targeted approach to storytelling, we'd be short-sighted not to vigorously and intentionally fuse them with our own human intrinsic powers to bring about brand stories the world has never seen before.

AI technology trends

Trends involving AI, ML and automation are defining new business strategies and competing priorities. The 2019 Enterprise Technology Trend report revealed the 10 top tendencies in IT that are driving business for consumers and B2B models today.

Though these trends are rooted specifically in technological offerings, we have already seen the beautiful synergy that innovation and storytelling can have if companies are empathetic and flexible enough to integrate them: advancing technology provokes the use of story, story is empowered by the use of technology, and round and round it goes.

For this reason, I'd like to quickly dive into these latest trends and leave you with some final instructions that along with design thinking principles, magic tricks, wands and ethics will take your brand story to places that you or your AI storyteller could only ever hope for.

Trend 1. Cutting-edge customer experience is a must-have

If it hasn't started yet, your company will most likely soon begin updating systems and technologies, increasing reliance on cloud-based innovations in order to provide a competitive customer experience. This is the time to pitch storytelling as yet another innovative approach to reaching customers. It is in essence a new technology. Leverage this momentum to propose your storytelling plan as part of the digital transformation efforts.

Trend 2. Increasing investment in employee experience

Companies are placing more focus and resources on talent retention and satisfaction. Take advantage of this growing tendency by suggesting implementation of employee advocacy efforts as well as the Reimagined Integrated Marketing Plan.

Trend 3. Enhanced developer support

Low-code or no-code tools are on their way out for organizations, while serverless computing continues to rise. This means your company's developers' lives will get a little easier, providing an opportunity for you and your storytelling team to engage in conversations about how your brand's story can become more *built in* and *not bolted on* as part of the organization's overall internal and external customer satisfaction strategies.

Trend 4. Mobile workplace

'Sixty-three per cent of the workforce uses their mobile devices for work tasks as much as personal tasks.' This raises the question: How can you leverage employee mobility to help your brand story reach them?

Trend 5. Connected systems

While connected experiences remain a lofty goal for organizations, brands are making concerted efforts to integrate their systems, especially customer relationship management (CRM) systems. Again, this is a great opportunity to begin getting involved and collaborating with teams leading this process from a brand storytelling platform and ensuring the systems are telling the brand story well too.

Trend 6. AI adoption and expansion

I dedicated an entire chapter to this very trend (Chapter 8) and hope you can truly capitalize on this ever-growing movement.

Trend 7. Voice technology for customer engagement

As AI enables voice- and text-first customer experiences, begin to brainstorm the possibilities of how this 'AI storyteller' will sound and align to your brand story attributes.

Trend 8. IT staff skillset diversification

This is a big one. I can personally attest to the increasing investment companies from every industry are making to help their engineers sharpen in-demand skills such as teamwork, collaboration and... you guessed it, storytelling. This is your stellar moment to make yourself available and train IT employees in the story craft. Prepare your materials. This opportunity is coming faster than you think.

Trend 9. Blockchain adoption

Still in its infancy, IT leaders believe that this new type of internet will play an important role in industries and companies in the near future, and, while its overall effects remain to be seen, the idea of more secure digital transactions is already a winning attribute in this record-keeping technology. From a storytelling perspective it is important to keep an eye on how this innovation will disrupt customer experience and transactions, as it will surely change the narrative for the brand once it's implemented.

Trend 10. Expanding the security mandate

A top priority for companies today is that of providing a trustworthy and secure digital environment for customers to connect and transact. So much so that 54 per cent of organizations in almost every sector have a dedicated IT security team. This trend, and the attention your brand is likely giving to it, is a great opportunity to add a layer of trust in your brand story. By incorporating evidence of how important security and trust are to your brand as part of the story, you will proactively help alleviate customer concerns and build trust.

The dawn of new technologies has brought forth incredible and exciting new opportunities for us as humans to evolve ourselves, our practices and our ingenuity. Today, we not only get to 'talk' to computers, but we can converse, play and cohabit with them. The machines are here. But perhaps they're not here to *disrupt* everything we've ever known about effective marketing and communication in business.

Perhaps they're here simply to take on the boring, robotic, operational parts of marketing and communications while *we* get to disrupt. Let's let the robots be robots and put them to work tirelessly on the mundane and mechanical things we actually don't enjoy, while we take back some precious hours of our ever-fleeting days and invest them in ourselves, our communities and our legacy, unlocking deeper levels of imagination, creativity and empathy.

Google 'storytelling' a few years from now and I hope you will find your name, along with that of your Sous Storyteller, listed among the great disruptors who in the tech era ventured to pioneer new and unchartered paths to marry the art and science of story – both for your organization and yourself.

And just to be clear, the paths aren't roads. Because as Doc predicted in *Back to the Future*: 'Where we're going, we don't need roads.'

I'm an 80s kid. I know. Lucky.

14

Inspire your brand story

Interviews with leading storytellers around the world

In this final chapter, it is my true honour and pleasure to invite some of the most talented and prominent allegorists from different walks of life and industries, who I also consider friends, to share their insights and fascinating stories about brand storytelling. I hope you enjoy their exquisite wisdom, witty humour and vulnerable personal accounts and that these serve to inspire you and your brand story as you go forward to tell it.

Interview with Dux Raymond Sy, CMO of AvePoint

Hi Dux. It's such a pleasure chatting with you today. Could you introduce yourself to our readers and tell us something curious about you they may find fascinating?

Hi, Miri – first off, I am very thankful for this privilege to share my story. I appreciate you including me in this much-needed brand story-telling guide.

I was born and raised in Manila, Philippines, by a wonderful, multi-cultural family. I have fond memories of loud conversations over dinner with my parents, five sisters and brother, learning to speak multiple languages and telling stories to keep my younger siblings occupied. Growing up in a big family, I've learned to easily adapt and pivot as the challenge (or opportunity) calls for it.

These days I serve as the Chief Marketing Officer of AvePoint. Over 16,000 customers and 6 million cloud users worldwide trust AvePoint software to migrate, manage and protect their data in the Microsoft cloud, on-premises, and in hybrid environments.

In my over 20 years of business and technology experience, I've supported digital transformation initiatives of private, educational and government organizations worldwide. I've had the opportunity to author the book *SharePoint for Project Management*; been recognized as a Microsoft Regional Director (RD) and Microsoft Most Valuable Professional (MVP); and delivered interactive presentations at leading industry events worldwide. I live in Washington, DC with my amazing wife and two children. In my free time, I frequently run along the Potomac River and sample the most exotic foods available (grilled scorpions, anyone?).

As you may have surmised, I am technical – in fact, I have a bachelor's degree in Telecommunications Engineering. I started my career as a developer, became a tech consultant and eventually a Chief Technology Officer. In 2016, I took on the role of Chief Marketing Officer. While I don't have a formal marketing background, this once in a lifetime opportunity is something I didn't want to pass up.

Since moving to the US in 1996, I've learned to embrace change – as it's inevitable and encourages personal development. That's why I can be coding in Assembler one day, pitching our software solution to a government customer the next and in a blink of an eye, be up on stage at a technical conference opening for Bon Jovi – essentially performing as the front act in front of 12,000 people.

Having these experiences enriches my journey and offers a wide variety of stories that I can tell.

The modern CMO today plays many roles, including brand storyteller. Can you share some insights on how you integrate storytelling in your day-to-day work and to drive business forward?

Have you been to Antarctica, Miri? It's actually on my bucket list. Other than being able to brag that I've been to seven continents, I am keen on visiting Scott Base. It's New Zealand's only Antarctic research station, perched on a low volcanic headland called Pram Point at the southern end of Ross Island.

You see, Scott Base does a lot of amazing research work and we had the great opportunity to address their needs. We provided them with a low-bandwidth data replication solution that allowed them to quickly access information that's based in Christchurch, New Zealand, which in the past they couldn't do efficiently as data connection is spotty in that part of the world.

It's stories like these that excite me every day – how we make an impact throughout our customers' business transformation journeys. While our software can certainly help, the challenge I pose to my peers is: how can we effectively surface these customer successes and translate them into compelling stories?

We came up with three core components for integrating brand storytelling in our business:

1   It's critical that we integrate our core values in everything we do. From how we promote our brand, to how are products are sold, to how we ensure customer satisfaction – we must be authentic in demonstrating agility, passion and teamwork.

    By centring on these three core values as our North Star, it allows us to have a shared set of values and ideals. It lets us focus on why AvePoint exists – it's not about our products, but it's all about the people we work with and the customers we serve.

2   We identify brand storytelling initiatives based on our business goals. It's critical for marketing organizations today to be in complete alignment with the overall corporate priorities. For example, our software helps customers migrate, manage and protect their data in the Microsoft cloud, on-premises, and in hybrid environments. But what does that mean? How can we translate that to a compelling brand story?

    When we deconstructed how our software helps our customers, it came down to 'we make it easy for people to do the right thing' with their Microsoft investments – plain and simple. As a result, every story that we highlight in our blog, marketing collateral and customer case studies revolves around that.

3   We take a multi-channel approach in telling our brand story. We position ourselves as industry experts with relevant content we produce in the form of blogs, ebooks, webinars and videos. We engage with customers and industry peers via social media platforms and regularly participate in global industry events. This keeps our brand top-of-mind and relevant in this fast-paced industry.

What piece of advice would you give new brand storytellers who need to convince their own CMOs (and top leadership) about the importance of implementing storytelling as part of their brand marketing and communication strategy?

In the age of increased business competition, constant streams of advertisements and social media feeds – people are suffering information overload, and fairly few messages are able to stick. Brands need to find better ways to cut through the noise to generate interest, engage their audience and compel them to take action. This is where storytelling is critical.

Storytelling isn't just about telling customers why your product or service is the best. It complements existing marketing initiatives and makes the 'picture complete'. Stories can move people. Stories can humanize, inform and inspire. Telling an authentic story can be the difference between a customer choosing your brand or your competitor's.

You don't need to look hard for proof that storytelling works – top organizations like Microsoft, Disney and Ritz Carlton have harnessed the power of storytelling as a key strategy in growing their businesses.

You're a real busy guy. How do you stay creative when designing stories and content? (What is your creative process?)

First, it's critical that I stay on top of industry trends and customer needs. Without a thorough understanding of the business I am in, I cannot be an effective storyteller. I keep up with who's who, the latest innovations and challenges that organizations face. For example, if you are a car salesperson for Honda, isn't it essential for you to know everything about Elon Musk, the latest car models from BMW and maybe developments on driverless vehicles? This enables you to understand where your potential buyer is coming from and craft your story that's relatable and with empathy.

Next, I design stories around the universal framework: Your Challenge, How We Can Help, Call to Action. By keeping it simple and concise, it helps me frame the story where the audience can genuinely feel that I know what they're going through, offer a solution that works and guide them to do something about it right away. By the way, I typically think about this when I go running.

Lastly, I work with my colleagues to A/B test stories to see which is really resonating with our audiences. We will typically test new stories in media that require less time investment and are quicker to market, like blogs or social media. We will build out the best-performing stories in longer-form content like eBooks, interactives and webinars. This allows us to be creative and make surprising discoveries but also maximize our efforts. By the time I tell a story on stage in front of hundreds of people, oftentimes it has been tested in front of multiple different types of audiences.

As one of the best brand storytellers in the industry I know, what tips can you offer our readers to also be successful when telling their brand story?

For me, three things I've learned that are critical when telling my brand story:

1   Ensure authenticity: Make sure every story you tell is not a marketing or sales pitch. It should always be in the best interest of your audience even if in some cases it may not seem like it's beneficial for you/your organization. Being authentic, transparent and showing vulnerability humanizes your story and is much more relatable than the constant chest thumping on how great you or your products are. For example, in my industry, I represent my personal brand, the AvePoint brand, and the Microsoft brand. I've spent time thinking about the overlap between the three, how these three separate but related aspects of my life can align to demonstrate value to the audience that I am speaking to.

2   Exude excellence: From ideation, to testing and promotion of your story – always aim for being the best in a world of compromise. If it means repurposing your PowerPoint slide into a video to make it more effective, *do it*! Every single detail matters when designing and delivering your story. Everyone is telling a story; for yours to be memorable, it needs to be excellent.

3   Develop standout public speaking skills: In order to be an effective storyteller, one of the first steps is to develop your public speaking and presentation prowess. Beyond that, make sure you stand out from the rest of the pack.

It took me over 10 years to learn these lessons the hard way. However, once I intentionally worked on being a better communicator, it greatly enhanced my storytelling abilities. In addition, I wanted to be memorable yet not cheesy – people's attention is more scarce than ever. I make sure that I 'edutain' every time I deliver a presentation – you can make a lasting impression when you educate and entertain at the same time. Here are some tips/tricks that you can get started with: http://dux.ai/rockstarpresenter (archived at https://perma.cc/E7NU-DY53)

Interview with Luz Maria Doria, two-time Emmy winner and Executive Producer of TV show *Despierta America*

Hello Luzma! Can you start by telling our audience who you are?
    I am a Colombian immigrant who always dreamed of living the life I live today. As a child, despite being very fearful and insecure, I wanted to

become a journalist. But I knew that journalists did not look like me. Then at age 13, I learned about a journalist named Cristina Saralegui, who at the time was the Editor-in-Chief for *Cosmopolitan* magazine and in it, she told many stories that helped and empowered me as a woman. At age 16, I graduated from high school and made the decision to move to Miami, Florida to study journalism. Shortly after graduating from Barry University and through a common friend, I asked Saralegui for an interview and she offered me my first job as editor of the same magazine I had always dreamed of working for. Cristina became my mentor and when she crossed over to television to host a talk show (eventually becoming the 'Latin Oprah'), I had the honour of serving as Editor-in-Chief of her magazine and continued to work alongside her for the next 10 years. I later made the jump to television myself, becoming an executive producer. I have been at Univision television network for 18 years, eight of which I have served as executive producer for the number one Spanish-language morning talk show in the United States: *Despierta America*. At age 50, I decided to give thanks to God and life for allowing me to become the woman I had always dreamed of, so I wrote my first book: *The Woman of My Dreams*. Writing this book changed my life as it propelled me from behind the cameras to a forefront platform where I was encouraged to share my stories with others. Soon after, I felt inspired to write a second book called *Your Starring Moment* and found myself travelling around the world, proving to myself – and others – that I could truly achieve anything I set my heart to, I just had to dare pursue it.

With your incredible background and pedigree in journalism, writing, magazine columnist and TV producer, you have certainly acquired a set of particular storytelling skills. Can you share with us what these skills are, how you acquired them and what have been your greatest challenges during this stunning career journey?

I've always been fascinated by stories. When I was a child, I refused to eat unless someone would tell me a story. My *nana*, Tatati, would share stories with me about her family. Then on my way to school, I'd ride the bus, imagine a narrative and share it with my friends. Every time someone caught my attention, I would pause and curiously imagine what their life was like. What I've always enjoyed most about journalism is the art of uncovering people's personal accounts and the 'life formulas' or methodologies they have employed throughout their lived journey that have served them well.

In order to tell a good story, you have to be curious because good stories require good research. However, it's important to investigate with sensitivity, being careful to touch the fibres of the human heart in the process so that the stories are captured in the most genuine way. To achieve this, you must remain respectful, persistent and diligent (apply yourself to learning and read a lot). When I was younger, I knew my biggest handicap was the fears that made me a timid person. Since I was fearful, I decided to combat those fears through learning. The more you learn, the more fearless and daring you become.

It's important for our readers to understand the power of storytelling. When I first met you, you told me something that really resonated with me. You said that you believe every person should write a book about their personal life story. Tell me, why do you have this conviction?

I believe we all are storytellers and have a story to tell, but not many people take the time to evaluate their life, the signs the universe sends them, the doors that have been closed for them or the coincidences they have lived. They miss out on the taste of the journey and lose sensibility to be able to tell the story. I always learn something from every person I meet. I learn that sometimes we sabotage our own stories. We lessen their importance of allegory and only focus on negative pieces of it, on what went wrong instead of the lessons learned. Imagine if every person would take time to share with others those life formulas that have endowed them with remarkable wisdom. The world would be a better place!

Besides encouraging our readers to write their own life story, what other advice would you give those storytellers who are just starting to design brand stories to take their business forward?

Your brand story must create a need in your audience. You should have a clear purpose for the brand. What are your brand's differentiators in the market? What is your brand's true mission? What will you do to ensure brand awareness with your stakeholders? What will you tell them about your product? Who will help you tell the story? Today we have a great tool called the internet. Social media serves as among the best plat-forms for audiences to consume stories. My books would not have been successful had it not been for my personal Instagram account. Leverage social media!

Before you go, is there a personal storytelling rule you never break and would like to share with the audience?

I always combine three key elements in story:

1 Real information and data. That requires in-depth research.

2 An emotional angle: stories have to make you cry, laugh, think. You decide. But it must reach and stay in the heart of your audience.

3 It must be compelling. Boredom is prohibited.

These three rules set the base and then the story can be constructed from there. It's futile to have a great message to share when the way you choose to share it is unengaging. The way you tell the message is as important as the message itself.

Interview with Derek E Baird, writer, social media expert and youth culture trend spotter

Hi Derek! I'm so excited you're sharing insights with this audience. To get started, can you tell me more about yourself?

Thanks for the invitation, Miri. So happy to be chatting with you today.

I help some of the biggest kidtech, education and entertainment brands in the world tell stories, build products and experiences, and gain credibility with youth audiences by aligning their brand with youth culture. In addition to my work in the kids and teen space, I've worked as an Adjunct Professor at Pepperdine University Graduate School of Education and Psychology (GSEP), advised early-stage education technology and kidtech start-ups, hold patents focused on child trust, safety and privacy (COPPA), and I'm the recipient of the Disney Inventor Award.

Impressive! You yourself are a brand storyteller and recently co-authored a book, The Gen Z Frequency – what inspired you to do this and can you offer our audience some highlights/insights of the book that they can apply to their brand storytelling?

The motivation to write *The Gen Z Frequency* was rooted in a desire to build a generational bridge between brands, educators, and anyone working with youth. While there has always been cultural tension between older and younger generations, the gap seems to be wider today more than ever. Our hope is to provide a path forward for intergenerational dialogue. In the book, we share key insights, strategies and tactics that any organization can deploy to build credibility to tune in with the unique cultural preferences of Gen Z. We conducted hundreds of interviews with Gen Z kids, tweens, teens and young adults and have distilled our findings into a youth culture playbook.

Because Gen Z (b. 1997–2010), and the Gen Alpha (b. 2010–2025) cohort right behind them, consume so much digital content, it's increasingly difficult for brands to reach them. This brings me to a Gen Z myth that I'd like to dispel – and it ties directly back to brand storytelling.

You often hear older folks say that younger people have 'the attention span of a goldfish'. This belief isn't exactly true. Every day younger people are processing an incredible amount of information – everything from tweets, news alerts, TikTok, texts and watching videos. As a result, they've become experts at quickly filtering the digital content that is filling their screens. This is often chalked up to having a 'short attention span'.

And this is where I'll tie it back to storytelling: If you want to reach Gen Z and Gen Alpha, you need to tell stories that capture their attention and make them stop scrolling. The scary part for brands is that you have mere nanoseconds to get them to tune in, or with a small flip of a thumb – you're off their radar.

What would you say is the most important thing storytellers need to consider when building a story and why?

Here are a few rules to keep in mind when building a story and creating content:

Rule 1: authenticity. If your audience doesn't trust you, they'll 'ghost' your brand. This is why creating content and stories that resonate is so crucial to building credibility with your audience. Trust is at the heart of authenticity. The best way to make sure your stories and content are aligned with the culture of your audience is to involve them in the process of creating it.

Rule 2: persona and voice. Create stories that resonate with your audience by identifying and then consistently applying the same voice, tone and persona. The most effective way to make sure the tone of your story is hitting the mark is to let your target segment co-create and participate in the creative process.

Rule 3: platform. If you're spending resources on creating and producing content, you want to see a return on that effort. Choosing the right platform and embracing the native platform features to help you create compelling stories is paramount. For example, if your goal is to reach tweens, putting your content on Facebook isn't going to help you reach your KPIs. Why? Because tweens and teens find Facebook inherently and completely uncool. To reach tweens, your content should live on Snapchat, TikTok or Instagram. Conversely, if you're trying to reach 40-something moms, you're not going to use a predominantly youthful platform like TikTok, you're going to use Facebook or Pinterest.

Rule 4: get creative. Your content and message must capture an audience's imagination and get them to tune in to your brand frequency. Your content can be as short and simple as a meme, GIF or Instagram Story, or as developed as an episodic video series, but needs to present relevant messages through themes, formats and platforms in moments that matter (see Rules 1–3). Marketing is not only about what you make, but about the stories you tell.

Any other storytelling 'musts' readers should consider when facing these challenges?

Stories must feel inclusive and diverse. When someone engages with a story, they need to see something reflected that looks like them. If they don't see themselves in your story, your brand won't become a part of their story. Representation matters.

Diversity means walking the talk. Diversity is showing an LGBTQ+ couple in a marketing campaign in February, not just during Pride Month in June. Identify and reach out to subgroups and build relationships with them. Develop content and experiences that connect them to their passions. Diversity is showing a Sikh wearing his turban. Diversity is including people in wheelchairs, in all social classes or ethnicities.

Stories are based on emotion. This human connection helps us to develop true cultural alignment, which fuels the most effective strategies for reaching consumers.

Any last piece of advice to our readers?

Look to new technologies such as augmented reality or new social content platforms such as TikTok or PopJam as places to experiment with storytelling. Push the envelope, and you might yield unexpected results.

Telling other people's stories can be messy. Even if you've included them in the creation process, things can go sideways. If you mess up or don't read the room right, apologize.

And then, listen.

Interview with Gregg L Witt, youth marketer and public speaker

Gregg! We met telling stories at National Geographic headquarters in Washington, DC. I was immediately impressed by your background. Can you share with our readers?

Always stoked to catch up with you and exchange 'stories'! For everyone else, I'm Co-Founder and Chief Strategy Officer at Engage Youth Co. where I lead brand strategy and consumer engagement programs for companies targeting youth audiences. It's a real privilege to be helping build and sustain some of the most successful youth-focused brands of today. In 2016, I was fortunate enough to be named a Top Youth Marketer To Follow by *Inc.* magazine, and in 2017 made the *Forbes* list of leading Gen Z experts.

When it comes to my relationship with this work, I never fall back on the 'know it when I see it' approach. I have always preferred a more immersive examination of the wisdom and authenticity inherent in today's youth culture, and encourage others to have the same respect for and curiosity about this powerful cohort.

Personally, I'm the father of four teens and pre-teens; as a former professional skateboarder, I still – against doctor's recommendations – actively play with skateboards on giant ramps and bowls, and am truly inspired by a long family history of entrepreneurship.

In this Brand Storytelling book, I talk a lot about the importance of empathy and authenticity to be able to reach your intended audience effectively. As a youth marketer you do the same but focus on specific insights about a younger cohort. Can you share some of those insights?

Absolutely! Empathy and authenticity are foundational, unignorable starting points to understanding and defining your relationship with any audience. The key word here is relationship. They are not a faceless target; your audience should be a group of people that you establish a rapport with. When it comes to Gen Z and the emerging Gen Alpha, they are particularly tuned in to that feeling of connection over need, and they want to be understood and heard.

The challenge is on us. We need to ask ourselves if our internal perceptions of our audience are accurate, and learn how to rise above our bias or preconceptions, so we can be open to the reality of how our product or service may be received by that audience. By getting ourselves out of the way, we can see what young people want and need more clearly. In order to do this, we need to know what informs their perceptions of the world. Once we understand what fuels youth opinions and preferences, we can better understand what motivates them. If we want their attention, we need to figure out how to appeal to them from their perspective. This is how you tell brand stories that work in reality and not just in cubicles and conference rooms.

To help brands focus on empathy and authenticity with younger audiences, use the following insights as a guide. Youth audiences:

- tend to reject companies without a clear and specifically relatable brand story and content;
- want to be listened to and respected by brands and be able to trust in the reliability of those brands they choose;
- are woke and demand to have their privacy protected;
- seek brands that connect with their passions and interests and contribute to their lives or support them in what they are trying to do;
- want more brands that inspire them to push forward, to reach further to achieve their dreams, and to find and inspire new and unique solutions that empower them;
- look for brands to provide experiences that create community, a place of belonging, or something for them to be part of and share.

What do you think is one of the biggest challenges marketers and communicators face today when it comes to storytelling, and how should they tackle it?

One of the biggest challenges that brands face is to identify and discover the inherent cultures most aligned with their brand, and then finding ways to authentically cultivate relevance. Unfortunately, too many brands default to demographic data that lead to fabricated storytelling and poor audience connection. Brands often think they have solved this problem with highly sophisticated social and digital targeting tools, but the accuracy and precision of age groups or geography still doesn't bring us close enough to the cultural nuances that drive effective storytelling. When brands or organizations align their stories with and contribute to youth culture, that's when the magic happens.

Carhartt Work In Progress (Carhartt WIP) is a great example of a successful apparel brand that has struck a balance between cultural relevance and commercial viability. Their approach to storytelling is unique and somewhat unconventional, with the story arc being a continued work in progress. Youth culture insiders who are part of the WIP family document and share their stories as they take place, weaving them into various collaborations, event experiences and products, so the audience is legitimately part of the story, rather than it being told to them. In order to maintain this organic style of storytelling, they have built strong relationships with unknown, inspiring, provocative and upcoming figures in music and sports, becoming an iconic and well-respected brand in underground scenes, from hip-hop to skate, graffiti to cycling, as well as working with labels such as APC, Neighborhood, Patta, Vans, Junya Watanabe and many more. Staying true to its roots of ruggedness, collaboration, survival and friendships, Carhartt WIP has built a fan base that is as strong to this day as it was years ago when it was originally established. Today it has grown beyond clothing to incorporate an in-house music label, European Skateboard Championships in Basel, Switzerland, and a Carhartt Skate Team, all successful in their own right, and relevant to the brand because they all contribute to the convergence of cultures that Carhartt WIP represents.

That takes a lot of creativity. We know creativity is something you can develop as a skillset. Can you share with our readers some tips and tricks on how to become more creative?
Oh yeah!

- Explore what's happening in other fields and genres, to help your brain get out of its habits and thought patterns. Constantly seek inspiration from relevant sources in and outside of your insular group of friends and colleagues.

- Playing is the key to creativity. It's how everyone learns most effectively. Allow your brain some no-stress, no-consequence time to have fun making mistakes and experimenting.

- Try singing about the things and events in your life or work, real and imagined. You may be surprised about where your mind goes when you mix the disciplines of music and words, and it might even get you out of a thinking rut. Plus, it's fun and hilarious.

- Have some guts when creating; sometimes you just need to be bold and brave. Learn to tune out those who laugh at you and be confident in what you've come up with, whether it leads to something or not. Question the status quo and find ways to responsibly break rules if needed.

- Know when you are most creative and protect that time. Give yourself a little extra time to ease into the creative process as well.

Anything else our readers should consider?

The brand's story is about the relationship between the brand and the audience. A brand's identity must be relevant to the audience, and consistently connected to that audience as the relationship evolves. To find that identity, you need to go far beyond the service, product and packaging, and really determine who you are and what you represent. It's the differentiator between successful brands, with strong audiences and proven staying power, and those that struggle to find their path. If you can build an identity that your audience cares about, you will have taken a significant first step towards the bigger goal of brand–audience alignment.

Second, find relevant ways to make the audience an active part of the story. What you build together will be more compelling and authentic than anything built in isolation.

Rapid-fire questions with Cindy Coloma, bestselling author and storyteller at Microsoft

Cindy, you're an award-winning author who's written over 25 critically acclaimed fiction and non-fiction books, some of which have been translated into eight languages. What are your best practices for storytelling?

Be a story hound

Always have your ears open for story wherever you are and in whatever you're doing. And ask questions. When someone is willing to ask questions and really listen, stories will be shared. Now this isn't always easy for me. Like many writers, I have an introvert nature, so sometimes it's difficult for me to step out of my comfort zone and talk with people I don't know or to follow through to get a story. But when I do, I'm never disappointed. Stories are everywhere: people around you in the market, the elderly man across the street, your co-workers, and often with old friends and family members whom we think we know and then discover are far more complex than we expected.

Know what makes a great story

What makes you engaged in a story? Why are others captivated by certain stories whether spoken, on a TED Talk, in an Academy Award-winning film? What are the engaging pieces and how are they woven into the structure of the beginning, middle and end? Write out what are your favourite stories, and then write down the harder part – why? And then practise, examine, iterate, and practise again. You will certainly see your storytelling skills develop and grow.

So, your best practice for storytelling is to practise storytelling. OK. I finally found a story, what do I do next?

Get the details

After you find great stories and know how to structure them and what makes them compelling, bring them further to life with details. You get details from a variety of ways:

- Museums, local historians, eyewitness interviews, biographies and memoirs, historical or location research.

- Interviews are a great way to get the details of a story. Record them if possible (with two devices), to preserve important details while you get to be an engaged listener. Take some notes, but do so carefully, while really paying attention and making eye contact as a listener should.

- Conduct interviews in a comfortable location. Bring props to help when things get tricky. One time I interviewed a Second World War veteran who encountered a lot of emotion when talking about their experiences. I brought an atlas of Europe during the war and when they seemed distressed, the map helped give them direction. I could see their expressions change and memories seemed to become more focused. Props such as maps, old photos, documents, books are among things that can serve as keys to a specific place and time. It also brings out the details.

- Bring along a friend. Having multiple angles to the story is also help-ful, whether it's an interview or researching a location, a museum or event. Another person can capture a nuance or find something that you missed.

- Have a list of questions longer than you'll ever get to. Have the top 3–5 that must get answered. The rest are for backup. But be ready to ask detailed questions connected to the five senses as you get answers. Follow your gut and be specific. 'What did that smell like?' 'How did that feel?' 'I can only imagine what that smelled like?'

- Always consider the five senses when gathering details. Stories come alive when people feel like you're really there.

- Carry a notepad. Always. You never know when you'll encounter a story or details you'll want to jot down.

Just a little warning: don't add too many details so that they drag your story down. Go have fun and see how storytelling changes not only the people listening, but how they'll change you most of all.

Rapid-fire questions with Park Howell, advertising industry veteran and owner of Business of Story

Park, you went from being a lead in the ad industry for over 30 years, including owning your own ad agency for 20 of those years, to becoming a full-time brand storyteller. Tell me more.

Well, Miri, I found in around 2006 that the brand marketing world stopped working the way we knew it. Brands owned the influence of mass media (the channels of TV, radio, print) but technology and the internet completely handed over control to the masses who have now become the media, and those folks, all of us, now own part of the brand stories. So, I set out to guide leaders and communicators at the brand level to leverage this direction and use the power of brand storytelling for business growth.

You have a saying that goes: Stop looking for your story, start finding scenes. What does that mean?

As you've seen, Miri, everybody nowadays is talking about storytelling. Everybody thinks they have to have this big 'tale to tell' in order to compete... and I say the opposite. Stop looking for the big story, and instead, go back and find the small moments that began the tale. When you knit those moments together, the story then finds you. Whether you're telling a brand or personal story, it's those stories of origin that really connect with people because they understand you at the human level.

One last tip for our readers.

Fuel your curiosity! Think back to the time you were a child or teenager and find a moment when your curiosity grabbed you and took you down a rabbit hole and you were so fascinated by it, that perhaps it surprised you but it took you to a whole other realm or world of understanding something. See if that curiosity is still alive at the same level today... if not – awaken it!

Rapid-fire questions with Candy Rasmijn-Reino, marketing and PR agency owner

Hi Candy. You've been in the marketing industry for over 18 years and currently lead a very successful PR agency in Aruba today, representing brands from all over the world. How are you using storytelling in public relations to enable the brand story in this medium?

Well Miri, first, you know well that the digital age has changed many things from what we now call 'traditional' PR and marketing strategies. In the past, you'd start by creating a communications and marketing approach and then you'd pitch it to television or newspapers to disseminate the messages. But honestly, there was no true way of measuring campaign success or if the content really landed with intended audiences. Today, digital channels have provided a platform that gives us visibility to instant responses from the audience so we can rapidly change the direction we're going with the message, if needed. Second, brands are now creating their own stories and PR is becoming more of an integration of new brand marketing trends, such as influencer marketing to reach target audiences. So, take time to find the right influencer in the market who will successfully help you take your story to market.

If I were to build my brand story from scratch and use it as a PR pitch to enlist influencers, what advice would you give me?

Tell a real story. Consider every aspect of what makes up your brand and insert the story of origin as part of the narrative. How did the brand get here? What were those lived experiences and learnings the brand had along the way? It is those little details that make the story human and connect us to the story.

Rapid-fire questions with Dona Sarkar, author, fashion designer, engineer and principal manager of Windows Insider Program at Microsoft

Dona, when we met for the first time, I was so curious about how you manage to do so many things at once. And do them well! In my mind, you truly embody what a master storyteller is because I know and believe the best storytellers are a 'jack of all trades'. But how do you keep a balance?

I fail. I'm really good at failing. So, I learn from the failures and do it better the next time. I also don't keep myself in a box. I think it's important for people to realize that we're all 'and' people. When we're young, we draw, we paint, we write, we play, we tell stories. As we grow up, we put ourselves in boxes: I'm a maths person, I'm a computer scientist, but actually, at the core, we remain 'and' people. So, do the thing that looks fun, and find that 'and'. Otherwise you are not being authentic to yourself or the story.

You've successfully published a total of eight fiction and non-fiction books. What's your secret for landing a good story? How long does it take for people to begin assimilating it?

Figure out which form and type of content works best for your niche audience. If your audience is visual, spend extra time building visual elements for your story. Choose your topics and stick to them. Choose what you want your brand to be known for. Don't be random, then people will automatically begin associating those topics to your brand. It happens really fast, in as little as three months! It happened for my personal brand in three months. I went from not knowing a lot about mixed reality and holograms. Then I started working on that team, so naturally, I talked about it every day for three months and suddenly I found out I had been included in a list of 'Fifty Top Influencers of Mixed Reality in the World', and wondered why am I on that list? Because I talked about it consistently for three months.

Last piece of wisdom to close us out.

Your brand story will continue to evolve. So, think ahead of time about what you want your brand to be next.

FURTHER READING

Chapter 1

Microsoft Corporation (2014) Microsoft Board Names Satya Nadella as CEO, https://news.microsoft.com/2014/02/04/microsoft-board-names-satya-nadella-as-ceo (archived at https://perma.cc/79R9-CTJQ)

The Walt Disney Company (nd) About The Walt Disney Company, www.thewaltdisneycompany.com/about (archived at https://perma.cc/NZ38-VNGF)

Chapter 3

Hartson, R and Pyla, P S (2012) *The UX Book: Process and guidelines for ensuring a quality user experience*, Morgan Kaufmann, Waltham, MA

Liedtka, J, Ogilvie, T and Brozenske, R (2011) *Designing for Growth: A design thinking tool kit for managers*, Columbia University Press, New York

Walker, T (2018) The effect of typography on user experience & conversions, *CXL* https://conversionxl.com/blog/the-effects-of-typography-on-user-experience-conversions (archived at https://perma.cc/22EB-K9B4)

Chapter 4

Baggs, M (2019) Gillette faces backlash and boycott over '#MeToo advert', *BBC News* www.bbc.co.uk/news/newsbeat-46874617 (archived at https://perma.cc/TZ37-57VU)

Bhargava, R (2016) *Non-Obvious 2017 Edition: How to think different, curate ideas and predict the future*, IdeaPress Publishing, Washington, DC

Ogilvy, R (2013) *Ogilvy on Advertising*, Multimedia Books, Singapore

Chapter 5

Agrawal, A J (2018) Millennials want transparency and social impact. What are you doing to build a millennial-friendly brand? *Entrepreneur* www.entrepreneur.com/article/314156 (archived at https://perma.cc/G3DA-H6EJ)

Bhargava, R (2016) *Non-Obvious 2017: How to think different, curate ideas and predict the future*, IdeaPress Publishing, Washington, DC

CMO Council (2014) Mastering adaptive customer engagements, CMO Council https://cmocouncil.org/thought-leadership/reports/mastering-adaptive-customer-engagements (archived at https://perma.cc/2BVM-8MMY)

Edelman Earned Brand (2018) Brands take a stand, *Edelman* www.edelman.com/
sites/g/files/aatuss191/files/2018-10/2018_Edelman_Earned_Brand_Global_
Report.pdf (archived at https://perma.cc/VDM4-GZR9)

Fagan, L (2016) Three ways to make your brand your consumer's best friend,
DigitalSurgeons, www.digitalsurgeons.com/thoughts/inspiration/make-your-brand-
your-consumers-best-friend (archived at https://perma.cc/52Z6-AQRE)

Feldman, B (2019) How to reach Millennials – your 2019 guide to effective
millennial marketing, *Taboola Blog* https://blog.taboola.com/marketing-to-
millennials (archived at https://perma.cc/7NDN-9NT9)

Fromm, J (2018) How much financial influence does Gen Z have? *Forbes* www.
forbes.com/sites/jefffromm/2018/01/10/what-you-need-to-know-about-the-
financial-impact-of-gen-z-influence/#6778ab3f56fc (archived at https://perma.cc/
M23F-ED6Z)

Giani, S (2019) Neuro-Insight's Shazia Ginai: Gillette example shows how socially
conscious ads can be double-edged, *More About Advertising* www.
moreaboutadvertising.com/2019/04/neuro-insights-shazia-ginai-gillette-
example-shows-how-socially-conscious-ads-can-be-double-edged (archived at
https://perma.cc/8A5R-DPUU)

Gibbons, G (2009) The social value of brands, in *Brands and Branding*, ed R
Clifton *et al*, pp 45–60, *The Economist*, London

Korschun, D (2017) Companies that stay silent on political issues can pay a hefty
price, *Fast Company* www.fastcompany.com/3067944/political-neutrality-can-
be-costly (archived at https://perma.cc/2YYH-M6JH)

Pearl, D (2018) As more consumers than ever make belief-driven purchases, it's
worth it for brands to take a stand, *Adweek*, www.adweek.com/brand-marketing/
as-more-consumers-than-ever-make-belief-driven-purchases-its-worth-it-for-
brands-to-take-a-stand (archived at https://perma.cc/8C6N-YVNB)

Chapter 6

Brown, B (2015) *Daring Greatly: How the courage to be vulnerable transforms the
way we live, love, parent, and lead*, Averly, New York

Tran, L (2016) Innovation: Better problem solving with the SCAMPER method
[Blog], *InLoox Blog*, 1 April www.inloox.com/company/blog/articles/
innovation-better-problem-solving-with-the-scamper-method (archived at
https://perma.cc/YZ2Z-AVJ6)

Chapter 7

Murphy, P *et al* (2007) *Ethical Marketing*, Routledge, London
http://ethicsupdates.net/theories (archived at https://perma.cc/BC5W-RKTW)
>www.wikihow.com/Develop-a-Code-of-Ethics (archived at https://perma.
cc/29GH-9RGC)

Chapter 8

Petrock, V (2018) Augmented reality marketing and advertising 2018, *e Marketer* www.emarketer.com/content/augmented-reality-marketing-and-advertising-2018 (archived at https://perma.cc/K8CG-54D3)

Chapter 9

Influencer Marketing Hub (2018) 20 Employee advocacy statistics that will blow your mind, *Influencer Marketing Hub* https://influencermarketinghub.com/20-employee-advocacy-statistics-that-will-blow-your-mind (archived at https://perma.cc/D5WC-WR7B)

Influencer Marketing Hub (2019) The State of Influencer Marketing 2019: Benchmark Report [+Infographic], *Influencer Marketing Hub* https://influencermarketinghub.com/influencer-marketing-2019-benchmark-report (archived at https://perma.cc/4X2G-G24U)

Hartson, R and Pyla, P S (2012) *The UX Book: Process and guidelines for ensuring a quality user experience*, Morgan Kaufmann, Waltham, MA

Kunsman, T (2019) 31 Eye-popping employee advocacy statistics that matter the most, *EveryoneSocial* https://everyonesocial.com/blog/employee-advocacy-statistics (archived at https://perma.cc/B86E-A2EK)

Chapter 10

Stone, T (2019) The psychological reason why brand consistency is so important, *Endeavor Creative* https://endeavorcreative.com/brand-consistency (archived at https://perma.cc/46RN-9ZVN)

Lucidpress (nd) The impact of brand consistency, www.lucidpress.com/pages/resources/report/the-impact-of-brand-consistency (archived at https://perma.cc/6GKV-CEP5)

de Bono, E (nd) Six Thinking Hats, The de Bono Group www.debonogroup.com/six_thinking_hats.php (archived at https://perma.cc/BB2F-5JSU)

Chapter 11

Andrivet, M (2015) What is branding? *The Branding Journal* www.thebrandingjournal.com/2015/10/what-is-branding-definition (archived at https://perma.cc/356Z-TP46)

Scherer, K (2009) The dynamic architecture of emotion: Evidence for the component process model, Taylor & Francis Online www.tandfonline.com/doi/abs/10.1080/02699930902928969?journalCode=pcem20 (archived at https://perma.cc/6ALR-ERLM)

Chapter 13

Whittaker, J (2018) *James Whittaker's Little Book of the Future*, self-published, Washington State

Emerging technology from the arXiv (2017) Experts predict when artificial intelligence will exceed human performance, *MIT Technology Review* www.technologyreview.com/s/607970/experts-predict-when-artificial-intelligence-will-exceed-human-performance (archived at https://perma.cc/PJ3Q-6D55)

Halber, D (2018) The anatomy of emotions, BrainFacts/SfN, www.brainfacts.org/Thinking-Sensing-and-Behaving/Emotions-Stress-and-Anxiety/2018/The-Anatomy-of-Emotions-090618 (archived at https://perma.cc/MD8T-J7BL)

Salesforce Research (2019) Enterprise technology trends, Salesforce Research, https://c1.sfdcstatic.com/content/dam/web/en_us/www/assets/pdf/platform/salesforce-research-enterprise-technology-trends.pdf (archived at https://perma.cc/S74A-UZZY)

INDEX

A/B testing 191
achievement pillars (Microsoft) 26–28
adaptation 17, 20, 85, 168, 183, 188
Adobe 115–20
advocacy 29, 109, 113, 115–23, 126–27,
    128–29, 184
affordances 123–24
African culture 89, 90
Airbnb 50
Alaska Airlines 42–43, 44
ambassadors 82–83, 85, 115–20
Angelou, Maya 22
antagonists 161–76
Antarctica 189
Apple 80, 111
'Art of Storytelling' (Microsoft) 177–78
artificial intelligence (AI) 42, 148, 168, 180,
    181, 183–87
assets 48–49, 56–57
attention span (attention-keeping) 8, 30,
    32, 34, 39, 196
attributes *see* brand attributes
audience 13, 15, 123, 140–42, *150*, *156*,
    160, 201
    see also design audience; Gen Alpha;
        Gen Z; millennials; younger
        audiences (youth culture)
augmented reality (AR) 100, 104, 109–10,
    197
authenticity 76, 81, 99, 107, 113, 192, 196,
    198–99
automation 56, 168, 183, 184
availability 57, 140–41
AvePoint 188–92

Baird, Derek E 195–97
Ballmer, Steve 6
Bambi 162–63
baseline setting 62, 116, *156*
belief-driven spending 66–67
believability 13, 15
benchmarking 116, 132, 133, 146–60, 171
Bhargava, Rohit 53, 64
Big Idea, the 53–54
blockchain 186
blogs 47, 64, 79, 117, 190, 191
boundary setting 81–82
brain studies 7–8, 17, 45, 47, 68, 72

brainstorming 35–36, 38, 83–86, 102, 144,
    176, 180, 185
brand, defined 80, 148
brand assets 48–49, 56–57
brand attributes 13, 15, 49, 51
    see also logos; slogans; tone
brand consistency 54–55, 133, 136, 164,
    169, 170, 205
brand culture activation journey *157*
brand identity 25–26, 48, 201
brand mentions 149–53, *156*, 170
brand mission statements 9–18, 25–26,
    35–36, 39, 43, 44, 50, 57, 70
brand positioning 158, 172
brand purpose 13, 65, 85, 194
brand reach 149–50, 152, 153
Brown, Brené 78
business functions 166

Camacho, Jose-Andres 115–20
campaigns 52, 58, 81
Carhartt Work in Progress 199–200
case studies 31, 47, 190
character flow 138–40
characters 21, 26–34, 82, 122–23, 138–40
Chia, T P 146
Clayton, Steve 26, 83, 172
cloud technology 5, 56, 60, 79, 179, 180,
    184, 188, 190
CMO Council (report) 69
Coca-Cola 16, 17
Coco 143
codes of conduct 66, 93, 94–95, 96–98
cognitive affordance *124*
collaboration 101, 108, 115, 120, 185,
    200
Coloma, Cindy 201–03
colour 45–46, 47
combined storytelling techniques 85
communication 58, 90
communications departments 58
companies 164–65
    see also organizations
competencies 74, 108
competitive edge 51, 67, 116
competitors 168–69
conclusions 50
conflict 27, 29, 30, 161

consistency 54–55, 133, 136, 164, 169,
         170, 205
content reach 149–50, 152, 153
contingency plans 137, 138
contractors *129*
converging ideas 33
conversion metrics *155–56*
Core Services Engineering and Operations
         (Microsoft) 16–17, 61
core values 66, 94, 137, 190
corporate social responsibility 65, 115,
         120
cortisol 8
Cosmopolitan 193
courage 78–79, 97
creativity 35, 191, 197, 200–01
culture (cultural norms) 92, 164
         see also African culture; culture
                  transformation; Hispanic culture;
                  Nordic culture
culture transformation *159–60*, 165
curiosity 198, 204
customer-centricity 63–75, 123
customer chair 73–74
customer experience 184
customer relationship management systems
         (CRM systems) 185
customers 21, 27, 29, 63–75, 109, 123, 184
         engagement 142–44, 152–53, *155–56*,
                  185
         see also UX (user experience)

defensibility test 132, 133, *135*
design affordances 123–24
design audience 59–61, 76, *106*, 175
design personas 114, 149
design thinking 21–38, 40, 58, 83–84, 86,
         174
designers 170–71
Despierta America 193
detail 192, 202–03, 204
developer support 185
digital transformation 6, 56, 57, 59–60, 79,
         104, 167, 184
Disney, Walt 11
Disney 11, 12, 16, 45–46, 139–40, 143,
         191
Disney Animation Studios 45–46
Distinguished Engineers (Microsoft)
         177–79
diversity 35, 197
Doc James *see* Whittaker, James
dopamine 8
Doria, Luz Maria 192–95

Earned Brand report (2018) 67
elimination, character 86
emails 9, 45, 54, 60, 179
embarrassment 24
emergent storytelling 107–09
         see also gamification
emotions 8, 17, 46, 58, 124–25, 146,
         147–48, 158, 195, 197
         metrics 149–53
         negative 68
         and visual elements 47
         see also happiness; love
empathy 22–28, 44, 59, 61–62, 70–73,
         137, 141, 174, 182–83, 198–99
employee advocacy 29, 113, 115–23,
         126–27, *128–29*, 165, 184
Employee Advocacy Learning Series 119
employee experience 184
employees 58–59, 82–83, *150*, 184
         see also employee advocacy
empowerment 7, 21, 26–27, 61, 136
endorphins 8
Engage Youth Co. 198
engagement 142–44, 152–53, *155–56*, 185
Enterprise Technology Trend Report (2019)
         184–87
entertainment industry 11, 100, 107, 143,
         195
         see also Disney
ethics 92–99
EveryoneSocial 116–19
excellence 192
execution test *135*
experience 114
         see also customer experience; UX (user
                  experience)
external audience *150*, *156*, *160*

Facebook 81, 113, 117, 197
Fagan, Lauren 65
fail fast 68, 137
failure stories 80, 205
false starts 33–34
Fast Company (report) 67
feedback 36–37, 59, 61, 137, 138, 141–42
feedback loops 37, 61, 137
'feel' 49
feelings 12, *13*, 15, 25–26, 28, 58, 92, 108
first-person point of view 47, 108
flexibility 86–87, 168
foundation, code of ethics 97
four pillars of achievement
                  (Microsoft) 26–28
4D experiments 132

functional affordance *124*
functionality 17–18

gamification 107–09, 118–19
Gates, Bill 6
Gen Alpha 196, 198–99
Gen Z 12, 53, 64, 65, 66, 195–96, 198–99
Gen Z Frequency (Baird) 195–96
Gestalt theory 47
Gillette 55, 68, 136
goal setting 35, 58–59, 62, 190
gold refining process 72
government 67, 92, *150*, *156*, *160*
Gregory (UX designer) 41, 171

guidelines 57, 81, 98, 126, 175–76
Hahn, Don 45–46
hands-on practice 165, 174
happiness 11
Haunted Mansion ride (Disney) 139–40
Haystack Method 53, 64
heroes 21, 27, 63–75
Hero's Journey 29, 64, 67
hierarchy of needs 24
Hispanic culture 76–77
'How to Optimize your LinkedIn Profile'
        (Adobe) 119
Howell, Park 203–04
human failure stories 80, 205
humanizing the brand 80

ideation *23*, 34–36, 175
IKEA 104
IMC plan (Reimagined Integrated
        Marketing Plan) 51–62, 184
immersive storytelling 42–43, 100–12
imposter syndrome 90
in medias res 32
inclusion 35, 70–73, 197
    see also immersive storytelling
inconclusive conclusions 50
indirect stakeholders 95
industry code of ethics 94–95, 98
industry trends *106*, 191
influencers (influence marketing) 110–11,
        113–15, 120–23, 125, 127–30,
        204
innovation 67–68
Instagram 81, 115, 118, 141, 178, 194, 197
integrated marketing plan 51–62, 184
interaction 43, 73–74, 107, 109
internal stakeholders (disciplines) 15, 44–
        45, 56–61, 94, 137, *150*, 154–55,
        159–60, 164–65, 172–76
    see also employees

interviews 202–03
IoT (Internet of Things) 179, 180
IT staff 185–86

Jobs, Steve 80, 114
journalism 193–94

key assumptions model 132–33, *134– 35*
key audiences 13, 15
key performance indicators (KPIs) 116–17
Korschun, Daniel 67

lasting action metrics 154, *157*, *159–60*
launch management task forces 138
laws 92
leaderboards (Adobe) 118–19
leadership 165, 166
    see also thought leadership; top
        management
Life is Good 17
LinkedIn 4, 61, 117, 118, 119, 151
LinkedIn About section 151
Lion King, The 46
listening tools 37–38, 138, 141, 172
live streaming 110–12
lived experiences 35, 87, 104, 132, *134*,
        169, 175, 182, 204
logos 45, 48, 57, 136, 148
love 154
Love vs Hate game 102–03, 108
Lyft 67

machine learning (ML) 180, 181, 184
Machu Picchu 71
management *128*
    see also leadership; middle management;
        top management
Marceline to Magic Kingdom Tour 139–40
marketing 56–57, 58
    influencer 110–11, 113–15, 120–23,
        125, 127–30, 204
    sports 118–19
marketing associations 98
marketing campaigns 52, 58, 81
Marvel Comics 50
Maslow, Abraham 23
master storytellers 22, 39, 174, 205
MasterCard 48
meaningfulness 12, 34, 38, 41, 47, 53, 112
measurement (metrics) 61–62, 116–17,
        149–57, *159–60*
    see also benchmarking
Medium 153
memory encoding 68
mentions 149–53, *156*, 170

#MeToo 55
micro influencers 122
Microsoft 6–7, 21, 136, 168, 172–73,
        177–78, 179–80, 191, 205
    audience 60–61, 123
    'customer chair' 73
    four pillars of achievement 26–28
    immersive storytelling 100–03, 107–08,
        111–12
    listening tools 138
    nested loops 31
    personal stories 47
    social media 152, 153
    vulnerability in storytelling 79
    see also Clayton, Steve; Coloma, Cindy;
        Core Services Engineering and
        Operations(Microsoft); Nadella,
        Satya; 'People of Action'; Sarker,
        Dona; Shared Service Engineering
        (SSE) Studio
middle management 128
millennials 12, 36, 53, 65, 66
mission see brand mission statements; story
        mission
mixed reality (MR) 109–10, 205
ML (machine learning) 180, 181, 184
mobile devices 110, 185
modifications 85
'Mom' ('Mother') 7, 22, 24, 63, 91, 162
monitoring processes 81–82
monomyths (Hero's Journey) 29, 64, 67
moral values 97
motivation, audience 123
Mount Rainier 42
mountain story structure 30
Murphy, Patrick 93–96
Myth, The 133, 134–35

Nadella, Satya 6–7, 73
napkin pitch model 36–37
National Geographic 115
negative emotions 68
nested loops 31
Nestlé 17
neurological studies see brain studies
Nike 17
Nordic culture 147
nostalgia 12, 161
notepads 203
Nowak, Lisa Marie 153–54

Ogilvy, David 53
opportunities charts 105–06
'Optimizing Your Social Media Presence'
        (Adobe) 119

organizations 93–94
    see also business functions; companies;
        culture (cultural norms); internal
        stakeholders (disciplines);
        leadership; processes; systems
Osborn, Alex Faickney 83
oxytocin 8

people-focused (personal) stories 31, 47,
        82–83, 183
'People of Action' 27
persistence 75, 80, 194
persona affordances 123–24
persona identity 125–26
personal brands 71, 76, 77, 151, 192, 205
personal ethics 95–99
personas 114, 122–26, 149, 196
petals 34
photographs 47, 107, 151, 202
physical affordance 124
Pinterest 197
Place 104
planning, contingency 137, 138
    see also Reimagined Integrated
        Marketing Plan (IMC)
playing 200
plot template 28
PopJam 197
posters 60
PR 204
Prada 25–26
Pram Point 189
preamble, code of ethics 96
presentation decks 174–75
Priceless (MasterCard) 48
printouts 174
processes 166–67
professional ethics (values) 98
prototyping 21 23, 36–40, 58, 101,
        103–04, 137–38, 144, 171,
        175
provisions of conduct 98
public speaking 89–91, 192
purchase decision-making 68
purpose 13, 65, 85, 194

Quechua 71
questioning 201, 202–03
    see also 'why' question

Rasmijn-Reino, Candy 204
reach 149–50, 152, 153
reaction metrics 153–54, 155–56
recycling 144, 145
Redditt 153

Reimagined Integrated Marketing Plan (IMC) 51–62, 184
relationship-building 8, 56, 65, 66
religious beliefs 92, 97
research 195
resources 57, 175–76
reward experiences 109
Ritz Carlton 191
Robin to Batman effect 21
Robopocalypse 17, 168
role reversal 86
rules setting 35

sales skills 74
Salesforce 166–67
Saralegui, Cristina 193
Sarkar, Dona 205
scalability 141
scale test 135
SCAMPER technique 83–86
Schultz, Howard 80
Scott Base 189
security, IT 186
self-calibration 71
sensory affordance 124
shareability 141
Shared Service Engineering (SSE) Studio 40–41
singing 200
skills 74–75, 82, 83, 185–86, 192, 193–94
    see also empathy; vulnerability
Slack 60
slogans 45, 48, 55, 183
small moments 203
SMART goals 58
Snapchat 197
social activism (value) 32, 53–54, 55, 64, 65, 66–67, 68
social advocacy 109
Social Ambassador Youth Program (Adobe) 115–20
social media 6, 43, 54, 67–68, 100, 138, 190, 194
    listening tools 37–38, 172
    Microsoft 152, 153
    see also Facebook; influencers (influencer marketing); Instagram; LinkedIn; Pinterest; PopJam; Slack; Snapchat; Social Ambassador Program (Adobe); Twitter; Yammer
social network groups 117, 138
'Social Value of Brands' (Gibbons) 68
socialpreneurs 113–14
society (societal laws) 92, 95, 97, 106, 171–72

soft skills 74, 82, 83
    see also empathy; vulnerability

sparklines 32
spherical video immersive storytelling 106–07
sports marketing 118–19
stakeholder conversations 132–33
stakeholders 36–37, 56–58, 59, 95, 132–33, 138, 150, 155–56, 159
Starbucks 17, 80
statement of professional values 98
status quo, challenging 200
stochastic processes 181
story arc 9–19, 30
story frameworks 191
story mission 13–15
story mission brief 13, 16
story setting 43–45
story structure 21, 29–34
storytellers 169–70
storytelling, defined 16
storytelling techniques 20, 57
Storytelling 2.0 72–73, 182–83
strategy 18
substitution 84–85
supervisors 129
Sy, Dux Raymond 188–92
systems 166–67

target audience 59–61, 76, 175
teams 35
technology 5, 106, 167–68, 177–87
    cloud 56, 60, 79, 188, 190
    see also artificial intelligence (AI); augmented reality (AR); automation; digital transformation; IoT (Internet of Things); mixed reality (MR); mobile devices; webinars
TED 17
testing 23, 37–38, 68, 81–82, 131–45, 175, 191
thought experiments 132
thought leadership 159–60
360°immersive storytelling 106–07
3D experiments 132
TikTok 196, 197
tone 13, 16
top management 128, 165, 166
'Toxic Masculinity' (Gillette) 55, 68, 136
training 74–75, 83, 172–76
TV screens 60
Twitter 113, 117, 118, 119, 151, 153
2D experiments 132
typography 36, 41, 46–47, 140

Uber 67
United States 98, 100–01, 177, 193
universal truth 11, 18, 24–26, 53, 56, 58,
        78, 108, 136
Univision 193
unused storytelling ideas 86
upcycling 144–45
user-generated content 50, 120
UX (user experience) 40–42, 114, 123, 171
UX designers 40–42, 114

value tests *134*
values 8, 66, 94, 97–98, 137, 190
Venezuela 177
videogames 107
villains 161–76
virtual reality (VR) 104, 109
visual elements 45–48
voice technology 185
vulnerability 76–88, 107, 137

Walt Disney Company (Disney) 11, 12, 16,
        139–40, 143, 191
webinars 111, 119, 190, 191
Weiler, Lance 100–01, 103–04
white papers 31, 47
Whittaker, James (Doc James) 62, 177–79,
        180–81
'why?' question 142
Windows Insider Program 153, 205
winning 64
Witt, Greg L 198–201
World Café 100–03
World Wildlife Fund 114

Yammer 60
younger audiences (youth culture) 143–44,
        198–201
    see also Gen Alpha; Gen Z; millennials

Ziglar, Zig 173

CPSIA information can be obtained
at www.ICGtesting.com
Printed in the USA
LVHW072104120723
752166LV00007B/159